Build With Steel
A Companion to the AISC Manual

LRFD

Paul W. Richards

Contents

Photo/Image Credits

Cover. Vector art simon2579/istockphoto.com and Paul Richards, background photo 4X-image/istockphoto.com.

Chapter 1. **xii** sdlgzps/istockphoto.com, **6** MIMOHE/istockphoto.com, all other photos and illustrations © Paul Richards.

Chapter 2. All photos and illustrations © Paul Richards.

Chapter 3. **16** doram/istockphoto.com and nadla/istockphoto.com, **25** hometowncd/istockphoto.com, all other photos and illustrations © Paul Richards.

Chapter 4. **30** samvalenbergs/istockphoto.com, **32** Joe_Potato/istockphoto.com, all other photos and illustrations © Paul Richards.

Chapter 5. **64** vavlt/istockphoto.com, all other photos and illustrations © Paul Richards.

Chapter 6. **84** tropicalpixsingapore/istockphoto.com, all other photos and illustrations © Paul Richards.

Chapter 7. **122** rodho/istockphoto.com, all other photos and illustrations © Paul Richards.

Chapter 8. All photos and illustrations © Paul Richards.

Chapter 9. **209** courtesy of Spencer Guthrie. All other photos and illustrations © Paul Richards.

Chapter 10. All photos and illustrations © Paul Richards.

Chapter 11. All photos and illustrations © Paul Richards.

Preface

A Beginner's Companion to the AISC Manual

Build with Steel is intended for students taking their first course in steel design or those trying to learn steel design on their own, perhaps in preparation for the FE or PE exam. This book concentrates only on the topics covered in an undergraduate steel design course and the FE/PE exams. Once you have mastered those topics, you will need to get another book to continue your journey. If you already know the basic principles of steel design there may be better books for your needs.

Build with Steel references a book published by the American Institute of Steel Construction (AISC) called the *AISC Steel Construction Manual* (hereafter called "the Manual"). You need to have the Manual (14th edition) with you as you go through this book.

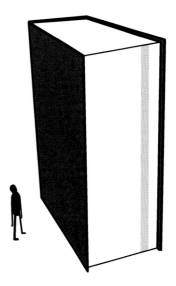

The Manual is thick and may be intimidating to some beginners. It contains specifications for steel design and tables to help steel designers. *Build With Steel* will help you learn steel design through the Manual. The layout, illustrations, and examples in *Build with Steel* will help you understand the world of steel design described in the Manual's text. *Build with Steel* will help you learn how to use the Manual to design steel structures.

Active Reading

The organization and layout of this book facilitate active reading. Each chapter starts with a *Consider This* box that poses questions which will be answered as you progress through the chapter.

Consider This

- What is active reading?
- What types of information boxes will be used throughout this book?
- How will reading questions help you identify important concepts?

One part of active reading is writing notes in the book as you read along. Every page has room for notes in the margin. As you read, write down things that come to mind, especially any questions.

Write notes and questions in the margins.

Throughout each chapter you will find *Study the Manual* boxes. These boxes direct you to specific pages in the Manual and explain what is going on and/or ask you questions about what you have read. Write in answers to all the questions in the *Study the Manual* boxes.

Study the Manual

Look at the first pages in the Manual.

- How many parts are there to the Manual?

- Which part is about bolt design?

The best part of *Build With Steel* is the examples. As you go through the book you will constantly encounter examples in blue boxes. The examples illustrate principles that are being discussed, highlight applications, and demonstrate solutions for typical design problems.

Example - Getting through the AISC Manual

If you read one page a day in the Manual, how many years would it take you to get through the entire thing?

Step 1 - Determine how many pages are in the Manual

It takes some effort to determine the number of pages in the Manual because the parts are individually numbered; there are seventeen parts plus the front matter and the index. Summing the pages in each part gives the total number of pages:

$$N = 2059 \text{ pgs}$$

Step 2 - Calculate the number of years

$$T = (2059 \text{ pgs}) \left(\frac{1 \text{ day}}{1 \text{ pg}} \right) \left(\frac{1 \text{ yr}}{365 \text{ days}} \right) = \textbf{5.64 yrs}$$

Each chapter in *Build With Steel* is divided into several sections. At the end of each section you will find a *You Should Know* box. This box contains questions about the material just covered. Write in answers to all the questions in the *You Should Know* box. If you can't answer a question, you need to go back and re-read the material you missed.

You Should Know

- Where will you find *You Should Know* boxes?
- What does it mean if you don't know the answer to a *You Should Know* question?

The last type of box you will encounter is a *Remember This* box. There is one at the end of each chapter that summarizes the main points of the chapter.

The Specification

The heart of the AISC Manual is the *Specification for Structural Steel Buildings* (AISC 360-10, "the Specification"). The Specification is found in Part 16 of the Manual and describes accepted methods for designing steel structures. All of the design tables in the Manual are based on the procedures described in the Specification. The Specification is the basis for everything that is discussed in *Build With Steel*.

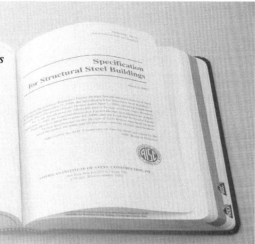

Study the Manual

Turn to page 16.1-iii of the Manual and read the first three paragraphs on the page.

- Why was the Specification written?

- Who wrote the Specification?

Turn through the first few pages of the Specification for Structural Steel Buildings to the Table of Contents (16.1-v).

- How are the chapters labeled? How many chapters are there?

Turn to the first page of the Commentary (16.1-241) and read it.

- Is the commentary part of the Specification (AISC 360-10)?

- What is the purpose of the commentary?

Turn through a few pages of the commentary.

- What is different about the coloring of the commentary pages?

Remember This

- *Build With Steel* helps beginners learn steel design through the AISC Manual.
- The information boxes in this book facilitate active reading. Active reading means that you: 1) write in answers to questions in the *Study the Manual* boxes, 2) write in answers to the questions in the *You Should Know* boxes, and 3) write notes and questions in the lined margins.
- The heart of the Manual is the Specification (AISC 360-10). The Specification is the basis for all of the design procedures and tables.

Molten metal glows and dances as it is cast. Steel has remarkable material properties and has played a major role in shaping the modern world.

Since the 1990s, most of the structural steel in the U.S. has been produced from scrap rather than ore.

1. Properties of Steel

Consider This

- What is steel? How is it related to wrought iron or cast iron?
- What are the mechanical properties of steel?
- How many different kinds of steel are there?
- What types of steel are used in structures?
- How do the properties of steel compare with other materials?

1.1 Chemical Composition

Steel is iron with small amounts of carbon (0.15 to 1.7% by weight). Less carbon results in wrought iron; more carbon results in cast iron.

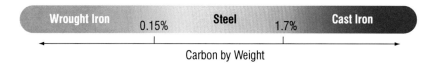

The amount of carbon in steel influences its strength and ductility. Strength is how much stress the steel can take before it yields or breaks. Ductility is the property that allows the steel to stretch and bend without breaking. Steels with high ductility are also generally easier to weld. In general, more carbon results in greater strength but lower ductility.

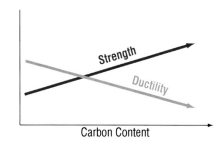

In addition to carbon, most steels contain small amounts of other elements to enhance the mechanical properties. These alloying elements may include: manganese, phosphorous, nickel, and silicon. The metal alloying elements can increase the strength of steel without decreasing ductility. However, compared with carbon, these elements are more expensive.

You Should Know

- How much carbon is in steel in general?
- What happens to the strength and ductility of steel when carbon content increases?
- How can a steel with 0.15% carbon be stronger than a steel with 0.7% carbon?

1.2 Tensile Strength

The usual test for determining the mechanical properties of steel is the direct tension test. In the direct tension test, a material sample (called a coupon) is pulled slowly in tension until it breaks.

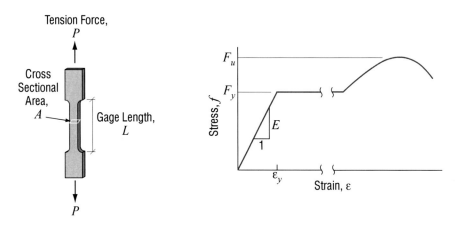

The stress in the coupon during testing, f, is calculated as the applied tension force, P, divided by the cross sectional area, A:

$$f = \frac{P}{A}$$

The strain in the coupon, ε, is calculated as the change in length, δ, divided by the gage length, L:

$$\varepsilon = \frac{\delta}{L}$$

The figure above shows the shape of the stress-strain curve for a typical structural steel. The stress and strain where the steel begins to yield are designated F_y and ε_y. For stresses less than F_y, the steel is elastic; the stress and strain are related linearly by Young's Modulus of Elasticity, E:

$$f = E\varepsilon$$

When the steel reaches F_y, it loses stiffness but maintains its strength. Once strains become large, hardening occurs and strength increases again. The stress when the steel reaches its maximum strength is designated F_u. The horizontal axis is spliced in the figure above because very large strains (10-20%) are required to reach F_u.

Example 1.1 Relationship Between Stress and Strain

The cross-sectional area of a steel coupon is 1.0 in.^{2}, and the gage length is 3.0 in. When a tension force of 5.0 kips is applied to the coupon it stretches 0.00052 in.
   What is the stress in the material?
   What is the strain?
   What is the modulus of elasticity?

Step 1 - Compute the stress

Assuming the steel remains elastic, the stress is:

$$f = \frac{P}{A} = \frac{5.0 \text{ kips}}{1.0 \text{ in.}^2} = 5.0 \text{ ksi}$$

Step 2 - Compute the strain

The strain is:

$$\varepsilon = \frac{\delta}{L} = \frac{0.00052 \text{ in.}}{3.0 \text{ in.}} = 0.00017$$

Step 3 - Compute the modulus of elasticity

Assuming the steel remains elastic, the modulus of elasticity is:

$$E = \frac{f}{\varepsilon} = \frac{5.0 \text{ ksi}}{0.00017} = 29,000 \text{ ksi}$$

The previous discussion has been about steel tested in tension. When steel is tested in compression, F_y and E are essentially the same as for tension. This characteristic of steel is convenient in design.

You Should Know

- What test is usually performed to determine steel mechanical properties?
- How would you compute Young's Modulus of Elasticity from tension test results?
- What properties of steel are the same for tension and compression loading?

1.3 Shear Strength

If a steel rod is torqued instead of stretched, the material will be in a state of pure shear rather than pure tension. Experimental testing has shown that the shear strength of steel is consistently about 60% of the tensile strength ($0.6F_y$). The Mises yield criterion, that is covered in many mechanics courses, agrees with experimental data and gives the theoretical shear strength of steel as $0.577F_y$.

Knowing the strength of steel in pure tension and shear is very helpful in steel design. Most of the critical locations in steel structures have stress states that are similar to either pure tension or pure shear.

You Should Know

- If you see the term $0.6F_y$ in an equation, what should come to mind?

1.4 Varieties of Structural Steel

More than thirty different types of steel are commonly used in buildings, bridges, and other structures. Each type of steel has unique chemistry and properties, but they all have less than 0.3% carbon. Steels are called by their ASTM designation. Three examples are ASTM A36, ASTM A992, and ASTM A325. Sometimes the designation provides information about the properties of the steel, but usually the designation is just a name.

The American Society for Testing and Materials (ASTM) publishes standards for various materials. For steel, these standards include requirements about chemistry and strength.

Example 1.2 ASTM A36 Steel

A36 steel is the standard material for steel plates and some shapes. In order for a material to be classified as A36, it must have a yield strength of at least 36 ksi and an ultimate strength (after strain hardening) of at least 58 ksi. A36 steel is generally 0.25-0.28% carbon.

Example 1.3 ASTM A992 Steel

A992 steel is the standard material for common "I-beams". In order for the material to be classified as A992 it must have a yield strength of at least 50 ksi but no greater than 65 ksi. The ratio of the yield to the ultimate strength cannot exceed 0.85. A992 has less than 0.23% carbon, but is stronger than A36 because of alloying elements.

Example 1.4 ASTM A325 Steel

A325 steel is a standard material for bolts. This material has less than 0.30% carbon, but has an ultimate strength of at least 105 ksi. This material is heat-treated to increase strength, but ductility is lost in the process.

The figure below shows tensile stress-strain curves for the three steels featured in the previous examples. Notice that the elastic slope (the modulus of elasticity) is similar for all three materials even though the strength and ductility is different. The modulus of elasticity, E, for all structural steels is about 29,000 ksi.

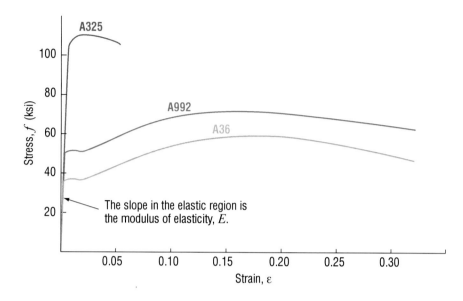

Study the Manual

Turn to §A3 in the Specification and read §A3.1 and §A3.1a.

• What is required as evidence that a material conforms to a particular ASTM standard?

• How many different types of steel are approved for use for steel plates? What is the first one listed?

You Should Know

• How many different kinds of structural steel are there?
• What is the difference between A36 and A992 steel?
• Why are bolts less ductile than structural shapes?
• What is the value for E for all structural steels, regardless of strength?
• Where in the Specification is the list of approved materials?

1.5 Production of Steel

The element iron (Fe) is rarely found in its pure metallic form naturally because it oxidizes in the presence of oxygen and moisture. In decades past, metallic iron was obtained by separating the oxygen from the iron in the ore hematite (Fe_2O_3) through a chemical process called reduction. In chemical reduction, hematite is heated in the presence of carbon (C) and the carbon combines with the oxygen in the ore, making CO_2 or CO gas and leaving the iron (Fe) behind. This chemical reduction is called smelting and can occur at temperatures below the melting point of iron; smelting is not necessarily the same as melting.

For more than a hundred years, smelting was the primary method for producing structural steel. However, beginning in the late 1970s, new mills were built that were specifically designed to produce steel shapes from scrap metal. Recycling scrap metal is more energy-efficient and environmentally-friendly than smelting ore. In the United States, most of the structural steel used today comes from recycled scrap metal.

Example 1.5 Development and Use of Steel

How long have people been making steel and using it in structures?

Steel has been used for bridges and buildings since the late 1800s (about 150 years). The list below summarizes some of the important events in the development and use of steel in structures.

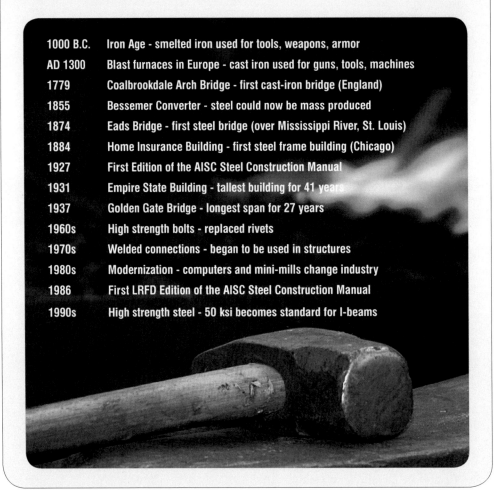

1000 B.C.	Iron Age - smelted iron used for tools, weapons, armor
AD 1300	Blast furnaces in Europe - cast iron used for guns, tools, machines
1779	Coalbrookdale Arch Bridge - first cast-iron bridge (England)
1855	Bessemer Converter - steel could now be mass produced
1874	Eads Bridge - first steel bridge (over Mississippi River, St. Louis)
1884	Home Insurance Building - first steel frame building (Chicago)
1927	First Edition of the AISC Steel Construction Manual
1931	Empire State Building - tallest building for 41 years
1937	Golden Gate Bridge - longest span for 27 years
1960s	High strength bolts - replaced rivets
1970s	Welded connections - began to be used in structures
1980s	Modernization - computers and mini-mills change industry
1986	First LRFD Edition of the AISC Steel Construction Manual
1990s	High strength steel - 50 ksi becomes standard for I-beams

You Should Know

- What is the difference between smelting and melting?
- Where was the first steel bridge built? When?
- How is most structural steel produced in the U.S. today?

1.6 Comparison with other Materials

Common materials for the construction of large structures are steel, concrete, and wood. The table below compares typical properties for each material.

Material	Tensile Strength (ksi)	Compressive Strength (ksi)	Modulus of Elasticity (ksi)	Coefficient of Thermal Expansion (for °F)	Density (lb/ft³)
Typical Steel	36-50	36-50	29,000	0.00065	490
Typical Concrete	≈0.3-0.5	3-5	3,000-4,000	0.00055	145
Typical Wood	≈0.5	≈1.5	≈1,600	0.00021	32

You Should Know

- How many times stronger is typical steel than typical concrete?
- How many times stiffer (modulus of elasticity) is typical steel than typical concrete?
- Which has the greatest strength/weight ratio: steel or concrete?
- What property is quite similar for both steel and concrete? What is the implication for reinforced concrete structures?

Remember This

- Structural steel consists of iron with small amounts of carbon and alloying elements.
- The most common test for determining steel properties is the direct tension test.
- The most commonly used mechanical properties are the modulus of elasticity, E, the yield stress, F_y, and the ultimate tensile stress, F_u.
- There are more than thirty different types of structural steel; each is defined by an ASTM designation that specifies requirements for the chemistry and mechanical properties.
- Most of the structural steel produced in the U.S. today is from recycled scrap metal.
- Steel is several times stronger and stiffer per pound than concrete or wood.

Hundreds of steel shapes are stacked in the yard of a steel service center. Service centers purchase most of the steel shapes that are produced in mills and maintain an inventory of shapes that can be supplied to steel fabricators as needed.

Steel structures are typically designed using off-the-shelf shapes, cut and drilled as needed.

2. Standard Steel Shapes

Consider This

- Why do we use standard shapes in steel structures?
- How many different standard shapes are there?
- How are the different shapes produced?
- What can you tell about a shape from its name?
- What are preferred materials for the different standard shapes?
- What information does the Manual have about each shape?

2.1 Background

In the late 1800s, mills began producing steel for railroads, ships, bridges, and buildings. Over time, a catalog of standard shapes (cross-sections) evolved that could be produced at various mills. Since the standard shapes are mass produced, they are generally less expensive than customized shapes and parts. Engineers need to be familiar with the standard shapes so they can use them effectively.

The standard shapes that are covered in the AISC *Steel Construction Manual* (the Manual) can be classified into three broad categories: Hot-rolled shapes, Cold-formed shapes, and Plates or bars. In the following sections, each of the categories of shapes will be discussed.

2.2 Hot-Rolled Shapes

Most steel shapes are produced by hot-rolling. In hot-rolling, a rough shape, called a *billet* or *blank*, is heated to around 2100 °F and then passed through a series of rollers that squeeze it into the desired shape. Hot-rolling is used to make a variety of structural steel shapes and reinforcing bar (rebar).

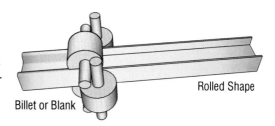

Rolled Shape

Billet or Blank

The various families of hot-rolled shapes are illustrated below.

Most hot-rolled shapes have names based on their depth and weight. For example, one of the standard wide flange shapes is named W14×22. The first letter of the name, W, indicates it is a wide flange. The first number, 14, indicates that the W14×22 is approximately 14 inches deep. The second number, 22, is the weight of the shape in pounds per foot of length. Likewise, an MC18×58 is a miscellaneous channel that is about 18 inches deep and weighs 58 lbs/ft, and an MT6×5.9 is a tee shape that is about 6 inches deep and weighs 5.9 lbs/ft. Tee shapes are made by cutting W, M, or S-shapes in half. For example, when you cut a W14×22 in half, you get two WT7×11s.

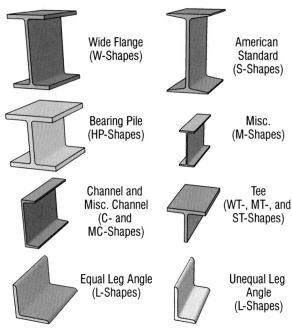

Wide Flange (W-Shapes)

American Standard (S-Shapes)

Bearing Pile (HP-Shapes)

Misc. (M-Shapes)

Channel and Misc. Channel (C- and MC-Shapes)

Tee (WT-, MT-, and ST-Shapes)

Equal Leg Angle (L-Shapes)

Unequal Leg Angle (L-Shapes)

For angles, the shape names are based on the cross-sectional dimensions. An L6×4×1/2 has a 6 in. leg and a 4 in. leg, both of which are ½ inch thick. The table below indicates the number of hot-rolled shapes in some of the families.

Shape Family	Number of Shapes	Range of Depths (in.)	Range of Weights (lbs/ft)
Wide Flange (W)	273	4 - 44	8.5 - 652
American Standard (S)	28	3 - 24	5.7 - 106
Miscellaneous (M)	18	3 - 13	3.7 - 12
Bearing Pile (HP)	21	8 - 18	36 - 204
Channel (C)	32	4 - 15	3.5 - 50
Miscellaneous Channel (MC)	40	3 - 18	7.1 - 58
Unequal Angle (L)	76	2.5 - 8	2.4 - 44
Equal Angle (L)	51	2 - 8	1.7 - 57

Example 2.1 The Difference Between W, S, M, and HP Shapes

What is the difference between the various families with I-shaped cross sections ?

From the table above, the majority of the hot-rolled shapes with "I" cross sections are wide flange shapes (W). Wide flange shapes are used for most general structural framing. The other families of hot-rolled I-shapes have their own specialty applications. American standard shapes (S) differ from wide flange shapes in that the flanges that are tapered and narrower. Miscellaneous shapes (M) differ from wide flange shapes in that the flanges are narrower and most of them are very light and small. Bearing piles (HP) differ from wide flange shapes in that the flanges are generally wider and the webs thicker.

2.3 Cold-Formed Shapes

Cold-formed shapes are produced by bending a steel plate at room temperature and welding the seam. The various families of cold-formed shapes are illustrated below.

Rectangular HSS   Square HSS   Round HSS   Pipe

The names of HSS shapes give information about the geometry. For example, an HSS3×1×1/8 is a rectangular hollow structural shape, about 3 inches by 1 inch, with 1/8 inch thick walls. These dimensions are called nominal dimensions; more exact dimensions are used for calculations. An HSS6.625×0.500 is a round HSS with an outside diameter of 6.625 inches and 0.5-inch thick walls.

HSS stands for Hollow Structural Section. These shapes were formerly designated TS (tube sections).

Pipe 8 Std.   Pipe 8 xx-Strong

Pipes have interesting names. The first term is always "Pipe"; the second term is the approximate diameter of the pipe (in inches); and the third term is either "std.," "x-strong," or "xx-strong" depending on the thickness of the walls. For example, a Pipe 8 Std. has an outside diameter of 8.63 inches and a wall thickness of 0.30 inches; but a Pipe 8 xx-strong has an outside diameter of 8.63 inches with a wall thickness of 0.82 inches.

Example 2.2 The Difference Between Round HSS Shapes and Pipe Shapes

What is the difference between Round HSS Shapes and Pipes?

Round HSSs and Pipes differ in what they are made of (material), and what sizes they come in.
Material: Round HSSs are made from material with F_y=42 ksi; Pipes are made from material with F_y=35 ksi.
Sizes: Round HSSs range in size from less than 2 inches in diameter all the way up to 20 inches in diameter with a variety of thicknesses. There are more than 120 round HSS shapes. Pipes range in size from 1 inch diameter up to 12 inches. There are 37 pipe shapes.

2.4 Plates and Bars

Bars and plates have solid rectangular or square cross sections. If a member has a solid rectangular section with a width of 8 inches or less it is called a bar. If the width is more than 8 inches, it is called a plate. Both are designated PL followed by the thickness, width (in inches), and length (in feet and inches). For example, a PL 1/2×5×2'-0" is a bar that is ½-inch thick by 5 inches wide, and 2 feet long.

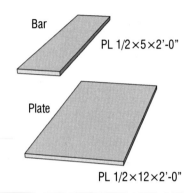

Bar
PL 1/2×5×2'-0"

Plate

PL 1/2×12×2'-0"

2.5 Cross-Sectional Properties

The first tables in the Manual provide dimensions and other information about the cross-sections of the various standard shapes. Table 1-1 provides information about W-Shapes.

Tables 1-2 through 1-14 are similar to Table 1-1 in that they provide dimensions and other cross-sectional information for standard shapes. Of course, each family of shapes has unique geometry and cross-sectional properties that need to be defined. In all cases, there is a figure at the top-left side of the page that illustrates the dimensions or axes that the listed information pertains to.

> **You Should Know**
>
> * What is the cross-sectional area for a W40x397?
> * What is the approximate flange width for a shape that falls in the group bounded by W40x593 and W40x199?
> * What is the moment of inertia about the Y-Y axis for a W40x264?

2.6 Preferred Materials

The standard shapes are mass produced using the preferred material for each shape. The preferred materials for the various shapes are given in Tables 2-3 and 2-4 of the Manual.

> **Study the Manual**
>
> Go to Table 2-4 of the Manual (page 2-48). Notice there are columns for the various standard shapes. The rows of the table are for different materials, each with an ASTM Designation (F_y and F_u for each material are given in the table). White boxes indicate the shape is not made from that material. The black box in each column indicates the preferred material for each shape.
>
> * What is the preferred material for most shapes?
>
> * What is the difference in preferred material for rectangular HSSs and round HSSs?
>
> * What is the preferred material for wide flange shapes?
>
> * What is F_y for a typical wide flange section?
>
> Go to Table 2-5 of the Manual (pg 2-49).
> * What is the preferred material for most plates and bars?
>
> * What is the one exception?

During design, we assume shapes are made from the preferred material unless we have a good reason for doing otherwise. The values for F_y and F_u that are used for design are the minimum values listed for the preferred material in Tables 2-4 or 2-5.

> **You Should Know**
>
> * Where can you look up material properties for standard steel shapes?

2.7 Built-up Shapes

Additional cross-sections can be created by combining standard shapes or plates. When two or more shapes are combined to act as a single member, that member is called a *built-up* shape. Perhaps the most common built-up shapes are double-angles. Other built-up shapes made from standard shapes include double channels, S-shapes with cap channels, plate girders, and box shapes made from channels, angles, or plates.

Study the Manual

Go to Table 1-15 of the Manual (page 1-102). Study the figures at the top of the table.
- What is the difference between LLBB and SLBB?

- What cross-sectional property is the same for both cases?

Look at Tables 1-16 through 1-20.
- What built-up shapes have properties tabulated in these tables.

Example 2.3 Plate Girders

Plate girders are custom I-shaped sections that are fabricated by welding plates together. The plate girder in this picture was fabricated for a highway interchange project.

Example 2.4 Box Columns

Plates can also be welded together to form rectangular (box shaped) cross-sections for use as beams or columns. This column was made from four plates stitch-welded together. A built-up column was used in this case to get a lightweight cross-section with a large moment of inertia.

- What are some examples of built-up shapes?

2.8 Manufacturing Tolerances

The cross-sectional dimensions of actual steel shapes will not be precisely those specified in Tables 1-1 through 1-14 of the Manual due to variability in manufacturing; in addition, the shapes will not be perfectly straight.

The permissible tolerances for standard shapes are given in Tables 1-22 through 1-29.

Study the Manual

Go to Table 1-22 of the Manual (page 1-119).

- What is the range of acceptable values for d, for a W40x503?

Turn to the next page.

- What is the difference between sweep and camber?

Go to Table 1-25.

- For an L8x8x1, what is the range of acceptable values for the leg length, B?

Go to Table 1-26.

- For an L2x2x3/8, what is the range of acceptable values for the thickness of the legs?

You Should Know

- What tables should you look at if you have questions about tolerances or acceptable variations from the ideal geometry?

Remember This

- Standard shapes are economical for steel design because they are mass produced.
- Three categories of standard shapes are: Hot-rolled, Cold-formed, and Plates/Bars.
- The name of a shape is based on its geometry and sometimes weight.
- Tables 1-1 through 1-17 of the Manual provide the dimensions and cross-sectional properties for all the standard shapes.
- Tables 2-4 through 2-5 of the Manual provide the preferred materials (and properties) for all the standard shapes.
- In design, assume a shape is made of the preferred material unless you know otherwise.
- Acceptable tolerances for standard shapes are explained in Tables 1-22 through 1-29 of the Manual.

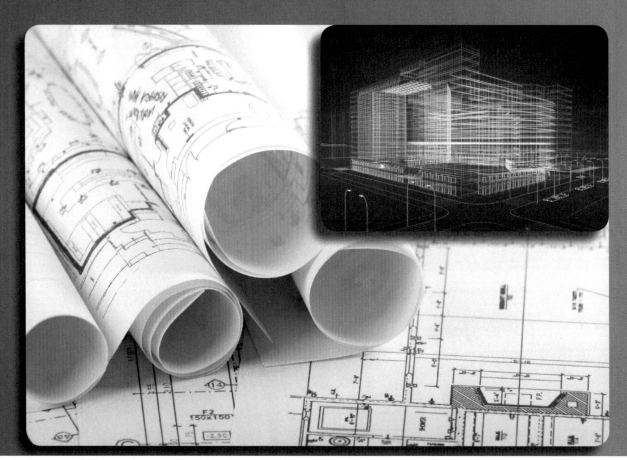

Structural designs are communicated through printed plans or computer models. The structural engineer decides how a building will be supported and selects appropriate shapes for the members so that the building can withstand gravity, wind, and earthquake loads.

Load and Resistance Factor Design (LRFD) can be used to pick appropriate shapes for steel structures.

3. Load and Resistance Factor Design

Consider This

- What is the underlying principle of all design methods?
- What are the "factors" in Load and Resistance Factor Design (LRFD)?
- What types of loads do steel structures carry?
- How is LRFD different from Allowable Stress Design?
- What is a limit state? How can you know how a member will fail?
- What is a general procedure for sizing members?

3.1 Basic Design Principles

The underlying principle of all design methods is that the capacity of a structural element should be greater than the demands that will be placed on it.

$$\text{Demands} < \text{Capacity}$$

This single principle can give rise to multiple design methods because there are different ways that demands and capacities can be defined and computed. In Load and Resistance Factor Design (LRFD), demands and capacities are computed using load factors and resistance factors (which will be explained later).

The courses you have taken in statics, mechanics, and materials, have prepared you to compute demands and capacities. Much of LRFD is simply applying the skills and knowledge you already have. Once you know how to determine demands and capacities, you are ready to engage in design. The remaining sections in this chapter discuss demands, capacity, and design in the context of LRFD.

The rest of the chapters in *Build with Steel* follow the same organization: demands, capacity, then design.

3.2 Overview of Loads

The demands on a structure come from various types of loads, including gravity, wind, and earthquake loads. The American Society of Civil Engineers (ASCE) publishes a document, called *ASCE 7*, that establishes standards for computing these various loads. *ASCE 7* is important because it is adopted into most of the building codes that regulate structural design. *Build With Steel* emphasizes gravity loading and includes much of the essential information from *ASCE 7* pertaining to gravity loads. Wind and seismic loads are much more complex and are only covered superficially in this book. Additional study of *ASCE 7* or other texts will be necessary for you to learn how to compute wind and seismic loads.

The table below describes the various loads that are considered when designing buildings. Gravity loads are subdivided into dead loads, live loads, roof live loads, snow loads, and rain loads.

Load	Symbol	Description
Dead	D	Gravity loads from a structure's self weight; also gravity loads from permanent components such as piping, ceilings, lights, carpet, roofing, and other similar things.
Live	L	Gravity loads from the weight of people, vehicles, furnishings (including partition walls), and moveable equipment.
Roof Live	L_r	Gravity loads on roofs from people and moveable equipment.
Rain	R	Gravity loads from rain due to the 50-yr. rain storm.
Snow	S	Gravity loads from snow due to the 50-yr. snow storm.
Wind	W	Lateral loads from the wind due to the 50-yr. wind storm.
Earthquake	E	Lateral loads that represent the earthquake that gives a 1% risk of collapse in 50 years.

3.3 Dead Loads

Large demands on a structure come from its own weight. Dead loads are estimated using a take-off which itemizes the various things that contribute to the dead load. The precise weight of each item cannot be known until after the design is complete, but reasonable estimates can usually be made based on previous experience. Average area loads, in pounds per square foot (psf), are generally used for design. The example below shows a weight take-off for a floor in a building.

Example 3.1 Typical Floor Dead Loads for a Steel Building

The table to the right is a typical floor weight take-off for a steel building. Note that the concrete slab-on-metal-deck and steel framing constitute most of the dead load.

Floor Weight Take-Off

Steel Framing	10 psf
3-1/2" Lightweight Concrete on 3" Metal Deck	40 psf
Mechanical, Electrical, Plumbing (MEP)	5 psf
Insulation	3 psf
Ceiling and Lights	4 psf
Floor Covering	5 psf
Miscellaneous	3 psf
	70 psf

When estimating dead loads, it is helpful to know how much various things weigh. Tables 17-12 and 17-13 in the Manual provide weights of common building materials. More detailed tables can be found in *ASCE 7*.

Study the Manual

Turn to Table 17-13 in the back of the Manual (page 17-26).

- What would the dead load be (in psf) for a hardwood floor (7/8 inch thick)?

- What would the dead load be (in psf) for asphalt shingles?

Turn to Table 17-12 in the Manual.

- How much does concrete masonry weigh (in pcf)?

- How much does steel weigh (in pcf)?

You Should Know

- Where is most of the weight of a building found?
- What are the units for average area loads?
- Where can you look up the weight of building materials that are not given in the back of the AISC Manual?

3.4 Live Loads

ASCE 7 specifies minimum live loads for various situations. These loads are based on studies of live loads in various types of buildings and locations within buildings. The table below indicates a few of the minimum live load values that are given in *ASCE 7*.

Example 3.2 Typical Floor Live Loads for a Steel Building

ASCE 7 has a table with minimum uniformly-distributed live loads for different situations. A few of the values from that table are summarized to the right. Notice that higher loads are specified for corridors. A value of 100 psf corresponds to people packed into an area (standing-room-only).

Minimum Live Loads (from ASCE 7)

Office Buildings	
Lobbies and first-floor corridors	100 psf
Offices	50 psf
Corridors above first floor	80 psf
Schools	
Classrooms	40 psf
Corridors above first floor	80 psf
First floor corridors	100 psf
Hotels and Apartments	
Private rooms and corridors	40 psf
Public areas and corridors	100 psf

For cases not given in the example above, you will need to refer to the minimum live load tables given in *ASCE 7*. The minimum loads specified in the tables should be conservative for most situations.

Example 3.3 Typical Office Live Loads

What is the live load (in psf) for the 12-foot x 12-foot office shown below?

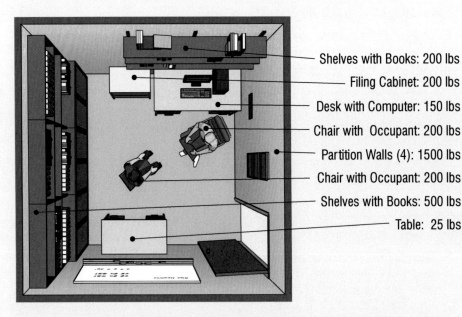

Shelves with Books: 200 lbs
Filing Cabinet: 200 lbs
Desk with Computer: 150 lbs
Chair with Occupant: 200 lbs
Partition Walls (4): 1500 lbs
Chair with Occupant: 200 lbs
Shelves with Books: 500 lbs
Table: 25 lbs

If the total live load (2975 lbs) is divided by the total floor area (144 ft^2), the average live load is 21 psf. This is a pretty typical live load for an office area. However, some offices are much more heavily loaded (think of the stereotypical professor with an office filled from floor to ceiling). To account for these occasional heavy loaders, *ASCE 7* specifies a minimum design load of 50 psf for offices.

3.5 Load Effects

It is important to understand the difference between loads and load effects. Gravity, wind, and earthquake loads will result in forces within the various parts of a structure. The internal forces in the structural members are called the load effects. The three most commonly considered load effects are: axial forces, bending moments, and shear forces. When we talk about demands on structural components, we are referring to the load effects. You learned how to compute load effects in Statics by using equilibrium equations.

Using standard notation in calculations is important so others can understand what you are doing. It is conventional to use the letter P to indicate axial load effects, the letter M to indicate bending moment load effects, and the letter V to indicate shear force load effects. It is conventional to use subscripts of D, L, Lr, R, S, W, and E to denote the loads that cause the effects. For example: P_D denotes the axial force in a member caused by the dead loads, while P_L denotes the axial force caused by the live loads.

Example 3.4 Computing Load Effects

Compute the load effects in member BC of the truss. Compute the effects separately for the dead and live load.

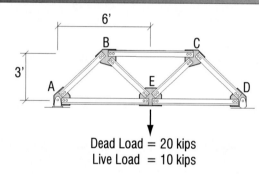

Dead Load = 20 kips
Live Load = 10 kips

Step 1 - Get support reactions from dead loads

First consider only the dead load applied. From symmetry, and summing forces in the y-direction, we observe:
$$R_A = R_D = 10 \text{ kips}$$

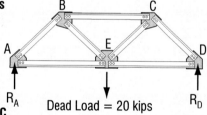

Dead Load = 20 kips

Step 2 - Compute internal forces in member BC

Cutting the system through member BC gives the free body diagram to the right. The unknown axial force in member BC is designated $P_{D,BC}$ since it is an axial force caused by dead loads (D). Summing moments about point E gives:
$$(10 \text{ kips})(6 \text{ ft}) + (P_{D,BC})(3 \text{ ft}) = 0$$
$$P_{D,BC} = -20 \text{ kips (compression)}$$

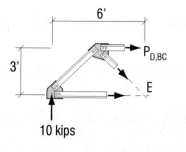

10 kips

continued on next page

---

example continued

Step 3 - Compute internal forces from the live load

Steps 1 and 2 could be repeated considering only the live load in order to compute $P_{L,BC}$. Another method to compute $P_{L,BC}$ is to simply recognize that the applied live load is 50 % of the dead load, so:

$$P_{L,BC} = (0.5)P_{D,BC} = -10 \text{ kips (compression)}$$

Step 4 - Summarize results

The load effects in member BC of the truss are:

$P_D = 20$ kips, compression
$M_D = 0$ (no moment)
$V_D = 0$ (no shear)
$P_L = 10$ kips, compression
$M_L = 0$ (no moment)
$V_L = 0$ (no shear)

You Should Know

- What is the difference between a load and a load effect?
- Is the self-weight of a beam a load or a load effect?
- What are the three most commonly considered load effects?
- What are the standard letters for designating the load effects?
- Are the "demands on structural components" the loads or the load effects?
- What would the symbol P_W denote?

3.6 Load Factors and Combinations

To determine the maximum demands on a member, we need to sum all of the load effects. As we sum up the load effects we need to consider two things: 1. there is a possibility for overload –actual loads might exceed calculated values; and 2. all of the load effects won't be at maximum value at the same time -severe loading of one type will likely occur when other loads are at moderate or minimal levels. For example, it is unlikely that the design earthquake will occur during a severe windstorm.

In Load and Resistance Factor Design (LRFD), we account for those two things by using load factors and load combinations. The LRFD load combinations are listed on page 2-10,11 of the Manual. Each of the seven load combinations represents a "worst-case-scenario" that we consider in design.

Turn to page 2-10 of the Manual and read the section on LRFD load combinations. The factors in the load combinations are the load factors of Load and Resistance Factor Design.

- What is the load factor for the dead loads (D) in combination 1?

Load factors that are greater than 1.0 account for overload. Load factors that are less than 1.0 recognize that different loads will not likely be at maximum values simultaneously.

- In load combination 2, which loads are considered to be at overload? Which loads are considered to be at less than maximum value?

- In load combination 2, why aren't roof live loads AND rain AND snow loads considered at the same time?

In some load combinations, the live load has a load factor of 0.5. Footnote 1 states that this load factor should equal 1.0 for garages, public assembly areas, and areas where the live load is greater than 100 psf.

The load combinations in the Manual are expressed in the most general form, where D, L, and the other symbols represent the load effects. A specific form of each combination can be written for each specific load effect. For example, the specific form of load combination 2 for axial loads would be: $1.2P_D + 1.6P_L$.

Load effects that have been factored and combined are designated with the subscript U (P_U, M_U, or V_U). The ultimate demands on a member are determined from the load combination that gives the greatest demand.

Example 3.5 Using Load Combinations

Compute the ultimate demands on member BC.

From the previous example,
$P_{D,BC} = 20$ kips and
$P_{L,BC} = 10$ kips.

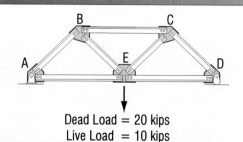

Dead Load = 20 kips
Live Load = 10 kips

Step 1 - Compute ultimate load effects from each load combination

$1.4(20 \text{ kips}) = 28 \text{ kips}$
$1.2(20 \text{ kips}) + 1.6(10 \text{ kips}) + 0.5(0) = 40 \text{ kips}$
$1.2(20 \text{ kips}) + 1.6(0) + 0.5(10 \text{ kips}) = 29 \text{ kips}$
$1.2(20 \text{ kips}) + 1.0(0) + 0.5(10 \text{ kips}) + 0.5(0) = 29 \text{ kips}$
$1.2(20 \text{ kips} + 1.0(0) + 0.5(10 \text{ kips}) + 0.2(0) = 29 \text{ kips}$
$0.9(20 \text{ kips}) + 1.0(0) = 18 \text{ kips}$
$0.9(20 \text{ kips}) + 1.0(0) = 18 \text{ kips}$

Step 2 - Identify the load combination that governs

Load combination 2 results in the greatest ultimate load so:

$P_u = \textbf{40 kips}$

When only dead and live loads are present, either load combination 1 or 2 will always govern. You may wonder why we compute the load effects for the various loads before we apply the load factors and combinations. In some situations, like the example above it might be faster to factor the loads first to determine ultimate loads, and then do the truss analysis to get the ultimate load effect. In the example above, that approach will result in a correct answer. But in some problems, you may get into trouble if you factor the loads instead of the load effects. By definition, *the load factors are for the load effects, not the loads.*

You Should Know

- Where do you look in the Manual to find load combinations?
- How can load factors account for overload?
- Do the load combinations apply to loads, or load effects?

3.7 Computing Demands in LRFD

The previous sections have discussed how to compute demands for load and resistance factor design (LRFD). The four general steps are:
1. Calculate the loads.
2. Calculate the load effects (structural analysis).
3. Combine the load effects using load factors and combinations.
4. Identify the maximum load effects.

In the chapters that follow, these steps will be applied to compute demands in tension members, columns, beams, and other structural members. More examples on computing demands that are specific to each type of structural member will be presented later.

This section has discussed member *demands*. The "bib" under the chapter name at the top of each page of this section has been labeled "demands." The next few sections of this chapter will talk about member capacities. Notice that the "bib" will change to capacities. Other than the introductory sections at the beginning of each chapter, each section will pertain to either demands, capacities, or design. The bibs will help you appreciate the context for the information you are reading.

You Should Know

- Which step in computing demands involves structural analysis?
- Which step in computing demands accounts for probability of overload?
- How is the rest of this Chapter structured?
- What do the bibs at the top of the page indicate? How many different kinds will there be?

3.8 Limit States

The previous sections have focused on computing demands using LRFD. The following sections will provide an overview on how capacities are computed using LRFD.

Structural members can fail in a variety of ways. Consider member AE of the truss shown to the right. This member will have tensile axial load effects. If the load on the truss were increased until AE failed, what would that failure look like?

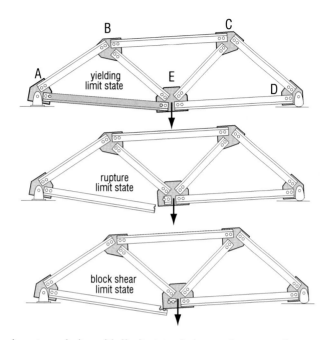

We can imagine a few possibilities. Member AE might yield causing the truss to sag (top); or member AE might fracture across a section that has been weakened by bolt holes (middle) causing the truss to collapse; or it might fracture in another mode (bottom). We call these different possible modes of failure *limit states*.

We can compare structural members to a chain, with limit states being analogous to the links. In order to find the capacity of a chain, we only need to know the capacity of the weakest link. In order to find the capacity of a member, we only need to know the capacity of the weakest limit state. However, in order to determine which limit state is the weakest, we usually need to compute the capacity for all of them.

The *nominal capacity* for each limit state is our best estimate of what the capacity would be for that limit state assuming perfect material and craftsmanship. The nominal capacity is denoted using the subscript n. For example, P_n is the nominal axial capacity for a member for a particular limit state and M_n would be the nominal moment capacity. Nominal capacities generally depend on the material and cross-sectional properties of a member.

Example 3.6 Computing Nominal Capacities for Limit States

If member AE in the truss were an L6×4×7/8, what is the nominal axial capacity for the yielding limit state (in kips)?

From Table 1-7, the cross sectional area of an L6×4×7/8 is 8.00 in.^{2}.
From Table 2-3, the standard material for angles is ASTM A36 with F_y= 36 ksi.

The cross section will yield if the axial load reaches (8.0 in.^{2})(36 ksi)= 288 kips.
The nominal capacity for the yielding limit state is P_n= **288** kips.

You Should Know

- How are structural members like chains?
- What two things do we assume to be perfect when computing nominal capacities?

3.9 Resistance Factors

We account for variability in materials and craftsmanship and for the type of failure by multiplying our nominal capacities by resistance factors. Resistance factors are denoted with the symbol ϕ. A resistance factor of 0.90 is used for limit states that involve yielding or buckling and a resistance factor of 0.75 is used for limit states that involve fracture.

The factored capacity for a limit state is equal to the nominal capacity multiplied by a resistance factor.

Example 3.7 Computing Factored Capacities for Limit States

If the nominal axial capacity of a member for the yielding limit state is 288 kips, what would be the factored capacity?

The factored capacity is obtained by multiplying the nominal capacity by the appropriate resistance factor. Since the limit state involves yielding, the resistance factor is: $\phi = 0.9$.
The factored capacity is: ϕP_n= (0.9)(288 kips)= **259** kips.

You Should Know

- What symbol is used to designate resistance factors?
- Are resistance factors applied to capacities or demands?
- What is the value of the resistance factor for limit states that involve fracture?

3.10 Governing Limit State

After the factored capacities have been determined for the pertinent limit states, they can be compared and the lowest value will be the design capacity of the member.

Example 3.8 Computing Design Capacity

The nominal capacities for a member for three limit states are:
P_n = 288 kips for yielding limit state
P_n = 325 kips for the fracture limit state
P_n = 320 kips for the block shear limit state
Which limit state governs and what is the design capacity?

Each nominal capacity must be multiplied by the pertinent resistance factor:
ϕP_n = (0.9)(287 kips) = 259 kips, for yielding limit state
ϕP_n = (0.75)(325 kips) = 244 kips, for the fracture limit state
ϕP_n = (0.75)(320 kips) = 240 kips, for the block shear limit state
Since the block shear limit state has the lowest factored capacity, it governs and the design capacity is **240** kips.

You Should Know

- If the *nominal* capacity for the yielding limit state and fracture limit state were the same, which limit state would have a lower *factored* capacity?

3.11 Allowable Stress Design (ASD)

Member design is picking economical sizes for each member so the capacities are greater than the demands.

$$\text{Demands} < \text{Capacity}$$

In LRFD, the demands are determined using load factors and load combinations, and the capacities are determined using resistance factors applied to nominal capacities.

$$\text{Demands} < \text{Capacity}$$
$$\textbf{(load factors)}\text{(service load effects)} < \textbf{(resistance factor)}\text{(nominal capacity)}$$

Most steel buildings have been designed using a different method. Prior to the 1990s, nearly all steel design was done using a method called Allowable Stress Design (ASD). ASD differs from LRFD in that the only factors in ASD are safety factors. In terms of the general formulation, ASD looks like:

$$\text{Demands} < \text{Capacity}$$
$$\text{(service load effects)} < \text{(nominal capacities)}/\textbf{(safety factor)}$$

LRFD is deemed a more rational approach since it reflects the fact that the uncertainty in capacities is different from the uncertainty in demands. The AISC Manual is designed to facilitate either method. *Build With Steel* will help you to learn LRFD. Once you know how to design with LRFD, it is easy to learn and work with ASD when necessary.

Study the Manual

Turn to page 2-11 of the Manual and read the section on Allowable Stress Design.

- How are the ASD load combinations different than the LRFD?

- How is overload accounted for in ASD?

You Should Know

- What types of factors are used in LRFD?
- What types of factors are used in ASD?
- Is it hard to learn ASD once you know LRFD?

3.12 Economical Design

Structural design is laying out a structure and picking economical sizes for each member so the capacities are greater than the demands. LRFD is an effective approach to ensuring that the design is safe, but what about economy?

To produce economical designs we must appreciate the fact that, for projects in the United States, labor costs are more than double the material costs for the steel structure. The most economical designs are *not* the ones that require the least material (use the lightest possible shapes); rather, the most economical designs are those that require the least labor (minimize fabrication and erection costs).

Example 3.9 Economical Design

What is a design principle that results in higher weight but lower overall cost?

Repeatability. Repeatability means using the same shapes throughout a project, even when they may be overly conservative in some applications. In the picture below you see sets of beams and columns that are all the same shape. In the final structure, the loads on these elements may vary dramatically and some beams and columns may be much stronger than what is really required. Repeating shapes may increase material costs, but tends to simplify fabrication and erection and results in the most economical designs.

In the following chapters, we will see how LRFD and principles of economic design are applied to various types of structural members. The general steps for designing a structural member are:

1. Compute demands.
2. Pick a shape to try, keeping in mind both capacity and economy.
3. Compute the capacity of the shape and compare with demands.
4. Finalize the design or iterate to find a better design.

In each of the following chapters you will see these four steps applied and learn how the Manual can help you to perform them quickly.

You Should Know

- Why isn't it best to minimize the weight of a steel structure?
- What are the four general steps for member design?

Remember This

- In Load and Resistance Factor Design (LRFD), demands and capacities are computed using load factors and resistance factors.
- ASCE 7 is a document that establishes minimum values for the various loads considered in design.
- The load effects we are most commonly concerned with are axial forces, bending moments, and shear forces.
- Load factors and load combinations account for the possibility of overload and reflect the fact that all load effects won't be at a maximum value simultaneously.
- Structural members can fail in a variety of ways; these different modes of failure are called limit states.
- Each limit state has a nominal capacity; resistance factors penalize the nominal capacity to account for variability in materials and craftsmanship.
- The weakest limit state is what governs the strength of a member.
- LRFD differs from ASD in that it has two types of factors - *load factors* that account for variability in demands, and *resistance factors* that account for variability in capacity; ASD has only one type of factor - safety factors.
- The most economical designs are those that minimize fabrication and erection labor costs.

The Golden Gate Bridge opened for traffic in 1937. For more than 25 years it was the longest-span bridge in the world, with a 4,200 foot main span that soars more than 200 feet above the water. The incredible tensile strength of steel is what makes this and other modern structures possible. The full potential of steel, from a material standpoint, is realized when it is used in tension members.

Trusses will have members that have only tension axial load effects.

4. Tension Members

4.1 Different Types

As discussed in the previous chapter, the most commonly considered load effects in structural members are axial forces, bending moments, and shear forces. In some structural members, the bending moments and shear forces are small enough to be negligible, and the axial forces are in tension. We refer to such members as *tension members*.

Most structures will have tension members of one kind or another. Examples include: hangers, truss members, braces in frames, and braces in diaphragms.

Example 4.1 Hangers

Hangers are used to suspend objects from structural floors or roofs. The picture shows a catwalk that is suspended from the roof of a field house. The vertical elements (one is indicated by the arrow) will have tension load effects resulting from the weight of the catwalk and people that may be on it. In this case, structural tees were used for the tension members.

Example 4.2 Truss Members

Trusses will have both tension and compression members. For simply-supported trusses with uniform downward loads, the bottom chord members will be in tension. When possible, the diagonal members are oriented purposefully so that they will be in tension. Consider the two trusses shown below. The truss on the left would have diagonal members in compression, while the truss on the right would have diagonal members in tension. The configuration on the right would be preferred (for the loading shown).

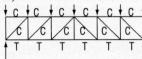
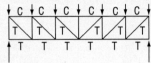

Freeway sign structures are purposefully designed to have diagonal members in tension. In the picture to the left, notice how the diagonal members are oriented down towards the center such that they will all be tension members.

Example 4.3 Braces in Frames

Braces in frames resist lateral loads from wind or earthquakes. The direction of these loads may alternate, so braces will sometimes be in compression and sometimes be in tension.

For relatively light loads, angles, HSS and pipe shapes are used for braces. For heavier loads, wide flange shapes may be used.

Example 4.4 Braces in Diaphragms

Tensioned cables or light angles may be used to brace roof diaphragms. These members are used in an x-configuration, so that one member will always be in tension, regardless of the direction of loading.

4.2 Computing Demands with Tributary Areas

Now that we know where tension members are found, let's discuss how tension member demands are computed. In the previous chapter, an approach was outlined for computing demands:

1. Calculate the loads.
2. Calculate the load effects (structural analysis).
3. Combine the load effects using load factors and load combinations.
4. Identify the maximum load effects.

When the loads are uniform, the concept of *tributary area* can be used for the structural analysis. The following examples explain tributary areas and how they are used when computing demands.

Example 4.5 Calculating Demands on a Hanger

A catwalk is to be designed for a uniform dead load of 10 psf and a uniform live load of 20 psf. Calculate the demands on one of the hangers.

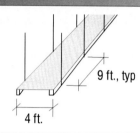

9 ft., typ

4 ft.

Step 1 - Calculate the loads
In this example the loads were given as: Dead=10 psf and Live=20 psf.

Step 2 - Calculate the load effects

2a - Calculate the tributary area for one hanger
In this problem, the loads are uniform, so tributary areas can be used for the structural analysis. The tributary areas for each hanger can be determined by drawing lines halfway between the hangers, in both directions (see the dashed lines in the figure to the right). These lines are the boundaries for the tributary areas for each hanger. Since the hangers are equally spaced, they will each have the same tributary area.

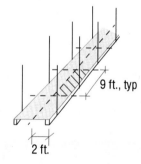

9 ft., typ

2 ft.

$$A_t = (2 \text{ ft})(9 \text{ ft}) = 18 \text{ ft}^2$$

2b - Get the load effects
The loads were given as: D=10 psf and L=20 psf. The axial load *effects* in the hanger can be computed as the loads multiplied by the tributary area:

$$P_D = (10 \text{ psf})(18 \text{ ft}^2) = 180 \text{ lbs}$$
$$P_L = (20 \text{ psf})(18 \text{ ft}^2) = 360 \text{ lbs}$$

Step 3 - Factor the load effects
Since only dead and live loads are present, load combination 1 or 2 will govern.

$$P_u = 1.4 P_D = 1.4(180 \text{ lbs}) = 252 \text{ lbs (Combo 1)}$$
$$P_u = 1.2 P_D + 1.6 P_L = 1.2(180 \text{ lbs}) + 1.6(360 \text{ lbs}) = 792 \text{ lbs (Combo 2)}$$

Step 4 - Identify the maximum load effect
Load combination 2 will govern because it gives the highest factored axial force.

$$P_u = \mathbf{792} \text{ lbs}$$

Example 4.6 Computing Demands in a Truss Member

The roof of a warehouse is supported by trusses that span 80 ft and are spaced 15 ft on center. The roof framing (represented by the grey plane) is such that the roof is only supported at the truss nodes. If the roof has a uniform dead load of 42 psf and a uniform live load of 20 psf, compute the factored demand on truss member AB.

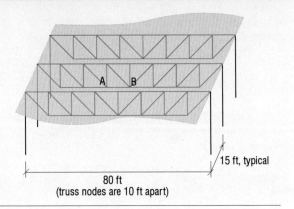

80 ft
(truss nodes are 10 ft apart)

15 ft, typical

Step 1 - Calculate the loads

In this example the loads were given as: Dead=42 psf and Live=20 psf.

Step 2 - Calculate the load effects

2a - Calculate the tributary areas for truss point loads

Tributary areas can be used to determine the magnitude of the load placed on the truss at each node. The tributary areas are determined by drawing lines midway between the nodes in both directions. The tributary area for an interior and edge node ($A_{t,i}$ and $A_{t,e}$) are illustrated to the right. Note that the tributary areas for all the nodes of all the trusses will add up to the total roof area.

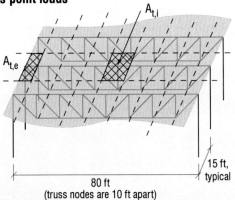

80 ft
(truss nodes are 10 ft apart)

15 ft, typical

The tributary areas for the internal and edge nodes are:

$$A_{t,i} = (10 \text{ ft})(15 \text{ ft}) = 150 \text{ ft}^2$$
$$A_{t,e} = (5 \text{ ft})(15 \text{ ft}) = 75 \text{ ft}^2$$

2b - Compute nodal loads based on tributary areas

The loads on the truss nodes can be determined by multiplying the uniform dead and live loads (which have units of psf) by the tributary areas (which have units of ft^2). The dead and live loads at each node are calculated as:

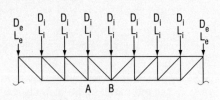

$$D_i = (42 \text{ psf})(150 \text{ ft}^2) = 6300 \text{ lbs} = 6.3 \text{ kips}$$
$$L_i = (20 \text{ psf})(150 \text{ ft}^2) = 3.0 \text{ kips}$$
$$D_e = (42 \text{ psf})(75 \text{ ft}^2) = 3.15 \text{ kips}$$
$$L_e = (20 \text{ psf})(75 \text{ ft}^2) = 1.5 \text{ kips}$$

It is customary to do the conversion from lbs to kips without explicitly stating it, as shown in the previous three equations.

Example Continued

2c - Get the dead load effects in member AB

The dead load effects in member AB can be determined by analyzing the truss under the dead loads only.

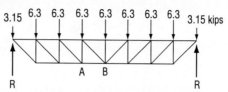

Recognizing symmetry, the support reactions can be computed by summing forces in the y-direction:

$$2R = 2(3.15 \text{ kips}) + 7(6.3 \text{ kips})$$
$$R = 25.2 \text{ kips}$$

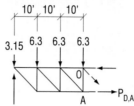

The method of sections is the fastest way to get the axial force in member AB. Cutting the truss as shown and summing moments about point O:

$$-(25.2 \text{ kips})(30 \text{ ft}) + (3.15 \text{ kips})(30 \text{ ft}) + (6.3 \text{ kips})(10 \text{ ft})$$
$$+ (6.3 \text{ kips})(20 \text{ ft}) + P_{D,AB}(10 \text{ ft}) = 0$$

$$P_{D,AB} = 47.3 \text{ kips (tension)}$$

2d - Get the live load effects in member AB

Step 2c could be repeated, but using the live loads instead of the dead; however, since the dead and live loads have the same proportions at all the nodes, it is easier to calculate $P_{L,AB}$ by using the ratio of live to dead loads:

$$P_{L,AB} = P_{D,AB}\frac{L}{D} = (47.3 \text{ kips})\frac{20 \text{ psf}}{42 \text{ psf}} = 22.5 \text{ kips}$$

Step 3 and 4 - Factor the load effects and identify the ultimate demand in AB

Since only dead and live loads are applied, load combination 1 or 2 will govern. Since the dead load is not more than eight times the live load, load combination 2 governs.

$$P_{u,AB} = 1.2P_{D,AB} + 1.6P_{L,AB} = 1.2(47.3 \text{ kips}) + 1.6(22.5 \text{ kips}) = \mathbf{93} \text{ kips}$$

Note that the ultimate demand can only be calculated to two significant figures because the loads were only given to two significant figures.

You Should Know

- When can tributary areas be used for computing demands?
- What are the steps for computing factored demands in tension members?
- If supports for a suspended ceiling were located every 4 ft in both directions, what is the tributary area for one support?
- If the ceiling weighs 4 psf, what is the factored tension demand in each support?

4.3 Limit States

The first step in computing the capacity of a tension member is to identify different ways it might fail. Three limit states that should be considered are:
1. Yielding in the gross section [also called the yielding limit state (YLS)]
2. Rupture in the net section [also called the fracture limit state (FLS)]
3. Block shear failure

These three limit states were illustrated for a truss member in the previous chapter. The Specification explains how the capacity of each of these limit states should be calculated. Yielding in the gross section and rupture in the net section are discussed in the Specification Chapter D while the block shear failure mode is discussed in the Specification Chapter J.

·yielding in gross section
·net section rupture
·block shear

You Should Know

- What are the three limit states that should be considered when computing tension member capacities?

4.4 Yielding

Imagine a steel bar that is subjected to increasing loads. While the bar remains elastic [(a) through (c)] the deformations are small because steel is so stiff (E=29,000 ksi). But when the material yields the stiffness is lost and the bar elongates dramatically without any increase in load. Eventually strain hardening occurs, but not until the bar is almost 10% longer than it was originally [case (d)].

If this bar were part of a structural system, the elongation associated with yielding might render the structure unusable.

The yielding limit state is called a ductile failure mode because there are large deformations before the strength is lost.

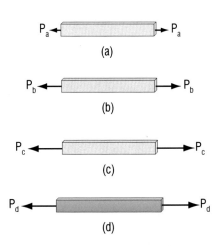

Study the Manual

Turn to Chapter D of the Specification (page 16.1-26).

Chapter D is all about computing the capacity of tension members. Section D1 talks about slenderness, which is a topic we'll return to when we discuss design. Section D2 includes the equations for computing the yielding limit state.

- What is the equation for the nominal capacity, P_n, for tensile yielding in the gross section?

- How would you get a value for A_g? (Read §D3.1 on page 16.1-27).

The φ factor has a subscript "t" to remind you that you are computing a tension capacity.

- What is the value of the φ factor for yielding in the gross section?

The equation for the capacity of yielding in the gross section is simply saying that a member will yield when the stress over the entire cross section is equal to F_y.

Example 4.7 Computing the Factored Capacity for Yielding Limit State

Compute the factored capacity of an L6×4×7/8 for yielding in the gross section.

Step 1 - Look up the necessary information

In order to compute yielding in the gross section you need to know the material yield stress, F_y, and the gross cross-sectional area, A_g. The typical material for angles is A36 steel with an F_y of 36 ksi (see Table 2-4). An $L6 \times 4 \times 7/8$ has a cross-sectional area of 8.00 in^2 (see Table 1-7).

Step 2 - Compute the factored capacity

Now we just plug in what we know:

$$\phi_t P_n = \phi_t F_y A_g$$
$$\phi_t P_n = (0.9)(36 \text{ ksi})(8.00 \text{ in}^2) = \textbf{259} \text{ kips}$$

The capacity for standard shapes for yielding in the gross section is tabulated in Tables 5-1 through 5-8. Looking up the capacity is typically faster than performing the calculation.

Example 4.8 Looking Up the Capacity for Yielding In the Gross Section

Determine the factored capacity of an L6×4×7/8 for yielding in the gross section.

Turn to Table 5-2 in the Manual. The table has several columns. On the left is a column with the shape designation. Towards the middle is a column labeled "Yielding" with a right subcolumn labeled "$\phi_t P_n$". This is the column that lists the factored capacity for yielding in the gross section.

The value listed for L6x4x7/8 is **259** kips, which is the same as the value calculated in the previous example.

Example 4.9 Visualizing Yielding in the Gross Cross Section

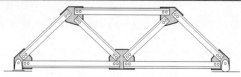

What would it look like if one of the bottom chord members yielded in the gross section? Would it be a catastrophic failure?

If a bottom chord member yielded, it would elongate and then begin to strain harden. It would not completely fail unless a greater load were applied, but the truss wouldn't look good (or safe) anymore. That is why yielding in the gross section is unacceptable.

elongation of the member might cause it to become unstable

4.5 Rupture of the Net Section

Each end of a tension member will be connected to something else. In these connection regions, stresses get concentrated in certain parts of the cross section. It is possible for tension members to fracture at the connection at loads that are lower than what would yield the gross section. This type of failure is called rupture of the net section.

Two things that cause stress concentrations in connections are bolt holes and shear lag. Bolt holes will be discussed first.

Consider a bar that is bolted and subjected to increasing axial load (a). At some load, the bar will begin to yield through a section at the leading bolt (b). The cross section is reduced at this location because of the bolt hole and is called the net section.

As the load increases, the yielding will spread across the net section (c). This yielding at the net section will always happen prior to yielding of the gross section but is not a problem. Since the yielding is confined to a small area, there is no excessive member elongation. The material in the region will simply strain harden and continue to hold the load (c).

If the load is increased further, one of two things will occur. Either the gross section will yield (as was discussed in the previous pages) or the material in the net section will reach F_u and fracture will occur (d). The fracture is called rupture of the net section.

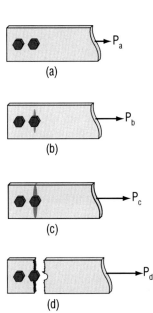

(a)

(b)

(c)

(d)

Example 4.10 Visualizing Rupture of the Net Section (Fracture Limit State)

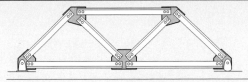

What would it look like if one of the bottom chord members ruptured in the net section? Would it be a catastrophic failure?

If a bottom chord member ruptured in the net section, the truss would look like the figure on the right. The truss would lose strength and fail catastrophically.

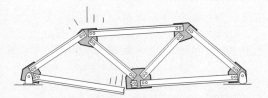

Study the Manual

Turn to page 16.1-26 of the Specification. At the bottom of the page you'll find the equation for computing the capacity for tensile rupture in the net section.

- What is the equation for the nominal capacity, P_n, for tensile rupture in the net section?

- How is this equation similar to the equation for yielding in the gross section?

The effective net area, A_e, accounts for stress concentrations caused by bolts and shear lag. We will learn how to compute A_e in the following sections.

The ϕ factor for rupture of the net section is lower than the ϕ factor for yielding in the gross section, partly to reflect that rupture is a more catastrophic failure mode.

- What is the value for the ϕ factor for tensile rupture in the net section?

You Should Know

- What two things cause stresses to be higher in connection regions?
- Why is it okay if the member yields near the bolt holes but not okay for a member to yield in the gross section?
- How do our calculations reflect that rupture of the net section is more catastrophic than yielding of the gross section?

4.6 Net Area

The first step in computing the effective net area, A_e, is to compute the net area, A_n. Look at the figure to the right. Two cross sections are shown, one in the body of the member and one through the leading bolt. The cross section through the leading bolt is where rupture may occur. The area of this section is called the net area, A_n, and is equal to the gross area, A_g, minus the bolt hole area. In cross section view, the bolt hole area is a rectangle not a circle!

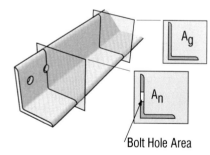
Bolt Hole Area

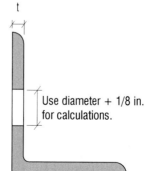
Use diameter + 1/8 in. for calculations.

For a bolt with diameter ϕ, the bolt hole area is computed as the thickness, t, multiplied by $\phi + 1/8$ in. The extra 1/8 in. accounts for two things. First, standard bolt holes are 1/16 in. bigger than the bolt diameter so the bolt will actually fit through the hole. In other words, the nominal hole diameter is 1/16 in. bigger than the bolt. Second, we consider another 1/16 in. of material to be damaged by the hole-making process (see B4.3b of the Specification).

Example 4.11 Computing the Net Area

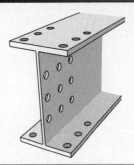

What is the net area for the W14×53 with 1 in. diameter bolts as shown?

Step 1 - Sketch the net area

Before the net area can be computed it must be visualized. Imagine a plane that passes through the leading line of bolts. If we sketch the section that results from cutting the member through this plane we can see there are four holes in the flanges and three holes in the web.

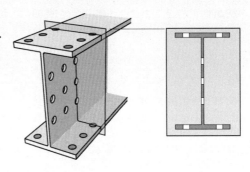

Step 2 - Look up the pertinent information

Look up properties for the W14×53 in Table 1-1. The needed properties are the gross area, the flange thickness, and the web thickness.

$A_g = 15.6 \text{ in.}^2$
$t_f = 0.660 \text{ in.}$
$t_w = 0.370 \text{ in.}$

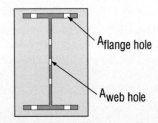

Step 3 - Calculate the hole areas

Calculate the areas of the holes in the flanges and the web by multiplying the material thickness by the effective hole diameter.

$A_{flange\ hole} = (0.660 \text{ in.})(1 \text{ in.} + \frac{1}{8} \text{ in.}) = 0.743 \text{ in.}^2$
$A_{web\ hole} = (0.370 \text{ in.})(1 \text{ in.} + \frac{1}{8} \text{ in.}) = 0.416 \text{ in.}^2$

Step 4 - Calculate the Net Area

Calculate the net area by subtracting the hole areas from the gross area.

$A_n = A_g - 4(A_{flange\ hole}) - 3(A_{web\ hole})$
$A_n = (15.6 \text{ in.}^2) - 4(0.743 \text{ in.}^2) - 3(0.416 \text{ in.}^2) = \textbf{11.4 in.}^2$

Final Note

With practice, all four steps can be combined into a single calculation.

$A_n = (15.6 \text{ in.}^2) - (1 \text{ in.} + \frac{1}{8} \text{ in.})[4(0.660 \text{ in.}) + 3(0.370 \text{ in.})] = \textbf{11.4 in.}^2$

4.7 Staggered Holes

When a member has multiple rows of bolts at the connection, these bolts can either be aligned or staggered. For both cases, the lines the bolts are positioned along are called gage lines. Dimensions that have to do with gage lines are usually designated with g. When the bolts are staggered, the longitudinal distance between any two consecutive bolts is called the pitch and designated s.

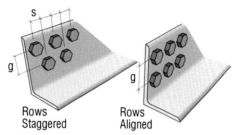

Rows
Staggered

Rows
Aligned

Study the Manual

For some shapes, standard gage lines have been established. Turn to page 1-48 of the Manual. At the bottom of the page you'll find a table that is titled *Workable Gages in Angle Legs*.

The figure on the left of the table, is the key for understanding the table. From the figure, the term g is the distance from the heel to the gage line if only one row of bolts is used. If an angle has a 7 in. leg and only one row of bolts, the gage line for the bolts would be located 4 in. from the heel.

- For an angle leg that is 5 in. and has one row of bolts, where is the gage line located?

Angle legs that are 5 in. or wider may have enough room for two rows of bolts. When two rows are used the figure indicates that one line is located a distance g_1 from the heel, and the other line is g_2 further.

- For an angle leg that is 7 in. and has two rows of bolts, where are the gage lines located?

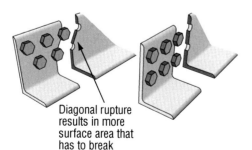

Diagonal rupture results in more surface area that has to break

When a rupture mode includes diagonal lines between holes it has more rupture area than if the lines between holes were vertical. In computing the net area for this mode we still use the gross area and hole areas but add in a bonus that accounts for the beneficial effects of the diagonal.

The equation for computing the net area for modes that include diagonal rupture lines is:

$$A_n = A_g - A_{holes} + Diagonal\ Bonus$$

For the equation above, the diagonal bonus has units of area and is equal to $(s^2/4g)t$ for each diagonal line, where s and g are the pitch and gage, and t is the thickness of the material. The following examples demonstrate how to use this equation to compute the net area for angles with staggered holes.

Example 4.12 Computing the Net Area with Staggered Holes

What is the net area for the L8×4×5/8 with 0.75 in. diameter bolts as shown?

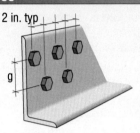

2 in. typ

g

Step 1 - Visualize the possible rupture modes
Before the net area can be calculated, the potential rupture modes must be visualized. One mode is rupture through the leading bolt hole. Another mode is rupture through the leading bolts of both rows. Both modes should be considered; the mode with the least net area will govern.

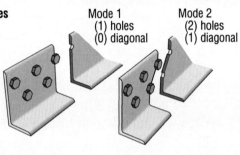

Mode 1
(1) holes
(0) diagonal

Mode 2
(2) holes
(1) diagonal

Step 2 - Look up pertinent information
Look up properties for the L8×4×5/8 in Table 1-7. The needed properties are the gross area and the distance between the bolt lines. The angle thickness is known to be 5/8 in. from the name of the shape.
$$A_g = 7.16\ \text{in.}^2$$
g (distance between bolt lines) $= g_2$(from page 1-46) $= 3$ in.

Step 3 - Calculate the hole area
$$A_{leg\ hole} = (0.625\ \text{in.})(0.75\ \text{in.} + \tfrac{1}{8}\ \text{in.}) = 0.547\ \text{in.}^2$$

Step 4 - Calculate the diagonal bonus
$$Bonus = \frac{s^2}{4g}t$$
$$Bonus = \frac{(2\ \text{in.})^2}{4(3\ \text{in.})}(0.625\ \text{in.}) = 0.208\ \text{in.}^2$$

Step 5 - Compute Net Area for each mode
$$A_{n,1} = (7.16\ \text{in.}^2) - 1(0.547\ \text{in.}^2) = 6.61\ \text{in.}^2$$
$$A_{n,2} = (7.16\ \text{in.}^2) - 2(0.547\ \text{in.}^2) + (0.208\ \text{in.}^2) = 6.27\ \text{in.}^2$$
Mode 2 governs:
$$A_n = 6.27\ \text{in.}^2$$

Final Note
Usually the diagonal bonus(es) are less than the area of a hole, and the mode of failure with the most holes will govern.

Example 4.13 Computing the Net Area with Staggered Holes in Two Legs

What is the net area for the L8×4×5/8 with 0.75 in. diameter bolts as shown?

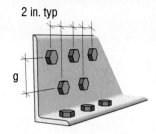

2 in. typ

g

Step 1 - Visualize the possible rupture modes

Before the net area can be calculated, the rupture mode must be visualized. The rupture mode that includes all the leading bolts will govern as discussed at the end of the previous example. This rupture mode includes two diagonals.

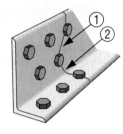

Step 2 - Get gross area and the distance between the bolt lines

Look up gross area for the L8×4×5/8 in Table 1-7.

$$A_g = 7.16 \text{ in.}^2$$

The locations of the gage lines can be looked up on pg. 1-48 of the Manual. Note that the bolt lines for the 8 in. leg are read from a different column in the table than the bolt line for the 4 in. leg. The figure to the right indicates the bolt line locations.

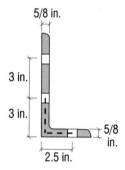

5/8 in.

3 in.

3 in.

5/8 in.

2.5 in.

To compute the diagonal bonuses, the transverse distances between the bolt lines are required. The transverse distance for diagonal 1 is simply:

$$g_{d1} = 3 \text{ in.}$$

The transverse distance for diagonal 2 is more difficult since it is part in one leg and part in another. The total transverse distance is the sum of the lengths of the dashed lines in the figure.

$$g_{d2} = (3 \text{ in.} - (\tfrac{1}{2})\tfrac{5}{8} \text{ in.}) + (2.5 \text{ in.} - (\tfrac{1}{2})\tfrac{5}{8} \text{ in.}) = 4.875 \text{ in.}$$

Step 3 - Calculate the hole area
$$A_h = (0.625 \text{ in.})(0.75 \text{ in.} + \tfrac{1}{8} \text{ in.}) = 0.547 \text{ in.}^2$$

Step 4 - Calculate the diagonal bonuses
$$Bonus\ 1 = \frac{s^2}{4g_{d1}}t = \frac{(2 \text{ in.})^2}{4(3 \text{ in.})}(0.625 \text{ in.}) = 0.208 \text{ in.}^2$$

$$Bonus\ 2 = \frac{s^2}{4g_{d2}}t = \frac{(2 \text{ in.})^2}{4(4.875 \text{ in.})}(0.625 \text{ in.}) = 0.128 \text{ in.}^2$$

Step 5 - Compute the Net Area
$$A_n = (7.16 \text{ in.}^2) - 3(0.547 \text{ in.}^2) + (0.208 \text{ in.}^2) + (0.128 \text{ in.}^2) = \mathbf{5.86} \text{ in.}^2$$

The Manual explains the net area and diagonal bonus in a slightly different way than what has been demonstrated in the previous examples.

Study the Manual

Turn to page 16.1-18 of the Specification. Read the first paragraph of §B4.3b.

The Manual explains net area as the product of a net width multiplied by a thickness. This approach is useful when computing the net area of bars and plates because the thickness is constant. But net width becomes cumbersome when working with rolled shapes because the thickness is different for different elements (for example flanges and webs); also, working with net width cannot account for the area of the fillets that are between the elements of a cross section.

Read the second paragraph of §B4.3b. The 1/16 in. mentioned here is in addition to the 1/16 in. difference between the bolt size and the nominal dimension of a standard hole. That is why we use 1/8 in. plus the bolt diameter to get the width of a hole.

Read the rest of Section §B4.3b.

- What is the difference between how the diagonal bonus is explained here and how it was applied in the previous two examples?

the diagonal bonus [added] to the An will lead to an increase to rupture capacity

You Should Know

- Why do staggered holes increase a section's rupture resistance?
- How is the beneficial effect of staggered holes applied in computing the net area?
- Where do you look in the Manual to find the standard gage lines for angles?

4.8 Shear Lag

In addition to bolt holes, there is a phenomenon called shear lag that causes stress concentrations in certain connections. Shear lag occurs when only some of the elements of a cross section are connected. For example, consider a channel. The cross section of a channel has three elements: the top flange, the web, and the bottom flange. However, when channels are used as tension members, only the web (one element of the cross section) is attached at the connection.

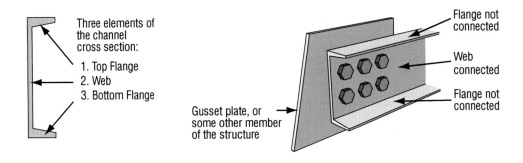

Three elements of the channel cross section:

1. Top Flange
2. Web
3. Bottom Flange

Gusset plate, or some other member of the structure

Flange not connected

Web connected

Flange not connected

When only one element of the cross section is connected, the force "flows" to that part of the cross section because that is the only way it can "get out" at the connection. Consider the channel again. Away from the connection (Section A), the stresses over the cross section will be uniform. But at a section near the leading lines of bolts (Section B), the stresses will increase in the web and decrease in the flanges. The force "flows" to the web because it needs to "get out" through the bolts. As a result, the flanges at the connection are somewhat ineffective. The flow of force to the connected element of the cross section is called *shear lag*. Shear lag makes it so only part of the cross section is effective.

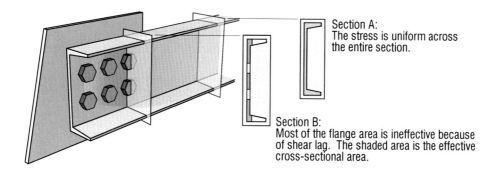

Section A:
The stress is uniform across the entire section.

Section B:
Most of the flange area is ineffective because of shear lag. The shaded area is the effective cross-sectional area.

There are two parameters that influence how much of the cross section is effective: connection length, and connection eccentricity. The figures below compare an angle connected through one leg when these parameters are adjusted.

The connection eccentricity, x-bar, is defined as the distance from the centroid of the cross section to the connected edge. When the eccentricity is small (right figure) that means that the unconnected element has relatively little area; this means there will be less shear lag and more effective area at the leading line of bolts.

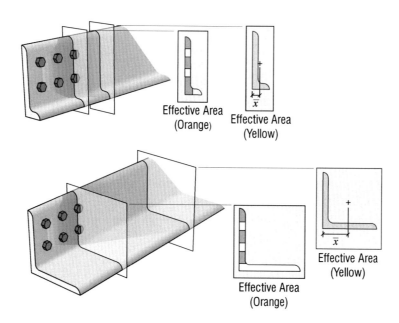

Effective Area
(Orange)

Effective Area
(Yellow)

Effective Area
(Orange)

Effective Area
(Yellow)

The connection length *l* is defined as the distance from the center of the leading bolt to the center of the trailing bolt. When *l* is large, the force has more length to flow into the connection, resulting in less shear lag and more effective area at the leading line of bolts.

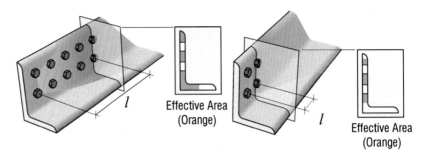

Effective Area
(Orange)

Effective Area
(Orange)

Study the Manual

Turn to §D3. (page 16.1-27) in the Specification and read it.
- What is the equation for the effective net area, A_e?

- Which table is used to determine the shear lag factor, U?

Turn to Table D3.1 (next page). The shear lag factor, U, is computed differently depending on the situation. There are 8 different cases that are covered in the table.
- When does Case 1 apply?

- What does it mean when $U=1.0$?

Case 2 applies to angles, wide flanges, and channels.
- What is U a function of in Case 2?

- How is *l* defined? (see the bottom of the table)

The distance x-bar is always a centroidal distance. The figure for Case 2 illustrates which centroidal distance is pertinent in various cases. For example, for a wide flange connected in the web, the centroidal distance, x-bar, is the distance from the centroid of half of the cross section (dividing the WF down the middle of the web) to the center of the web.

Computing x-bar as illustrated in the table can be tedious for cases where it can't just be looked up. As an alternative, Cases 7 and 8 can be used to more quickly compute U for wide flanges and angles. Cases 7 and 8 will give similar or lower values for U than what would be computed using Case 2.

Cases 3 through 6 are for situations where members are welded rather than bolted at the connection.
- Which cases apply to hollow sections welded to gusset plates?

The following examples will demonstrate how to use Table D3.1 to compute the shear lag factor, U, and the effective net area, A_e, for various situations.

Example 4.14 Computing the Shear Lag Factor When All Elements Connected

What is the shear lag factor for the L8×4×5/8 connected as shown?

The cross section of an angle has two elements (two legs). Since there are bolts in both legs at the connection, both elements of the cross section are considered to transmit loads. Case 1 applies; the shear lag factor, U, is equal to 1.0. This means there is no shear lag, and all of the net area is effective.

Example 4.15 Computing the Shear Lag Factor for a Channel

What is the shear lag factor for the C10×30 connected as shown?

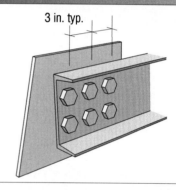

3 in. typ.

Step 1 - Identify which case of Table D3.1 applies

Since the channel is connected through the web only, Case 2 applies.

Step 2 - Get the connection length and eccentricity

The connection length is the distance from the first to last bolt. Since the bolts are 3 in. apart:

$$l = (2)(3 \text{ in.}) = 6 \text{ in.}$$

The connection eccentricity will be the distance from the centroid of the channel to the far edge of the web. This distance can be looked up for a C10×30 in Table 1-5.

$$\bar{x} = 0.649 \text{ in.}$$

Step 3 - Compute U

$$U = 1 - \frac{\bar{x}}{l} = 1 - \frac{0.649 \text{ in.}}{6 \text{ in.}} = \mathbf{0.891}$$

Final Note

The answer means that 89% of the net area will be effective. A longer connection would have resulted in a higher value for U and a greater effective net area.

Example 4.16 Computing the Shear Lag Factor for an Angle

What is the shear lag factor for the L8×4×5/8 connected as shown?

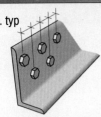

2 in. typ

Step 1 - Identify which cases of Table D3.1 apply

For angles connected through one leg, Case 2 applies. Since this angle has four or more fasteners in the line Case 8 may also be used. Case 2 will take longer to calculate but will give a more precise value for U. Case 8 is quick and will give a conservative answer.

Step 2 - Get the connection length and eccentricity

The connection length is the distance from the first to last bolt. Since the bolts are 2.0 in. apart:

$$l = (4)(2.0 \text{ in.}) = 8.0 \text{ in.}$$

The connection eccentricity will be the distance from the centroid of the angle to the far edge of the attached leg. This distance can be looked up for a L8×4×5/8 in Table 1-7.

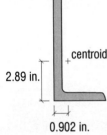

2.89 in.

centroid

0.902 in.

$$\bar{x} = 0.902 \text{ in.}$$

Step 3 - Compute U using Case 2

$$U = 1 - \frac{\bar{x}}{l} = 1 - \frac{0.902 \text{ in.}}{8.0 \text{ in.}} = \mathbf{0.887}$$

Step 4 - Get U using Case 8

$$U = \mathbf{0.80}$$

Final Note

In this example U was computed twice using Case 2 and Case 8. In practice either is acceptable and only one needs to be determined. Case 8 is faster but is more conservative than Case 2.

What if the short leg had been the one connected rather than the long one?

If the short leg were connected rather than the long leg, the calculation using Case 2 would be different. The value for $\bar{x}$ would be the distance from the centroid to the edge of the **short** leg rather than the distance to the long one. This distance can be looked up in Table 1-7, but it may be a little confusing because it is designated $\bar{y}$ in the Table.

$$\bar{x} \text{ (for calculating } U\text{)} = \bar{y} \text{ (from Table 1-7)} = 2.89 \text{ in.}$$
$$U = 1 - \frac{\bar{x}}{l} = 1 - \frac{2.89 \text{ in.}}{8.0 \text{ in.}} = \mathbf{0.639}$$

From this result, the shear lag is much worse when the short leg is attached. In general, when angles with unequal legs are used they are oriented so the longer of the two legs will be attached at the connection. It is inappropriate to use Case 8 if the angle is connected through the short leg.

Example 4.17 Computing the Shear Lag Factor for WF Connected in Web

Compute the shear lag factor for a W14×90
tension member that is attached through the
web only with the connection detail shown.

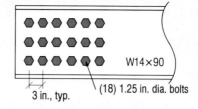

W14×90

(18) 1.25 in. dia. bolts

3 in., typ.

Step 1 - Identify which cases of Table D3.1 apply

For a wide flange connected through the web only, Case 2 or Case 7 may be
used. Both calculations will be done in this example to show the difference.

Step 2 - Get the connection length and eccentricity

The connection length is the distance from the first to last bolt. Since the bolts
are 3 in. apart and there are five spaces:

$$l = (5)(3 \text{ in.}) = 15 \text{ in.}$$

The connection eccentricity, $\bar{x}$, for this case is illustrated in the example
column of Table D3.1. The eccentricity is defined as the distance from the
center of the web to the centroid of half the area (dividing the W14×90 down
the center of the web). This distance is not tabulated in the Manual, and needs
to be computed. The procedure for computing the centroid of a composite
area is covered in Statics.

$$\bar{x} = \frac{A_1 \bar{x}_1 + A_2 \bar{x}_2 + A_3 \bar{x}_3}{A_1 + A_2 + A_3}$$

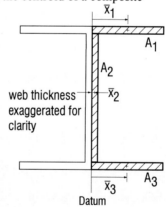

$\bar{x}_1$

A_1

A_2

web thickness
exaggerated for
clarity

$\bar{x}_2$

$\bar{x}_3$ A_3

Datum

The following properties from
Table 1-1 are needed to compute the
areas and centroidal distances:

$b_f = 14.5$ in.
$t_f = 0.710$ in.
$d = 14.0$ in.
$t_w = 0.440$ in.

Now doing the calculations:

$$A_1 = \frac{b_f}{2} t_f = \frac{14.5 \text{ in.}}{2}(0.710 \text{ in.}) = 5.148 \text{ in.}^2$$

$$\bar{x}_1 = \frac{1}{2}\frac{b_f}{2} = \frac{14.5 \text{ in.}}{4} = 3.625 \text{ in.}$$

$$A_2 = \frac{t_w}{2}(d - 2t_f) = \frac{0.440 \text{ in.}}{2}(14.0 \text{ in.} - 2(0.710 \text{ in.})) = 2.768 \text{ in.}^2$$

$$\bar{x}_2 = \frac{1}{2}\frac{t_w}{2} = \frac{0.440 \text{ in.}}{4} = 0.11 \text{ in.}$$

$A_3 = A_1$ and $\bar{x}_3 = \bar{x}_1$

$$\bar{x} = \frac{(5.148 \text{ in.}^2)(3.625 \text{ in.}) + (2.768 \text{ in.}^2)(0.11 \text{ in.}) + (5.148 \text{ in.}^2)(3.625 \text{ in.})}{(5.148 \text{ in.}^2 + 2.768 \text{ in.}^2 + 5.148 \text{ in.}^2)}$$

$$\bar{x} = 2.88 \text{ in.}$$

continued on next page

Example Continued

Step 3 - Compute U using Case 2

$$U = 1 - \frac{\bar{x}}{l} = 1 - \frac{2.88 \text{ in.}}{15 \text{ in.}} = \mathbf{0.810}$$

Step 4 - Get U using Case 7

Case 7 has several sub-cases for different types of connections. For the case of the web being connected with 4 or more fasteners:

$$U = \mathbf{0.70}$$

Final Note

In this example U was computed twice using Case 2 and Case 7. In practice, either is acceptable and only one need be determined. Case 7 is faster, but is more conservative compared to Case 2.

What if the wide flange had been connected in the flanges only rather than the web?

If the flanges were connected, rather than the web, the calculations for Case 2 and 7 would be different. From the picture in Table D3.1, the value for $\bar{x}$ would be the distance from the outside edge of the flange to the centroid of half the cross section (dividing the WF into a top and bottom half). It is easy to obtain the value for $\bar{x}$ in this case because it is tabulated in the Manual in Table 1-8. If a W14×90 is cut into top and bottom halves, each half is a WT7×45. From Table 1-8, the distance from the centroid of a WT7×45 to the edge of the flange is:

$\bar{x} = 1.09$ in. (note that this dimension is called $\bar{y}$ in the table)

$$U = 1 - \frac{\bar{x}}{l} = 1 - \frac{1.09 \text{ in.}}{15 \text{ in.}} = \mathbf{0.927}$$

In general, the shear lag is less when the flanges are connected. This is reflected in Case 7 where the values for U are higher when the flanges are connected. For the W14×90, Case 7 gives a shear lag factor of $U = 0.9$ since the flange is wider than two thirds of the depth.

The preceding examples have demonstrated how Table D3.1 can be used to compute shear lag factors for channels, angles, and wide flanges. Computing shear lag factors for plates and HSS shapes using Cases 4 through 6 is straightforward but will not be demonstrated here.

You Should Know

- What are the elements of a cross section?
- When will shear lag occur?
- Will a longer connection increase or decrease shear lag?
- Will a greater connection eccentricity increase or decrease shear lag?
- Which table in the Manual shows how the shear lag factor, U, is calculated?
- If you want to minimize shear lag, which leg of an unequal angle should you connect?
- In design, do you have to compute shear lag factors using multiple cases?

4.9 Effective Net Area

The effective net area, A_e, is defined as the net area, A_n, multiplied by the shear lag factor, U (see Eqn. D3-1). Sections 4.6 and 4.7 of this book have discussed how to compute A_n. Section 4.8 explained how the shear lag factor U is computed.

Once the effective net area is known, it is easy to determine the capacity for tensile rupture of the net section using Eqn. D2-2.

Example 4.18 Computing the Capacity for Tensile Rupture of the Net Section

Compute the capacity for tensile rupture on the net section for the L8×4×5/8 angle with 0.75 in. dia. bolts.

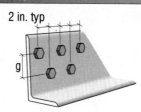

Step 1 - Visualize the failure mode

Tensile rupture will occur through the leading line of bolts. This is where the stresses are highest because material has been removed for the bolt holes, and shear lag is making some of the other material ineffective.

Step 2 - Calculate the Net Area

The net area was computed for this connection in Example 4.12. Recall that the net area was calculated by starting with the gross area, subtracting out the bolt hole areas, and then adding a bonus because there is a diagonal on the fracture path.

$$A_n = (7.16 \text{ in.}^2) - 2(0.547 \text{ in.}^2) + (0.208 \text{ in.}^2) = 6.27 \text{ in.}^2$$

Step 3 - Calculate the Shear Lag Factor

The shear lag factor was computed for this connection in Example 4.16. The value obtained from Case 2 is the most precise.

$$U = 1 - \frac{\bar{x}}{l} = 1 - \frac{0.902 \text{ in.}}{8 \text{ in.}} = 0.887$$

Step 4 - Compute the nominal capacity for Tensile Rupture of the Net Section

The equation for P_n is:

$$P_n = F_u A_e = F_u (A_n U)$$

Table 2-3 indicates the standard material for angles is A36 steel with $F_u = 58$ ksi. Values for the other terms were determined in Steps 2 and 3.

$$P_n = (58 \text{ ksi})(6.27 \text{ in.}^2)(0.887) = 322.6 \text{ kips}$$

Step 5 - Compute the factored capacity for Tensile Rupture of the Net Section

$$\phi P_n = (0.75)P_n = (0.75)(322.6 \text{ kips}) = \textbf{242 kips}$$

Block shear
failure mechs
-Shear
-tension

You Should Know

- How do you compute the capacity for tensile rupture of the net section?
- Which step takes the most time?

4.10 Block Shear

Up to this point in the chapter, two limit states have been discussed for tension members: yielding in the gross section and tensile rupture in the net section. One final limit state that should be considered is called *block shear* failure. Block shear is similar to tensile rupture of the net section in that fracture occurs, but it is different because the fracture does not propogate through the entire cross section. Rather, block shear failures look like something "took a bite" out of the tension member. Examples of block shear failure modes are shown below.

Block shear failures always involve some areas failing in tension and some failing in shear. Consider the bar below that has failed in block shear. The failure surfaces perpendicular to the direction of loading (colored red) ruptured due to tension. The failure surfaces parallel to the direction of loading (colored yellow) ruptured due to shear.

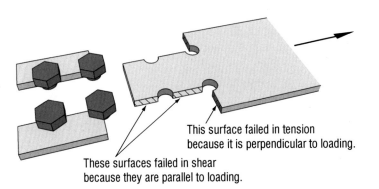

This surface failed in tension
because it is perpendicular to loading.

These surfaces failed in shear
because they are parallel to loading.

In order to compute the capacity associated with block shear limit states, the areas of material failing in tension and shear need to be identified. The following example illustrates how this is done.

Example 4.19 Computing Tension and Shear Areas for Block Shear

Compute the gross and net areas in
tension and shear for the block shear
failure mode shown. The plate is 3/8
in. thick and the bolts are 5/8 in.

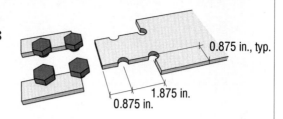

0.875 in., typ.

1.875 in.

0.875 in.

Step 1 - Identify the tension and shear failure surfaces

It is essential to have a sketch (2D or 3D) or picture in mind when computing
block shear areas. In this problem a sketch of the failure mode is provided. The
surfaces that are perpendicular to the direction of loading are tension failure
surfaces; the others are shear failure surfaces.

Step 2 - Compute the gross tension area and gross shear area

Gross areas are computed by ignoring the
missing material from the bolt holes.
Dimensions for computing gross areas are
based on centerline dimensions of the bolt
holes. The gross tension area is shaded red
on the figure to the right. Based on the given
dimensions it is:

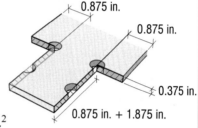

0.875 in.

0.875 in.

0.375 in.

0.875 in. + 1.875 in.

$$A_{gt} = 2(0.375 \text{ in.})(0.875 \text{ in.}) = \textbf{0.656 in.}^2$$

The gross shear area is shaded yellow. Based
on the given dimensions it is:

$$A_{gv} = 2(0.375 \text{ in.})(0.875 \text{ in.} + 1.875 \text{ in.}) = \textbf{2.06 in.}^2$$

Step 3 - Calculate the net tension and net shear areas

The net areas are obtained by subtracting out
bolt holes. The procedure is similar to what
has been done in previous examples. One
thing to be aware of is that holes that are in a
corner of the block shear tear-out look as if
they have lost $\frac{1}{4}$ of their area. But remember
that in section view, these corner holes have
$\frac{1}{2}$ the cross-sectional area of a whole hole.

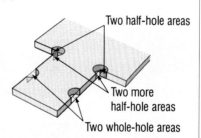

Two half-hole areas

Two more
half-hole areas

Two whole-hole areas

$$A_{nt} = A_{gt} - 2(\text{half-holes})$$
$$A_{nt} = 0.656 \text{ in.}^2 - 2\frac{(0.375 \text{ in.})(0.625 \text{ in.} + \frac{1}{8} \text{ in.})}{2} = \textbf{0.375 in.}^2$$

A similar procedure is used to get the net
shear area.

$$A_{nv} = A_{gv} - 2(\text{whole-holes}) - 2(\text{half-holes})$$
$$A_{nv} = A_{gv} - 3(\text{whole-holes})$$
$$A_{nv} = 2.06 \text{ in.}^2 - 3(0.375 \text{ in.})(0.625 \text{ in.} + \frac{1}{8} \text{ in.}) = \textbf{1.22 in.}^2$$

Study the Manual

Turn to §J4.3 in the Specification (page 16.1-129).

This section provides the equations for computing the capacity for block shear limit states. The nominal capacity is designated R_n because block shear is considered a connection failure mode.

- Write Eqn. J4-5 for R_n.

- What is the value of the ϕ factor for block shear limit states? How does it compare with the ϕ factor for tension rupture on the net section?

The equation for R_n has two parts (separated by a less-than-or-equal sign). This is to be understood to mean that R_n is equal to the left part as long as it is less than the right. Or in other words, R_n is equal to whichever side that gives the smallest number.

Look at the left part of the equation.

- Why is the shear area multiplied by $0.6F_u$ while the tension area is multiplied by F_u?

- What value should you usually use for U_{bs} if the tension stress is uniform?

The user note says to look in the commentary for cases where U_{bs} should be taken as 0.5. Go to the commentary.

- What are those cases?

The commentary also explains the second part of the equation for R_n.

- From the commentary, what does it mean physically if the second part of the equation for R_n governs?

The following example shows how the capacity for a block shear limit state is calculated using equation J4-5.

Example 4.20 Computing Block Shear Capacity

What is the factored capacity for the block shear failure mode of Example 4.19?

Step 1 - Get values for the various terms in Eqn. J4-5

The areas were computed in the previous example. Standard plate material is A36 with $F_y = 36$ ksi and $F_u = 58$ ksi. U_{bs} will be equal to 1.0 for all tension members.

Step 2 - Calculate the nominal capacity with Eqn. J4-5

$$R_n = 0.6F_u A_{nv} + U_{bs}F_u A_{nt} \leq 0.6F_y A_{gv} + U_{bs}F_u A_{nt}$$
$$R_n = 0.6(58 \text{ ksi})(1.22 \text{ in.}^2) + 1.0(58 \text{ ksi})(0.375 \text{ in.}^2) \leq$$
$$0.6(36 \text{ ksi})(2.06 \text{ in.}^2) + 1.0(58 \text{ ksi})(0.375 \text{ in.}^2)$$
$$R_n = 64.2 \text{ kips} \leq 66.2 \text{ kips}$$

Since the left side is smaller, it governs.

$$R_n = 64.2 \text{ kips}$$

Step 3 - Calculate the factored capacity

$$\phi R_n = (0.75)(64.2 \text{ kips}) = \textbf{48.2 kips}$$

Calculating areas and using equation J4-5 are relatively easy tasks. The hardest part about block shear is identifying what the possible failure modes are and using judgment to determine which will govern without having to run calculations on all of them.

The figures below and on the next page illustrate several common cases, show the possible block shear modes, and give suggestions for determining which will govern.

Case 1: Angle with One Leg Bolted

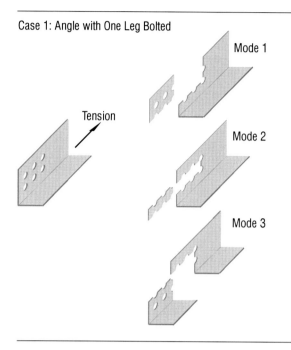

Modes 1 and 2 should be calculated. Either may govern depending on the locations of the bolt rows.

By inspection, Mode 3 has the same shear area as Mode 1, but much greater tension area. It does not need to be calculated.

Case 2: Channel Bolted Through Web

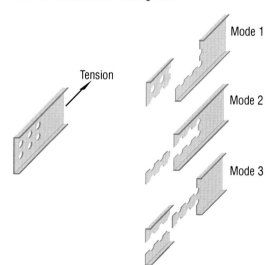

Mode 2 will usually govern over Mode 1 because the flange has a lot of tension area.

By inspection, Mode 3 has the same shear area as Mode 2 and more tension area, so it does not need to be calculated.

Case 3: Wide Flange Bolted Through Web

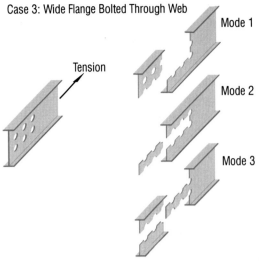

By inspection, Mode 2 will govern because Modes 1 and 3 would require fracture through the flange. Only calculate Mode 2.

Case 4: Wide Flange Bolted Through Flanges

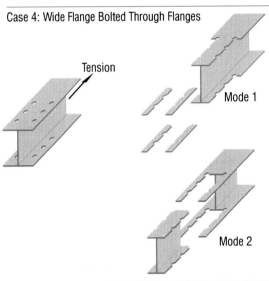

By inspection, Mode 1 will govern since the tension area is much less. Mode 1 is all that needs to be calculated.

Case 5: Wide Flange Bolted Through Both

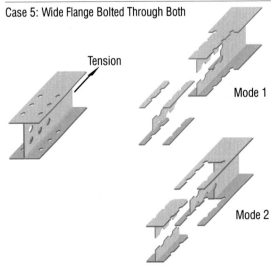

These modes involve a lot of surfaces rupturing. By inspection, the shear area is the same for both modes. The tension area will most likely be less for Mode 1, but it depends on the location of the bolts.

Computing the capacity of a tension member involves computing the factored capacity of the three limit states (yielding of gross section, tensile rupture of net section, and block shear) and determining which is the least. The limit state with the lowest factored capacity governs. This is illustrated in the following example.

Example 4.21 Computing the Capacity of a Tension Member

A 2L6×6×1 is used as the bottom chord of a truss. The connection detail at each end of the member is the same and shown in the detail. Compute the tension capacity of the 2L6×6×1.

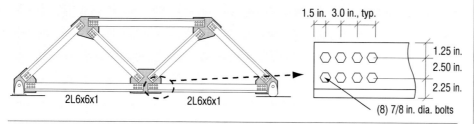

Step 1 - Get the capacity for yielding of the gross section

The capacity for yielding of the gross section can be looked up for a 2L6×6×1 in Table 5-8:

$$\phi_t P_n = 713 \text{ kips}$$

Step 2 - Calculate the capacity for tensile rupture of the net section

First compute the net area. The net area of interest is from the section that passes through the leading line of bolts. It is important to visualize this cross section, especially when dealing with double angles. From the picture to the right it is clear that there are four bolt holes through the net section.

Don't forget there are (2) angles

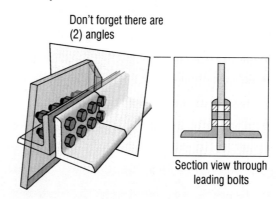

Section view through leading bolts

$$A_n = (22.0 \text{ in.}^2) - 4(1 \text{ in.})(0.875 \text{ in.} + \tfrac{1}{8} \text{ in.}) = 18.0 \text{ in.}^2$$

Next compute the shear lag factor. The shear lag factor for the double angle will be the same as it would be for a single. Case 2 is easy to apply in this situation and yields the most precise value.

$$U = 1 - \frac{\bar{x}}{l} = 1 - \frac{1.86 \text{ in.}}{9} = 0.793$$

The factored capacity for tensile rupture of the net section is:.

$$\phi_t P_n = \phi_t F_u A_e = (0.75)(58 \text{ ksi})(18.0 \text{ in.}^2)(0.793) = 621 \text{ kips}$$

Step 3 - Calculate the block shear capacity

Two block shear modes will be checked to determine which governs. Both angles will be accounted for when computing the gross and net areas.

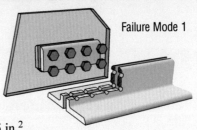

Failure Mode 1

For Mode 1:

$A_{gt} = 2(1.0 \text{ in.})(1.25 \text{ in.} + 2.5 \text{ in.}) = 7.5 \text{ in.}^2$

$A_{gv} = 2(1.0 \text{ in.})[1.5 \text{ in.} + 3(3.0 \text{ in.})] = 21.0 \text{ in.}^2$

$A_{nt} = 7.5 \text{ in.}^2 - (2 \text{ angles})(1.5 \frac{\text{holes}}{\text{angle}})(1.0 \text{ in.})(0.875 \text{ in.} + \frac{1}{8} \text{ in.}) = 4.5 \text{ in.}^2$

$A_{nv} = 21.0 \text{ in.}^2 - (2 \text{ angles})(3.5 \frac{\text{holes}}{\text{angle}})(1.0 \text{ in.})(0.875 \text{ in.} + \frac{1}{8} \text{ in.}) = 14.0 \text{ in.}^2$

$R_n = (0.6)(58 \text{ ksi})(14.0 \text{ in.}^2) + 1.0(58 \text{ ksi})(4.5 \text{ in.}^2) \leq$
$\qquad\qquad (0.6)(36 \text{ ksi})(21.0 \text{ in.}^2) + 1.0(58 \text{ ksi})(4.5 \text{ in.}^2)$

$R_n = 748.2 \text{ kips} \leq 714.6 \text{ kips}$

$R_n = 714.6 \text{ kips}$

Failure Mode 2

For Mode 2:

$A_{gt} = 2(1.0 \text{ in.})(2.5 \text{ in.}) = 5.0 \text{ in.}^2$

$A_{gv} = 2(2)(1.0 \text{ in.})[1.5 \text{ in.} + 3(3.0 \text{ in.})] = 42.0 \text{ in.}^2$

$A_{nt} = 5.0 \text{ in.}^2 - (2 \text{ angles})(1.0 \frac{\text{holes}}{\text{angle}})(1.0 \text{ in.})(0.875 \text{ in.} + \frac{1}{8} \text{ in.}) = 3.0 \text{ in.}^2$

$A_{nv} = 42.0 \text{ in.}^2 - (2 \text{ angles})(7.0 \frac{\text{holes}}{\text{angle}})(1.0 \text{ in.})(0.875 \text{ in.} + \frac{1}{8} \text{ in.}) = 28.0 \text{ in.}^2$

$R_n = (0.6)(58 \text{ ksi})(28.0 \text{ in.}^2) + 1.0(58 \text{ ksi})(3.0 \text{ in.}^2) \leq$
$\qquad\qquad (0.6)(36 \text{ ksi})(42.0 \text{ in.}^2) + 1.0(58 \text{ ksi})(3.0 \text{ in.}^2)$

$R_n = 1148.4 \text{ kips} \leq 1081.2 \text{ kips}$

$R_n = 1081.2 \text{ kips}$

Mode 1 governs. The factored capacity for block shear is:

$\phi R_n = (0.75)(714.6 \text{ kips}) = \textbf{536 kips}$

Note: The gusset plate between the angles at the connection could also experience a block shear failure. The calculation is beyond the scope of this particular problem.

Step 4 - Identify the governing limit state and summarize the factored capacity

It is good to summarize all the limit states that have been calculated:

Yielding: $\phi_t P_n = \textbf{713 kips}$

Rupture of Net Section: $\phi_t P_n = \textbf{621 kips}$.

Block Shear: $\phi R_n = \textbf{536 kips}$.

Since the block shear limit state has the lowest capacity, it governs. The tension capacity is **536 kips**.

- How is block shear different from rupture through the net section?
- How can you tell which limit state governs the capacity of a tension member?

the smallest when all 3

limit states are calculated

4.11 Design

The previous sections have described how to compute demands and capacities of tension members when the geometry and member sizes (shapes) are known. But the job of the designer is to determine what the geometry and member sizes should be. The general steps of member design were outlined in the previous chapter:

1. Compute demands.
2. Pick a shape to try.
3. Compute the capacity of the shape and compare with demands.
4. Finalize the design or iterate to find a better design.

Step 1 is generally a straightforward application of structural analysis. Statics is used for the problems in this book. Most designers will approach Step 1 in essentially the same way for a given problem.

Step 2 is where designers express their style. Some designers like to do preliminary calculations as part of Step 2, so that when they pick a shape to try they are almost guaranteed to pick something that works. This approach is elegant and appeals to many engineers.

Another style for Step 2 is to use rough judgment and tables to quickly pick a shape. Often this shape will turn out not to work, but by doing the calculations for the trial shape the designer can quickly determine an appropriate shape for the second guess. This style feels more iterative and less elegant but is faster for some types of problems. This is the style that I will use in the examples.

Once a shape is selected in Step 2, all that remains is to verify that the factored capacity exceeds the demand. If it does, then the design is adequate.

Study the Manual

Turn to Part 5 of the Manual, Design of Tension Members.

This part of the Manual has information and tables to assist in the design of tension members. Read the paragraph under Slenderness (page 5-3).

The ratio l/r is the slendernss, where r is the least radius of gyration for a cross section.

- What is the recommended limit for the slenderness of tension members?

Go to the commentary for Section D1 (page 16.1-282).

- Why is there a recommended upper limit for the slenderness of tension members?

Read the two paragraphs under DESIGN TABLE DISCUSSION (page 5-3).

- Which tables list values for the capacities for yielding of the gross section and tensile rupture of the net section?

- The tables list capacities assuming that the effective net area is equal to $0.75A_g$. Why is $0.75A_g$ assumed?

- If the effective net area turns out to be greater than $0.75A_g$ can you still use the tables?

The example that follows illustrates how the steps of design are applied and how the tables in Part 5 of the Manual can be used to design tension members.

Example 4.22 Design of a Truss Tension Member

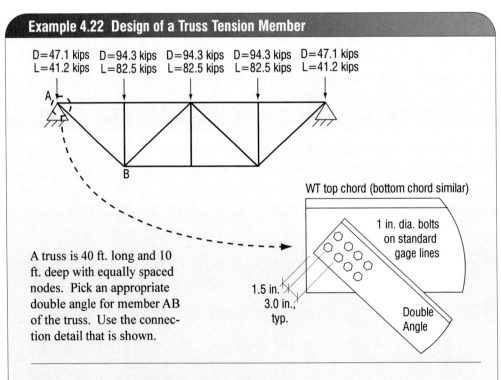

A truss is 40 ft. long and 10 ft. deep with equally spaced nodes. Pick an appropriate double angle for member AB of the truss. Use the connection detail that is shown.

Step 1 - Get the factored demands for AB

1a - Compute dead load effects for AB

Considering only the dead loads, the vertical support reaction at point A would be:

$$R_y = \tfrac{1}{2}(47.1 \text{ kips} + 94.3 \text{ kips} + 94.3 \text{ kips} + 94.3 \text{ kips} + 47.1 \text{ kips})$$
$$R_y = 188.6 \text{ kips}$$

Example Continued

The vertical component of the axial force in member AB, $P_{D,AB}$, will be equal to the vertical support reaction, R_y.

$$P_{D,AB}(\cos 45) = R_y - D$$

so

$$P_{D,AB} = \frac{188.6 - 47.1 \text{ kips}}{(\cos 45)} = 200 \text{ kips}$$

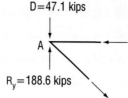

D=47.1 kips

A

R_y=188.6 kips

$P_{D,AB}$

1b - Compute live load effects for AB

Since the point live loads are all 87.5% of the point dead loads

$$P_{L,AB} = 0.875 P_{D,AB} = (0.875)(200 \text{ kips}) = 175 \text{ kips}$$

1c - Factor the load effects to get the ultimate demand

By inspection, load combination 2 will govern.

$$P_{U,AB} = 1.2 P_D + 1.6 P_L$$
$$P_{U,AB} = 1.2(200 \text{ kips}) + 1.6(175 \text{ kips}) = \mathbf{520} \text{ kips}$$

Step 2 - Pick a shape to try

Use Table 5-8 to identify double angles that have yielding capacities and approximate rupture capacities greater than $P_U = 520$ kips.
From Table 5-8, the following angles seem like good possibilities:

$2L6 \times 6 \times \frac{3}{4}$ with $A_g = 16.9$ in.^{2}
$2L6 \times 6 \times \frac{7}{8}$ with $A_g = 19.5$ in.^{2}
$2L8 \times 4 \times \frac{3}{4}$ with $A_g = 16.9$ in.^{2}
$2L8 \times 4 \times \frac{7}{8}$ with $A_g = 19.5$ in.^{2}
$2L8 \times 6 \times \frac{5}{8}$ with $A_g = 16.7$ in.^{2}
$2L8 \times 6 \times \frac{3}{4}$ with $A_g = 19.9$ in.^{2}
$2L8 \times 8 \times \frac{9}{16}$ with $A_g = 17.4$ in.^{2}

In general, the angles with unequal legs will be more efficient for tension members because they will have less shear lag.

~~$2L6 \times 6 \times \frac{3}{4}$ with $A_g = 16.9$ in.^{2}~~
~~$2L6 \times 6 \times \frac{7}{8}$ with $A_g = 19.5$ in.^{2}~~
$2L8 \times 4 \times \frac{3}{4}$ with $A_g = 16.9$ in.^{2}
$2L8 \times 4 \times \frac{7}{8}$ with $A_g = 19.5$ in.^{2}
$2L8 \times 6 \times \frac{5}{8}$ with $A_g = 16.7$ in.^{2}
$2L8 \times 6 \times \frac{3}{4}$ with $A_g = 19.9$ in.^{2}
~~$2L8 \times 8 \times \frac{9}{16}$ with $A_g = 17.4$ in.^{2}~~

Of the remaining, the lightest will be the $2L8 \times 6 \times \frac{5}{8}$ since it has the smallest cross-sectional area. But it is possible that block shear will govern and the $2L8 \times 6 \times \frac{5}{8}$ won't work. The heavier angles with thicker flanges will have greater block shear capacity. It is not obvious which is the best choice. At this point, just try something.

continued on next page

Example Continued

$$\text{Try } 2L8 \times 4 \times \tfrac{3}{4}$$

Step 3 - Check the capacity of the trial shape

3a - Yielding of gross section

The yield capacity is read directly from Table 5-8.

$$\phi_t P_n = 548 \text{ kips} > 520 \text{ kips (OK)}$$

3b - Rupture of the net section

Table 5-8 only gives an approximation for the rupture capacity by assuming $A_e = 0.75A_g$. The actual values for A_e and the rupture capacity need to be computed.

$$A_g = 16.9 \text{ in.}^2$$
$$A_n = 16.9 \text{ in.}^2 - 4(\tfrac{3}{4} \text{ in.})(1.0 \text{ in.} + \tfrac{1}{8} \text{ in.}) = 13.53 \text{ in.}^2$$
$$U = 1 - \frac{0.949 \text{ in.}}{9 \text{ in.}} = 0.895$$
$$A_e = (13.53 \text{ in.}^2)(0.895) = 12.1 \text{ in.}^2$$
$$\phi_t P_n = (0.75)(58 \text{ ksi})(12.1 \text{ in.}^2) = 527 \text{ kips}$$
$$\phi_t P_n = 527 \text{ kips} > 520 \text{ kips (OK)}$$

3c - Block shear capacity

For Mode 1:

$$A_{gt} = 2(\tfrac{3}{4} \text{ in.})(2.0 \text{ in.} + 3.0 \text{ in.}) = 7.5 \text{ in.}^2$$
$$A_{gv} = 2(\tfrac{3}{4} \text{ in.})[1.5 \text{ in.} + 3(3.0 \text{ in.})] = 15.75 \text{ in.}^2$$
$$A_{nt} = 7.5 \text{ in.}^2 - (2 \text{ angles})(1.5 \tfrac{\text{holes}}{\text{angle}})(\tfrac{3}{4} \text{ in.})(1.0 \text{ in.} + \tfrac{1}{8} \text{ in.}) = 4.97 \text{ in.}^2$$
$$A_{nv} = 15.75 \text{ in.}^2 - (2 \text{ angles})(3.5 \tfrac{\text{holes}}{\text{angle}})(\tfrac{3}{4} \text{ in.})(1.0 \text{ in.} + \tfrac{1}{8} \text{ in.}) = 9.84 \text{ in.}^2$$
$$R_n = (0.6)(58 \text{ ksi})(9.84 \text{ in.}^2) + 1.0(58 \text{ ksi})(4.97 \text{ in.}^2) \leq$$
$$(0.6)(36 \text{ ksi})(15.75 \text{ in.}^2) + 1.0(58 \text{ ksi})(4.97 \text{ in.}^2)$$
$$R_n = 630.7 \text{ kips} \leq 628.5 \text{ kips}$$
$$R_n = 628.5 \text{ kips}$$

Mode 2 was calculated (not shown here) and found to have greater capacity. Mode 1 governs.

$$\phi R_n = (0.75)(628.5 \text{ kips}) = 471 \text{ kips} < 520 \text{ kips (No Good)}$$

The $2L8 \times 4 \times \tfrac{3}{4}$ will not work because the block shear capacity is less than the demand.

3d - Slenderness

Even though the trial shape will not work due to block shear, it won't be a waste to check the slenderness. The radius of gyration for the double angle can be looked up in Table 1-15

$$r = 1.69 \text{ in. (assuming the gusset plate between the angles is } \tfrac{3}{4} \text{ in.)}$$

The length of the member is obtained from the geometry of the truss.

$$l = \sqrt{(10 \text{ ft})^2 + (10 \text{ ft})^2} = 14.14 \text{ ft}$$

Example Continued

The length needs to be expressed in the same units as the radius of gyration.

$$l = (14.14 \text{ ft.})(\tfrac{12 \text{ in.}}{\text{ft}}) = 170 \text{ in.}$$
$$l/r = 170 < 300 \textbf{ (OK)}$$

Step 4 - Iterate to find an acceptable design

Even though the $2L8 \times 4 \times \frac{3}{4}$ did not work, the previous calculations are still useful. In fact, very little additional effort is required to identify an acceptable design.

Try $2L8 \times 4 \times \frac{7}{8}$

The $2L8 \times 4 \times \frac{7}{8}$ will be okay for yielding, rupture, and slenderness since it has more area than the $2L8 \times 4 \times \frac{3}{4}$. For the block shear calculation, the only thing that is different from the previous calculation is that the thickness is $\frac{7}{8}$ rather than $\frac{3}{4}$. The block shear capacity for the $2L8 \times 4 \times \frac{7}{8}$ can be obtained by scaling the previous result.

$$\phi R_n = (471 \text{ kips})\frac{\left(\frac{7}{8}\right)}{\left(\frac{3}{4}\right)} = \textbf{550 } \text{kips} > 520 \text{ kips } \textbf{(OK)}$$

Use $2L8 \times 4 \times \frac{7}{8}$

You Should Know

- What is the difference between "elegant" and "more iterative" design styles?
- What part of the Manual has design charts for tension members?
- What is the yield capacity for a W16x31?
- What do you do when A_e is not equal to $0.75A_g$?

Remember This

- Most steel structures have tension members. The most common types are hangers, truss members, and braces.
- Computing demands in tension members usually involves some sort of structural analysis (Statics). The concept of tributary area is helpful in determining loads on hangers and truss nodes.
- Three limit states to consider for tension members are: yielding of the gross section (yielding), rupture of the net section (rupture), and block shear.
- Yielding of the gross section is unacceptable because it results in excessive deformation.
- Rupture of the net section may occur because bolt holes and shear lag reduce the effective area. To compute the capacity for rupture of the net section, an effective area needs to be determined.
- Block shear failure is when a chunk gets torn out at the connection.
- In block shear failures some surfaces fail in tension while others fail in shear.
- Design is always a guess-and-check exercise. Some engineers prefer to do preliminary calculations to ensure a good first guess. Others prefer to quickly check a roughly selected member, and then make a final selection based on those calculations.

Connections in steel structures are generally either bolted or welded. Some connections, like the one above, may require hundreds of bolts to transfer the loads. Basic principles of connection design hold true whether a connection has a few, a few dozen, or a few hundred bolts.

Bolts are often the most economical way to assemble structures in the field.

5. Simple Bolted Connections

Consider This

- Why are bolts used for connections in most steel structures?
- In what situations will all the bolts of a connection resist the loads equally?
- How can you tell if a bolt is in tension, shear, or both?
- How are bolt capacities calculated?
- How is excessive bearing defined?
- What are slip-critical connections and when are they used?

5.1 Background

From the late 1800s through the early 1960s, rivets were used almost exclusively for connections in steel structures. Riveting provided strong connections but was labor intensive. A team of four skilled workers was required for installation.

Rivets were used to create built-up shapes and connect members to each other.

If a structure has rivets, it was probably built before the 1960s.

By the 1960s, high-strength bolts were being used instead of rivets in most civil structures. The primary advantage of bolts over rivets is the reduced labor for construction. Another advantage is that they are safer to install since they don't need to be put in hot.

The most common materials for bolts are A325 and A490 steel. When bolts are produced, the material type is imprinted on the head of the bolt, so it is easy to know what they are (see picture). The bolt on the top of the picture is called a twist-off bolt. These are often used when a tensioned bolt is required. They do not have a hex-head, but are tightened by a tool that twists and pulls on the tail of the bolt. The tail twists off when the proper tension has been achieved.

Bolts are usually placed through standard holes that are 1/16 in. greater in diameter than the size of the bolt. However, in some cases it is helpful to use bigger holes. There are three different types of enlarged holes. These are oversized holes, short-slotted holes, and long-slotted holes. The dimensions for these various enlarged holes are given in Table J3.3 of the Specification.

Example 5.1 Enlarged Bolt Holes

The picture shows the base plate for a street-light post. Slotted holes were used to facilitate the connection. Slotted or oversized holes are often used for base plates because it is difficult to precisely position anchor bolts that are embedded in concrete. Enlarged holes provide some flexibility in positioning at the connection.

You Should Know

- What do you know about the age of a structure if it has rivets? *made b/w 1800's → 1960's*
- How can you tell what material a bolt is made from? *imprinted on head*
- What is the diameter of an oversized hole for a 3/4 in. bolt? *13/16"*

5.2 Bolt Demands in Simple Connections

Consider the two connections to the right. In the connection on top, the line of action of the member force passes through the centroid of the bolt group. The load is transferred from the member to the bolts without any sort of eccentricity. Connections of this type are called *simple connections*, and it is reasonable to assume that all of the bolts share the load equally.

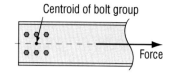

Compare this with the other connection. In this case, the line of action of the force (which acts through the centroid of the member) does not pass through the centroid of the bolt group. There is some eccentricity between the lines that induces a moment that needs to be resisted by the bolt group. In this type of connection it cannot be assumed that the bolts have equal demands. It is not a simple connection.

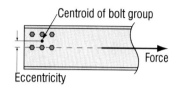

Simple connections are common in steel structures. This section will explain how bolt demands are calculated in simple connections. For connections with eccentricities, you will need to refer to other texts and Tables 7-7 through 7-14 of the AISC Manual.

Simple bolted connections may have bolts in shear or tension. The figure to the right shows a wide flange that is attached to another wide flange by two angles. If an axial force were present, as shown, the bolts on line A, would be loaded in shear because the load acts perpendicular to the shaft of the bolts. The bolts on lines B and C would be loaded in tension because the load acts parallel to the shaft of the bolts.

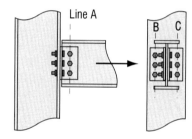

Example 5.2 Bolt Demands

For the connection shown immediately above, compute the demands on the bolts if the axial force is equal to 100 kips.

Step 1 - Calculate demands on the bolts on Line A

The bolts on Line A will be in shear. There are three bolts that will equally resist the 100 kip force. The demand on each bolt is **33.3** kips shear.

Step 2 - Calculate the demands on the bolts on Lines B and C

The bolts on Lines B and C will be in tension. There are six bolts that equally resist the 100 kip force. The demand on each bolt is **16.7** kips tension.

Demands

Example 5.3 Bolt Demands under Multiple Loads

The beam below is 30 ft long and supports a uniform dead load of 0.5 k/ft and a uniform live load of 0.6 k/ft. This beam is also used to transfer forces during earthquake loading and has an axial load effect from the earthquake of 150 kips. Compute the demands on the bolts shown.

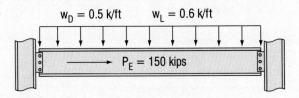

$w_D = 0.5$ k/ft $w_L = 0.6$ k/ft

$P_E = 150$ kips

Step 1 - Get the factored resultants at the connection

The bolts at the left and right connections will have the same demands. The bolts will resist a vertical force equal to the support reaction for the beam under the factored vertical loads. The bolts will also resist a horizontal force equal to the factored axial load.

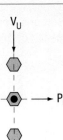

V_U

P_U

By inspection, either load combination 2 or 5 will govern. For load combination 2:

$$V_u = 1.2(0.5 \text{ k/ft})(30 \text{ ft})(1/2) + 1.6(0.6 \text{ k/ft})(30 \text{ ft})(1/2) = 23.4 \text{ kips}$$
$$P_u = 1.2(0 \text{ kips}) + 1.6(0 \text{ kips}) = 0 \text{ kips}$$

For load combination 5:

$$V_u = 1.2(0.5 \text{ k/ft})(30 \text{ ft})(1/2) + 0.5(0.6 \text{ k/ft})(30 \text{ ft})(1/2) = 13.5 \text{ kips}$$
$$P_u = 1.2(0 \text{ kips}) + 1.0(150 \text{ kips}) + 0.5(0 \text{ kips}) = 150 \text{ kips}$$

Now by inspection it is clear that load combination 5 will govern.

Step 2 - Calculate the bolt demands

Both the horizontal and vertical forces put the bolts into shear because they act perpendicular to the shaft of the bolts. The resultant of V_u and P_u is:

$$R_u = \sqrt{P_u^2 + V_u^2} = \sqrt{(150 \text{ kips})^2 + (13.5 \text{ kips})^2} = 151 \text{ kips}$$

The bolts resist force equally, so the demand in each bolt is:

$$R_u = \frac{151 \text{ kips}}{3} = \textbf{50.2 kips/bolt, shear}$$

line of action goes through center of bolt

You Should Know

- How can you tell if a bolted connection is simple?
- How do you compute demands on bolts in simple bolted connections?

bolt share load equally

5.3 Bolt Capacity

In the previous section, we found that computing bolt demands in simple connections is not very complicated. Computing bolt capacity is also straightforward, although there are some things to be aware of. Before discussing bolt capacity, we will consider the capacity of steel rods in general.

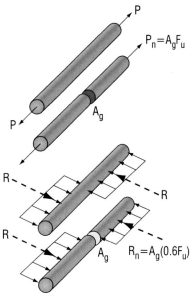

In general, the capacity of a rod depends on the cross-sectional area of the rod, the material, and how the rod is loaded. Consider the rods shown on the right that are in tension. The axial load that will cause the rod to break, P_n, will be equal to the cross-sectional area (A_g) multiplied by the ultimate strength of the material (F_u).

For a rod in shear, the load that will cause it to break, R_n, will be equal to the cross-sectional area multiplied by the ultimate shear strength of the material (commonly taken as $0.6F_u$).

·6 comes from shear strength = 60% of tension strength

Bolts are different than the cases above because of the threads. The figure below shows a typical bolt. The "bolt diameter" is defined as the diameter of the un-threaded portion of the bolt. When bolts fail in tension or shear in the threaded region, the area that is fracturing is less than the full cross-section area calculated using the bolt diameter (because of the threads).

The procedure in the Specification for computing bolt capacity accounts for the reduced cross section in the threaded part of the bolt, by using an adjusted value for the material strength.

Turn to Table J3.2 (page 16.1-120). This table provides the values F_{nt} and F_{nv} for various types of bolts and threaded parts.

- How many different types of fasteners are listed in the left column?

- For most of the fasteners, there are two rows given for each. What is the difference in these two rows?

The phrase "threads are not excluded from the shear planes" means that the bolt will fail through the threaded portion. We might expect this to occur for a connection like the one on the left (below), where threads are at the interface of the two parts being connected. The phrase "threads are excluded from the shear planes" means there are no threads at the interface; this is illustrated in the figure to the right.

Threads not excluded
(threads included)
in failure plane

Threads excluded
(threads not included)
in failure plane

Engineers specify bolt diameters, but don't usually specify the length of the bolts or the threaded portions; the steel fabricator usually makes these decisions. Thus, during design, the engineer typically conservatively assumes that the threads are not excluded (assumes the case on the left).

The other two columns of Table J3.2 give values for F_{nt} and F_{nv}. F_{nt} is the stress used to compute the capacity of a bolt in tension. F_{nt} has been adjusted so that when it is multiplied by the unthreaded cross-sectional area of the bolt, it will give the tension capacity of the threaded part, which is where the bolt will actually fail in tension. Similarly, F_{nv} is the stress used to compute the capacity of the bolt in shear. For the case where threads are not excluded, F_{nv} has been adjusted so that when it is multiplied by the unthreaded cross-sectional area of the bolt, it will give the shear capacity of the threaded part.

Read the commentary for subsection 6. on page 16.1-402, then go back to Table J3.2.

- Compare F_{nt} and F_{nv} for the case of an A325 bolt when threads are excluded. Does the difference in tension and shear strength match what we typically assume for steel?

- Compare F_{nv} for the two cases of A325 bolts (threads not excluded, threads excluded). Based on these numbers, what is the percentage difference in the cross-sectional area for the threaded and unthreaded portions of an A325 bolt?

The bolt on the right is said to be in *double shear*. In order for it to fail, two planes will have to rupture. Thus, the capacity of a bolt in double shear will be twice the capacity of the bolt in single shear.

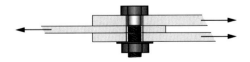

Example 5.4 Calculating Bolt Capacity

What is the design strength of a 7/8 in. dia. A325 bolt in single shear?

Step 1 - Compute the cross-sectional area of the unthreaded part of the bolt

$$A_b = \frac{\pi d_b^2}{4} = \frac{\pi(7/8 \text{ in.})^2}{4} = 0.601 \text{ in.}^2$$

Step 2 - Get F_n from Table J3.2

The value of F_n depends on whether the bolt will break through the threaded or unthreaded region. Since we do not know, we will conservatively assume that the threads are not excluded:

$$F_n = F_{nv} = 54 \text{ ksi}$$

Step 3 - Compute the factored capacity using Eqn J3-1

$$\phi R_n = \phi F_n A_b = (0.75)(54 \text{ ksi})(0.601 \text{ in.}^2) = \textbf{24.3} \text{ kips}$$

The calculations demonstrated in Example 5.4 have already been done for standard bolts. The capacities for typical bolts are listed in Tables 7-1 (shear capacity) and 7-2 (tension capacity).

Study the Manual

Turn to Table 7-1 (page 7-22). This table provides the shear strength for typical bolts.

The top row on the table indicates the various bolt diameters and the row below indicates the cross-sectional area.

- Look at the cross-sectional area for a 7/8 in. bolt. How does it compare with the value calculated in Example 5.4?

The left-most column is the material designation for the bolt. The next column has the symbols N or X. N stands for "threads Not excluded"; this is the case that we will use most of the time.

The N and X rows are further subdivided into S and D rows. S stands for Single shear loading; D is for Double shear.

The values of interest to us are the factored capacities, ϕr_n. Lowercase r_n is used to emphasize that the values are for a single bolt.

- What is ϕr_n for a 7/8 in. A325 bolt in single shear?

- How does this compare with the value calculated in Example 5.4?

Now look at Table 7-2. The layout is similar but it is less complicated than Table 7-1 because bolts in tension will always fail through the threads and there will always be only a single failure plane.

> ### You Should Know
>
> * How do you determine the capacity of a bolt?

5.4 Excessive Bearing Limit States

When the thickness of a part being connected is small relative to the size and strength of the bolts, excessive bearing may occur. There are two modes of excessive bearing failure. The first mode is called bolt-by-bolt block shear. The second is called hole elongation.

Bolt-by-bolt block shear failure   *Hole elongation*

We will consider block shear first. The capacity against bolt-by-bolt block shear can be computed for each bolt individually based on the area of material that would fail and the strength of the material. From the pictures below, the area of material that would fail for one bolt is approximately $2L_c t$ because there are two failure surfaces, each with a length L_c, and a thickness t.

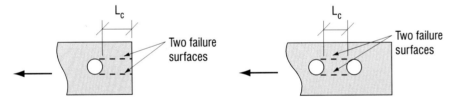

For the case on the right, the interior bolt would probably only fail in block-shear if the edge bolt did too; but the capacity is computed separately for each bolt. For bolts on the edge, L_c is taken as the distance from the edge of the bolt hole to the edge of the member. For interior bolts, L_c is taken as the distance from the edge of one bolt to the edge of the adjacent bolt (NOT the center-to-center distance for the bolts). In either case, when the failure area is multiplied by the shear strength of the material, $0.6F_u$, the resulting capacity is: $R_n = (0.6F_u)(2L_c t) = 1.2L_c t F_u$.

The other excessive bearing mode is hole elongation. The capacity against excessive hole elongation is a function of the diameter of the bolt, the thickness of the part being connected, and the strength of the part being connected. Experiments have shown that elongation greater than 1/4 in. will begin to develop as the bearing force is increased beyond $2.4dtF_u$ (see commentary on Page 16.1-410 of the Manual). In other words, the capacity for a bolt based on hole elongation is $R_n = 2.4dtF_u$.

Study the Manual

Read §J3.10 of the Manual (page 16.1-127).

- What is the ϕ factor for bearing limit states?

- Why are there three different equations for the bearing strength, R_n?

The equations for R_n have two parts, separated by a less-than-or-equal-to sign. This should be interpreted to mean that R_n is equal to whichever of the two parts is lowest.

- How does the theory discussed on the previous page (of *Build With Steel*) compare with Eqns. J3-6a, J3-6b, and J3-6c?

- Which of Eqns. J3-6a or J3-6b will give the lowest capacity?

Excessive bearing capacity for a connection is computed by summing the bearing resistances of the individual bolts. This procedure is demonstrated in the following example.

Example 5.5 Calculating Bearing Capacity

What is the factored capacity for excessive bearing?

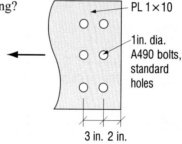

PL 1×10

1in. dia. A490 bolts, standard holes

3 in. 2 in.

Step 1 - Compute Lc for each bolt

For the bolts closest to the edge (Line A), L_c will be equal to the distance from the edge to the center of the bolt hole minus half of the bolt hole diameter:

$$L_c = 2\text{in.} - \frac{1\text{ in.} + 1/16\text{ in.}}{2} = 1.469 \text{ in.}$$

Note that 1/16 in. was added to get the actual diameter of the holes. For this limit state it is not required to add another 1/16 in.

For the bolts on Line B, L_c will be equal to:

$$L_c = 3\text{in.} - (1\text{ in.} + 1/16\text{ in.}) = 1.938 \text{ in.}$$

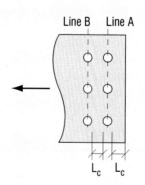

Line B   Line A

L_c L_c

continued on next page

Example Continued

Step 2 - Compute the nominal capacity for each bolt

The nominal capacity for each bolt for excessive bearing is determined using Eqn. J3-6a or J3-6b since the holes are standard size. The problem does not state whether or not deformation at the service load is a consideration, so we will conservatively assume that it is; Eqn. J3-6a applies.

For the bolts on Line A, Eqn J3-6a gives:

$$R_n = 1.2L_c t F_u \leq 2.4 dt F_u$$
$$R_n = 1.2(1.469 \text{ in.})(0.75 \text{ in.})(58 \text{ ksi}) \leq 2.4(1.0 \text{ in.})(0.75 \text{ in.})(58 \text{ ksi})$$
$$R_n = 76.7 \text{ kips} \leq 104.1 \text{ kips}$$
$$R_n = 76.7 \text{ kips (per bolt)}$$

For the bolts on Line B, Eqn J3-6a gives:

$$R_n = 1.2L_c t F_u \leq 2.4 dt F_u$$
$$R_n = 1.2(1.938 \text{ in.})(0.75 \text{ in.})(58 \text{ ksi}) \leq 2.4(1.0 \text{ in.})(0.75 \text{ in.})(58 \text{ ksi})$$
$$R_n = 101 \text{ kips} \leq 104.1 \text{ kips}$$
$$R_n = 101 \text{ kips (per bolt)}$$

Step 3 - Sum the bolt capacities and apply the resistance factor

The capacity of the connection for the excessive bearing limit state will be equal to the sum of the capacities of all the bolts, multiplied by the resistance factor:

$$\phi R_n = (0.75)[(3 \text{ bolts})(76.7 \text{ kips/bolt}) + (3 \text{ bolts})(101 \text{ kips/bolt})]$$
$$\phi R_n = \textbf{400} \text{ kips}$$

Note that the capacity for excessive bearing is linearly related to the thickness of the material (t shows up on both sides of Eqn J3-6). If the plate in this example were 3/8 in. thick rather than 3/4 in. thick, the bearing capacity would be half as much (200 kips).

In the example above, the left side of Eqn. J3-6a governed for all the bolts of the connection. This means that the governing mode of failure for all the bolts was bolt-by-bolt block-shear. In other connections, it is possible that some of the bolts may have capacity limited by the right side of Eqn. J3-6a while others are limited by the left side, implying that some bolts are limited by block shear and others by hole elongation. Still, the procedure given in the Specification is to determine the bolt capacities individually and then sum them up, even if that means mix-and-matching specific bearing modes of failure.

You Should Know

- What are the two modes of excessive bearing failure? *elongation & tearout*
- How are the capacities of these two modes calculated?
- How do you compute the capacity of an entire connection?

5.5 Slip-Resistant Connections

The previous two sections have explored limit states for bolts that involve either fracture of the bolt or excessive bearing. Some bolts are designed with an additional criteria in mind: slip resistance. Slip resistance may be needed for a variety of reasons. The most common is to protect connections from high-cycle fatigue failure. Fatigue failures may occur in connections that experience repeated load reversals. This is often the case for connections in steel bridges.

Bolted connections slip because the holes are slightly larger than the bolts. Slip resistance can be provided by friction forces.

In Statics you encountered a block on a surface that is subjected to an increasing lateral load, P. A friction force, F, between the block and the surface develops to balance the lateral load. The maximum friction force that can develop is equal to the normal force, N, multiplied by the static coefficient of friction, μ_s.

$$F_{max} = \mu_s N$$

If the lateral force, P, exceeds the maximum friction force, then the block will slip. The slip resistance of the block might be increased by either increasing the normal force or changing the surface such that the coefficient of friction is greater.

In a bolted connection, normal forces are generated when a bolt is tensioned and squeezes the parts together. The normal forces generated by one bolt are equal to the tension in the bolt as shown in the free body diagram to the right. The greater the bolt tension, the greater will be the normal force. And the greater the normal force, the greater will be the slip resistance.

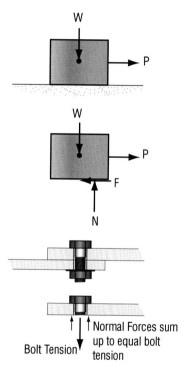

Normal Forces sum up to equal bolt tension

Bolt Tension

Study the Manual

Read §J3.8 of the Manual (page 16.1-126).

Look at Eqn. J3-4, which gives the slip resistance for one bolt. In that equation, μ is the coefficient of friction, and the other terms combined are the effective normal force.

- What will μ be equal to?

- What is the D_u factor? What will it be equal to?

- What will the h_f factor be equal to if you have no fillers?

T_b is the tension that is in the bolt. There are minimum levels of tensioning required for a bolt to be considered tensioned. The minimum tension depends on the bolt size and bolt material; values are given in Table J3.1.

- What is the minimum tension for a 1 in. diameter, A490 bolt?

n_s is the number of slip planes. It will be equal to 1 when bolts are in single shear.

The following example shows how the slip resistance of a connection is computed.

Example 5.6 Computing Slip Resistance

Compute ϕR_n for slipping for the connection shown.

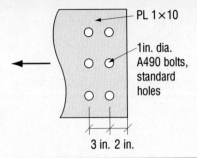

PL 1×10

1in. dia. A490 bolts, standard holes

3 in. 2 in.

Step 1 - Look up the bolt tension

The minimum bolt pretension is given in Table J3.1 for a 1 in. A490 bolt (Group B):

$$T_b = 64 \text{ kips}$$

Step 2 - Compute the slip resistance for a single bolt

The slip resistance of a single bolt is given by Eqn. J3-4:

$$R_n = \mu D_u h_f T_b n_s$$

The type of surface is not specified, so we will conservatively assume a Class A surface:

$$\mu = 0.30$$

D_u is always equal to 1.13 and h_f will be equal to 1.0 for no fillers. The number of slip planes is not specified so we will conservatively assume only one making $n_s = 1$.

$$R_n = (0.30)(1.13)(1.00)(64 \text{ kips})(1) = 21.7 \text{ kips/bolt}$$

Step 3 - Sum the bolt capacities and apply the resistance factor

The capacity of the connection for slipping will be equal to the sum of the capacities of all the bolts, multiplied by the resistance factor. For standard size holes, $\phi = 1.0$.

$$\phi R_n = (1.0)[(6 \text{ bolts})(21.7 \text{ kips/bolt})]$$
$$\phi R_n = \mathbf{130} \text{ kips}$$

In some situations a slip-critical connection may have an applied tension that reduces the clamping force of the bolts. Eqn. J3-5 gives an adjustment factor that accounts for such effects.

You Should Know

- Why do some connections need to be slip resistant?
- If the slip resistance of a connection is inadequate, what can you do to increase it?
- Where are minimum bolt pretensions tabulated?

conditions have high cycle of fatigue

increase number force or change surface

5.6 Bolt Layout

The previous sections have discussed the demands and capacities on bolted connections. The final two sections in the chapter cover bolt design. When we design a bolted connection we specify: the type of bolts, how many bolts will be used, what size the bolts will be, and how the bolts will be positioned.

There are standards for bolt positioning that should be followed when designing a connection. These standards include minimum and maximum edge distances and bolt-to-bolt spacing.

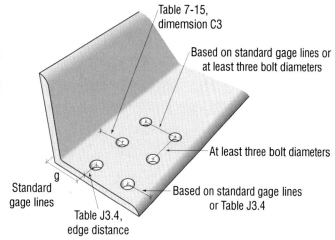

The figure above summarizes some of the standards pertaining to bolt layout. The various distances will be discussed in turn, beginning with *edge distances*, the distances from the center of the bolt holes to the edge. Table J3.4 provides minimum edge distances for bolts.

Study the Manual

Read §J3.4 of the Specification (page 16.1-122).

- True or False: It is okay to use edge distances less than those listed in Table J3.4 as long as excessive bearing limit states are checked.

Read §J3.5 of the Specification (page 16.1-122).

- What is the maximum distance a bolt can be positioned from an edge?

Read the commentary for §J3.5 of the Specification (page 16.1-402).

- Why is there a maximum edge distance for bolts?

The Specification also prescribes minimum and maximum *bolt-to-bolt* spacing. Minimum spacing requirements facilitate construction. If bolts are positioned too close to each other, it is difficult to get tools in to tighten them.

Study the Manual

Read §J3.3 of the Specification (page 16.1-122).

- What is the preferred center-to-center spacing of bolts?

When designing bolted connections, you should provide at least the preferred spacing.

Example 5.7 Bolt Spacing Requirements

A PL 3/4×8×3'-0" is to be connected at each end with (12) 3/4 in. bolts. Lay out the connection such that the length of the connection is minimized.

Step 1 - Envision the options

It is helpful to start by picturing what the choices would be for the layout. At this point, it will be unclear if some of them will actually work, but you need to envision the layouts before you can check them. The choices are:

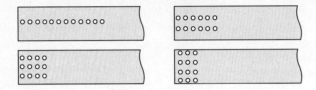

Step 2 - Compute the number of rows that can fit

The width of the bar is given as 8 inches. The minimum edge distance for a 3/4 in. bolt can be read from Table J3.4:

$$e_{min} = 1 \text{ in.}$$

The minimum preferred bolt spacing is 3 times the bolt diameter:

$$g_{min} = 3(3/4 \text{ in.}) = 2.25 \text{ in.}$$

The connection length will be minimized if the maximum possible number of rows is used. It looks like three rows might fit. The required width for three rows would be equal to two edge distances plus two bolt-to-bolt spacings:

$$w_{req} = 2(1 \text{ in.}) + 2(2.25 \text{ in.}) = 6.5 \text{ in.}$$

Sinice this required width is less than the available 8 in. it will work. We can see that adding another row will not work since 6.5 in. plus 2.25 in. will exceed 8 in.

Step 3 - Specify the design

Once we know three rows will fit, all that is left is to specify exactly where we want the bolts to be. There is not one right answer. Some positioning may provide better block shear resistance than others. The positioning shown below satisfies minimum edge distance and spacing requirements. It could now be checked for excessive bearing, block shear, and rupture of the net section.

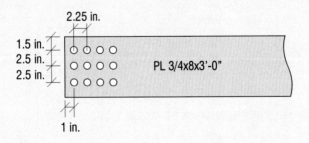

- What are the rules for bolt spacing and edge distances? *no less than $2^2/3$ bolt dia*

($3 \times$ is preferred) bolt dia

5.7 Design

When tension members are designed, information about the connection is required to compute the rupture limit state and block shear limit states. When connections are designed, information about the part geometry is required to lay out the bolts. Thus the connection design and member design are tied to each other and usually occur simultaneously. It can be difficult to know where to start. There is not one magic procedure that will lead you directly to the best solution every time.

To begin with, the engineer needs a rough idea about what the members and connections should look like for the particular thing being designed. Engineers get this rough idea by looking at similar things that have been designed and built. If the engineer is doing something completely unprecedented, which may not be a good idea until after they have a few years of experience, they may just guess something to get the design process rolling.

For bolted connections, it is usually necessary early in the design to assume a bolt material and size. If for some reason it needs to be adjusted later, the calculations can be updated.

The following example shows how the bolted connection for a tension member is integrated with the design of the tension member.

Example 5.8 Bolt Spacing Requirements

A short span road bridge will be made from wide flange members with gusset plates at the nodes. The wide flange members will be bolted to gusset plates through both flanges as indicated in the rough connection detail.

Specify a member for AB and design the bolted connection at each end of the member. The ultimate axial force in the member has already been determined and is indicated in the figure.

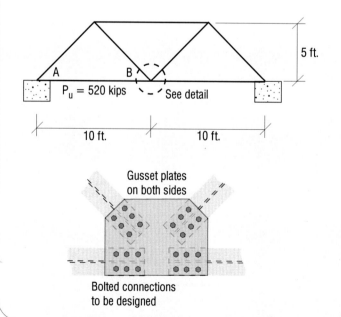

Gusset plates on both sides

Bolted connections to be designed

continued on next page

Example Continued

Step 1 - Get the factored demands

The first step in design is always to get the factored demands. In this problem the factored demands for AB are given:

$$P_u = 520 \text{ kips}$$

Step 2 - Estimate a member size and a bolt size

Going to Table 5-1, there are many wide flange shapes that may work for member AB. In determining which to try, we might consider the context of the design. First, the "thickness" of the truss is going to be equal to the depth of the wide flange shape we pick, so we may prefer to pick a wide flange with small depth. Second, the flange of the wide flange should be wide enough to comfortably fit a line of bolts on each side of the web. There are several shapes that would be equally good to try; we'll just pick one.

> Try W8×48

The W8×48 is a reasonable shape to try because its capacity for the yielding limit state is 634 kips (greater than P_u) and its capacity for the rupture limit state will probably be in the neighborhood of 520 kips (about equal to P_u). At this stage it is too early to know for sure what the rupture capacity will be (since the connection has not been designed).

We also need to estimate what bolt size to use. 7/8 in. and 1 in. are common sizes, and usually not a bad place to start. From Table 7-1, $\phi_v r_n = 24.3$ kips/bolt for a 7/8 in. dia. A325. This would mean we'd need 520/24.3=22 bolts. If A490 bolts were used, we'd need 520/30.7=17 bolts, which would give us a slightly shorter connection length. Either is fine, and it is unclear at this point which might be better. We just need to try something and move forward.

> Try (20) 7/8 in. A490 bolts.

Step 3 - Lay out the bolts

Now we need to lay out the connection. This step is required before we can compute excessive bearing of the bolts, block shear, or the rupture limit state.

The minimum edge distance can be determined from Table J3.4. For a 7/8 in. bolt it is 1 1/8 in. Bolts should be spaced at least 3(7/8)=2.625 in. apart. The gage distance for a W8×48 is given in Table 1-1.

> $g = 5.5$ in. (see the column in Table 1-1 labeled "Workable Gage")

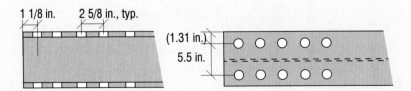

Step 4 - Compute the capacity of all pertinent limit states

Now that the connection layout has been determined, we can compute the capacity for all pertinent limit states.

Bolt shearing:

$$\phi R_n = (20 \text{ bolts})(30.7 \text{ kips/bolt}) = \textbf{614} \text{ kips (OK)}$$

Excessive bolt bearing:

End bolts
$$L_c = 1.125 \text{ in} - \frac{7/8 \text{ in.} + 1/16 \text{ in.}}{2} = 0.66 \text{ in.}$$
$t = 0.685$ in. (flange thickness of W8×48)
$R_n = 1.2(0.66 \text{ in.})(0.685 \text{ in.})(65 \text{ ksi}) \leq 2.4(0.875 \text{ in.})(0.685 \text{ in.})(65 \text{ ksi})$
$R_n = 35.3 \text{ kips} \leq 93.5 \text{ kips}$
$R_n = 35.3$ kips (per bolt)

Other bolts
$L_c = 2.625 \text{ in} - (7/8 \text{ in.} + 1/16 \text{ in.}) = 1.69 \text{ in.}$
$t = 0.685$ in. (flange thickness of W8×48)
$R_n = 1.2(1.69 \text{ in.})(0.685 \text{ in.})(65 \text{ ksi}) \leq 2.4(0.875 \text{ in.})(0.685 \text{ in.})(65 \text{ ksi})$
$R_n = 90.3 \text{ kips} \leq 93.5 \text{ kips}$
$R_n = 90.3$ kips (per bolt)

Total
$$\phi R_n = 0.75[(4 \text{ bolts})(35.3 \text{ k/bolt}) + (16 \text{ bolts})(90.3 \text{ k/bolt})] = \textbf{1190} \text{ kips (OK)}$$

Rupture Limit State:

$A_n = (14.1 \text{ in.}^2) - 4(7/8 \text{ in.} + 1/8 \text{ in.})(0.685 \text{ in.}) = 11.36 \text{ in.}^2$
$\bar{x} = 0.777$ in.
$l = 4(2.625 \text{ in.}) = 10.5 \text{ in.}$
$U = 1 - \frac{\bar{x}}{l} = 1 - \frac{0.777 \text{ in.}}{10.5 \text{ in.}} = 0.926$
$A_e = UA_n = 0.926(11.36 \text{ in.}^2) = 10.5 \text{ in.}^2$
$\phi R_n = 0.75(10.5 \text{ in.}^2)(65 \text{ ksi}) = \textbf{512} \text{ kips (NO GOOD)}$

We note that the rupture limit state capacity is less than the demand. That means that the W8×48 will not work for the member. Even though we know it doesn't work, we will go ahead and check the block shear capacity of the W8×48. That way before we pick a new shape to try, we will know if block shear is going to be an issue.

Block shear:

$A_{gt} = 4[(1.31 \text{ in.})(0.685 \text{ in.})] = 3.59 \text{ in.}^2$
$A_{gv} = 4[(1.125 \text{ in.} + 4(2.625 \text{ in.}))(0.685 \text{ in.})] = 31.85 \text{ in.}^2$
$A_{nt} = 3.59 \text{ in.}^2 - 4(0.5)[(7/8 \text{ in.} + 1/8 \text{ in.})(0.685 \text{ in.})] = 2.22 \text{ in.}^2$
$A_{nv} = 31.85 \text{ in.}^2 - 4(4.5)[(7/8 \text{ in.} + 1/8 \text{ in.})(0.685 \text{ in.})] = 19.52 \text{ in.}^2$

continued on next page

Example Continued

$$R_n = (0.6)(65 \text{ ksi})(19.52 \text{ in.}^2) + 1.0(65 \text{ ksi})(2.22 \text{ in.}^2) \leq$$
$$(0.6)(50 \text{ ksi})(31.85 \text{ in.}^2) + 1.0(65 \text{ ksi})(2.22 \text{ in.}^2)$$

$$R_n = 905.6 \text{ kips} \leq 1098 \text{ kips}$$
$$R_n = 905.6 \text{ kips}$$
$$\phi R_n = 0.75(905.6 \text{ kips}) = \mathbf{679} \text{ kips (OK)}$$

The block shear capacity is fine for the W8×48, so it will be fine for the next heavier shape as well.

Step 5 - Try another shape and finalize the design

Even though our first try didn't work out, it is not as if all of our previous calculations are wasted. In fact, we can finalize the design at this point with very little additional work. Since the W8×48 was barely inadequate for the rupture limit state, we can be fairly confident that the next heavier W8× will work.

Try W8×58

Rupture Limit State:

$$A_n = (17.1 \text{ in.}^2) - 4(7/8 \text{ in.} + 1/8 \text{ in.})(0.0.810 \text{ in.}) = 13.86 \text{ in.}^2$$
$$\bar{x} = 0.874 \text{ in.}$$
$$l = 4(25/8 \text{ in.}) = 10.5 \text{ in.}$$
$$U = 1 - \frac{\bar{x}}{l} = 1 - \frac{0.874 \text{ in.}}{10.5 \text{ in.}} = 0.917$$
$$A_e = UA_n = 0.917(13.86 \text{ in.}^2) = 12.7 \text{ in.}^2$$
$$\phi R_n = 0.75(12.7 \text{ in.}^2)(65 \text{ ksi}) = \mathbf{619} \text{ kips (OK)}$$

Note that for the W8×58 bolt shearing will be the lowest limit state (see previous calcs). So the limiting capacity for the member and connection is:

$$\phi R_n = \mathbf{614} \text{ kips (Bolt Shearing)}$$

We note that the W8×58 has excess tension capacity. It is possible that there is another wide flange shape (perhaps a W10×54) that is lighter and would do the job. But the design that we've arrived at is reasonable and has the benefit of providing a "thinner" truss.

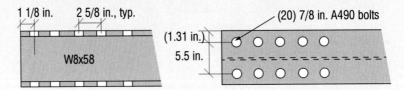

1 1/8 in.   2 5/8 in., typ.   (20) 7/8 in. A490 bolts

W8x58   (1.31 in.)   5.5 in.

Design

You Should Know

- Why can't connections be designed independently of the member? → need info on one or other for design
- How do you know what size/material of bolt to use?
- Why doesn't it matter too much if you guess the wrong size to start with?

[handwritten annotation connected to second bullet:] assume from other designs or similar problems then adjust later

Remember This

- Bolted connections are usually the most economical way to assemble a structure in the field, because they require less labor than welded or riveted connections.
- When the centroid of a bolt group is in line with the line-of-action of the member force, the connection is "simple" and the bolts can be assumed to resist the demand equally.
- Bolts may be loaded in shear, tension, or both. This chapter has focused on situations where bolts were in shear. You should refer to other materials and learn more before designing connections with bolts in tension or shear+tension.
- The capacity of a bolt in shear depends on whether it is failing through the threaded or unthreaded portions of the bolt.
- If the thickness of a part is thin, relative to the size of a bolt, then excessive bearing in the form of bolt-by-bolt block shear or hole elongation may occur.
- Tensioning the bolts increases the friction between parts and can provide slip resistant connections.
- The design of a bolted connection is typically integrated with the design of the member being connected.

Columns are one of the most basic structural elements and have been used for centuries. Compared to the stone columns of the Parthenon, steel columns are remarkably light and slender. While stone columns crack when overloaded, the capacity of steel columns is governed by buckling considerations.

Columns are often made from wide flange or HSS shapes.

6. Columns

Consider This

- How can tributary areas be used to compute column load effects?
- What is live load reduction? When can it be used?
- How are exterior wall loads different than floor loads?
- What are the limit states for columns?
- What is the difference between global and local buckling?
- Why are global and local slenderness so important for columns?
- What design aids are in the Manual to help with column design?

6.1 Overview

Columns in steel buildings collect loads from the various levels and transmit them down to the foundation. The demands on the columns under gravity loads depend on the magnitude of the floor and roof loads and the column spacing (in plan view). Column demands are relatively easy to compute when uniform floor and roof loads are assumed.

With regards to capacity, the strength of a column depends on four things:

1. The geometric properties of the cross-section
2. The length
3. The end connections (constraint)
4. The strength of the steel

The structure of this chapter is similar to the previous ones. Sections 6.2 through 6.6 will discuss how to compute column demands. Then Sections 6.7 through 6.14 will discuss how to compute the capacity of a column. Finally, Sections 6.15 and 6.16 will explain how to efficiently design columns.

6.2 Computing Demands with Tributary Areas

Consider a simple structure with four columns supporting a roof (a). When a uniform load is applied to the entire roof, intuition tells us that all of the columns will share the load equally (b). The load effects in each column would be equal to the total load divided by four.

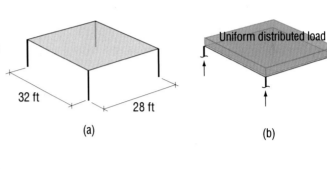

(a)   (b)

We reach the same conclusion using the idea of tributary areas. Tributary areas for columns are defined by lines running halfway between all of the columns in both directions, as shown in (c). The tributary area for one column is indicated in (d).

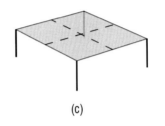   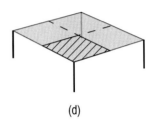

(c)   (d)

Once the tributary area for a column has been determined, the load effect is calculated as the uniformly-distributed load (usually given in psf) multiplied by the tributary area (usually in ft^2).

Example 6.1 Computing Column Demands Using Tributary Area

Calculate the factored demands for a column of the system discussed above if there is a uniformly-distributed roof dead load of 80 psf and a roof live load of 40 psf.

Step 1 - Calculate the tributary area for the column

The tributary area for one column is indicated in figure (d) above.

$$A_t = \left(\tfrac{32\,\text{ft}}{2}\right)\left(\tfrac{28\,\text{ft}}{2}\right) = 224 \text{ ft}^2$$

Step 2 - Calculate the dead and roof live load effects

The dead and live load effects are calculated by multiplying the uniform loads by the tributary area:

$$P_D = (80 \text{ psf})(224 \text{ ft}^2) = 17,900 \text{ lbs} = 17.9 \text{ kips}$$

It is common practice to convert from lbs to kips without formally stating the units conversion, as shown in the next equation.

$$P_{Lr} = (40 \text{ psf})(224 \text{ ft}^2) = 8.96 \text{ kips}$$

Step 3 - Compute the factored demand

By inspection, load combination 3 will govern (see page 2-10 of the Manual).

$$P_U = 1.2(17.9 \text{ kips}) + 1.6(8.96 \text{ kips}) + 0.5(0) = \textbf{36 kips}$$

For buildings with more than one story, the tributary areas for columns increase as you move down the frame. First-story columns will have the most tributary area because they have tributary area from all the floors above. Top-story columns will have the least tributary area since they have only the roof above. The general procedure for computing tributary areas and load effects for columns in multi-story buildings is demonstrated in the following example.

Example 6.2 Computing Column Demands in Multi-story Buildings

Compute the factored demands for the interior column at the first story given the following loads:

Floor Dead Load: 75 psf
Floor Live Load: 50 psf
Roof Dead Load: 42 psf
Roof Live Load: 20 psf

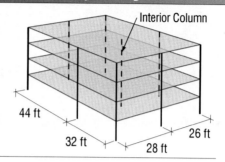

Step 1 - Calculate the tributary area (per floor) for the interior column

The tributary area for the interior column is determined by drawing lines midway between all the columns in both directions. These lines and the bounded area around the interior column are shown for the roof level to the right.

Tributary area at other levels is similar, but not shown for clarity

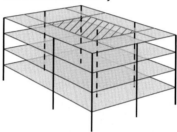

$$A_{t,level} = \left(\frac{44\text{ ft}}{2} + \frac{32\text{ ft}}{2}\right)\left(\frac{28\text{ ft}}{2} + \frac{26\text{ ft}}{2}\right)$$
$$A_{t,level} = 1026\text{ ft}^2 \text{ per floor/roof level}$$

Step 2 - Account for the appropriate number of floors and roof

The problem is asking about the interior column at the *first* story. The first story column has tributary area from three floors above and the roof. It is best to compute the tributary area from the floors and the roof separately since floor loads are different than roof loads.

$$A_{t,floors} = 3(1026\text{ ft}^2) = 3078\text{ ft}^2$$
$$A_{t,roof} = 1(1026\text{ ft}^2) = 1026\text{ ft}^2$$

Step 3 - Calculate the dead, live, and roof live load effects

Load effects are calculated by multiplying the uniform loads by the pertinent tributary areas.

$$P_D = (75\text{ psf})(3078\text{ ft}^2) + (42\text{ psf})(1026\text{ ft}^2) = 273.9\text{ kips}$$
$$P_L = (50\text{ psf})(3078\text{ ft}^2) = 153.9\text{ kips}$$
$$P_{Lr} = (20\text{ psf})(1026\text{ ft}^2) = 20.5\text{ kips}$$

Step 4 - Calculate the factored demand

By inspection, load combination 2 will govern.

$$P_U = 1.2(273.9\text{ kips}) + 1.6(153.9\text{ kips}) + 0.5(20.5\text{ kips}) = \textbf{585}\text{ kips}$$

Floors and stories are two different things. Floors are horizontal elements in a building and are supported by columns. The term "story" means the space between the floors. The "first-story columns" are those that are between the first and second floors. First-story columns carry load from all the floors and roof above.

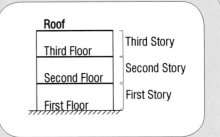

$A_{TC} = \left(\frac{w}{2}\right)\left(\frac{l}{2}\right) =$

You Should Know

- How do you compute the tributary area for a column?
- Why do we calculate the tributary roof area separately from the tributary floor area? (see Example 6.2, step 2)
- If a building has ten stories, how many floors does the fifth story column support?

5

6.3 Floor Live Load Reduction

The live loads that we use for design come from the document *ASCE 7* and represent fairly heavy loading (see Section 3.4). For columns that receive loads from large areas, it is unlikely that heavy live loading is present over the entire area at the same time. To account for this in design, *ASCE 7* provides a method for reducing the design live load for members that receive loads from large areas.

Live load reduction for columns is based on the area of influence of the column. To explain what the area of influence is, consider again the simple one-story building with four columns (a). If a point load were applied anywhere on the roof (other than the edge), all of the columns

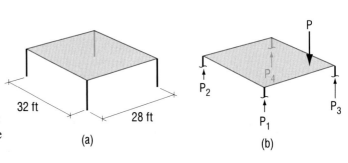

would have some load effect (b), but the columns won't share the load equally unless the point load were placed in the center. Since each of the columns has some load effect when the point load is placed anywhere on the roof, we say the area of influence for one column is equal to the entire roof area (896 ft²).

The area of influence is different than the tributary area. In the example above, if point loads were placed everywhere (a uniform distributed load), then the load effects in the columns would equalize, and the load effects could be calculated using the tributary area method. But the whole concept of tributary area is irrelevant except when there are uniform distributed loads. The area of influence of a column will overlap that of other columns, and will be equal to four times the tributary area (as long as the slab does not cantilever).

ASCE 7 provides an equation for live load reduction as a function of the area of influence. For columns that have areas of influence greater than 400 ft², the live load may be reduced using the equation:

$$L = L_o \left(0.25 + \frac{15}{\sqrt{K_{LL}A_t}} \right)$$

where L_o is the unreduced live load (usually in psf) and $K_{LL}A_t$ is the area of influence (in ft²) for the total *floor* area supported by the column. For the case of a column, K_{LL} is equal to 4 since the area of influence is four times bigger than that tributary area (as long as the slab does not cantilever).

There is a limit to how much the live load can be reduced. For a column supporting only one floor, the live load may only be reduced to 50% of the unreduced live load. For a column supporting more than one floor, the live load may be reduced only to 40% of the unreduced live load. If the formula above indicates a reduction greater than these values, use the maximum reductions just explained.

Example 6.3 Computing Reduced Floor Live Load

If the unreduced floor live load for the building is 40 psf, what is the reduced floor live load for the indicated column?

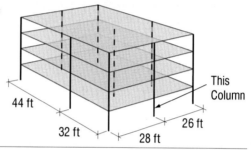

Step 1 - Calculate the tributary area (per floor) for the column

The tributary area for one level will be determined as a first step. The tributary area for one level is:

$$A_{t,level} = \left(\tfrac{32 \text{ ft}}{2} \right) \left(\tfrac{28 \text{ ft}}{2} + \tfrac{26 \text{ ft}}{2} \right)$$
$$A_{t,level} = 432 \text{ ft}^2 \text{ per level}$$

Step 2 - Calculate the total tributary floor area

The first story column is what we are considering. Summing the tributary areas for all the *floors* above the first story column:

$$A_t = (3 \text{ floors})(432 \text{ ft}^2 \text{ per floor}) = 1296 \text{ ft}^2$$

The area of influence will be four times this tributary area. Since the area of influence will be greater than 400 ft², the live load may be reduced.

Step 3 - Calculate the reduced live load

$$L = L_o \left(0.25 + \frac{15}{\sqrt{4(1296)}} \right) = L_o(0.46)$$

The formula indicates the reduced live load is 46% of the unreduced live load. This is greater than the 40% lower limit, so the reduced live load *is* $L_o(0.46)$. If the equation had yielded a reduced live load of less than 40%, we would have just used 40%.

$$L = L_o(0.46) = (40 \text{ psf})(0.46) = \textbf{18.3 psf}$$

6.4 Roof Live Load Reduction

Roof live loads may also be reduced, but the equation is different than for floor live loads. The equation for roof live load reduction given in ASCE 7 is:

$$L_r = L_o R_1 R_2$$

where L_o is the unreduced live load (usually in psf), R_1 is a factor related to the tributary area (A_t), and R_2 is a factor related to the pitch of the roof.

$R_1 = 1$	for $A_t \leq 200 \text{ ft}^2$
$R_1 = 1.2 - 0.001A_t$	for $200 \text{ ft}^2 < A_t < 600 \text{ ft}^2$
$R_1 = 0.6$	for $A_t \geq 600 \text{ ft}^2$

$R_2 = 1$	for roof slope of less than 4 in. of rise per foot.
$R_2 = 1.2 - 0.05F$	for roof slope, F, between 4 in. and 12 in.
$R_2 = 0.6$	for roof slope greater than 12 in. of rise per foot.

The roof live load may not be reduced to less than 12 psf. If a smaller value is calculated using the equation, use 12 psf. The following example shows how the reduced roof live load is computed.

Example 6.4 Computing Reduced Roof Live Load

If the unreduced roof live load is 20 psf, what is the reduced roof live load (in psf) that should be used when computing the demands on the indicated column.

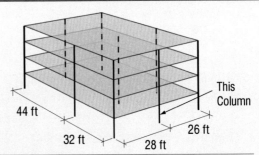

This Column

44 ft

32 ft   28 ft   26 ft

Step 1 - Calculate the tributary roof area for the column

$$A_t = \left(\tfrac{32 \text{ ft}}{2}\right)\left(\tfrac{28 \text{ ft}}{2} + \tfrac{26 \text{ ft}}{2}\right) = 432 \text{ ft}^2$$

Step 2 - Calculate the reduced live load

$R_1 = 1.2 - 0.001A_t$	since $200 \text{ ft}^2 < A_t < 600 \text{ ft}^2$
$R_1 = 1.2 - 0.001(432) = 0.768$	
$R_2 = 1$	since the roof is flat
$L_r = L_o R_1 R_2 = (20 \text{ psf})(0.768)(1) = 15.4 \text{ psf}$	

The computed value is greater than 12 psf, so we use the computed value.

$$L_r = \mathbf{15.4} \text{ psf}$$

6.5 Exterior Wall Loads

Most buildings have exterior walls of some kind. The weight of the exterior walls can be significant.

Example 6.5 Computing Exterior Wall Loads

If the exterior wall weighs 25 psf, what is the total weight of the exterior walls?

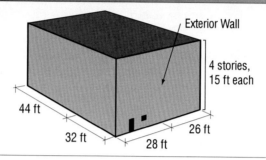

Exterior Wall

4 stories, 15 ft each

44 ft

32 ft

28 ft

26 ft

Step 1 - Calculate the surface area of the exterior wall

The weight of the walls is given in pounds per square foot, so the first step is to determine the surface area of the exterior walls. The total surface area will be equal to the building perimeter multiplied by the building height.

$$perimeter = 2(44\text{ ft} + 32\text{ ft}) + 2(28\text{ ft} + 26\text{ ft}) = 260\text{ ft}$$
$$height = (4\text{ stories})(15\text{ ft/story}) = 60\text{ ft}$$
$$area = (260\text{ ft})(60\text{ ft}) = 15{,}600\text{ ft}^2$$

Step 2 - Calculate the weight

The total wall weight is the weight (in psf) multiplied by the total surface area.

$$W_{wall} = (25\text{ psf})(15{,}600\text{ ft}^2) = \mathbf{390}\text{ kips}$$

If the exterior walls sat on the ground (a), then none of the exterior wall weight would need to be supported by the columns. But most of the time, the exterior walls are supported by the floors. Figure (b) illustrates a common case where the exterior wall at each story "sits" on the floor below and "hangs" from the floor above.

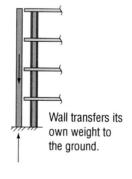

Wall transfers its own weight to the ground.

(a)

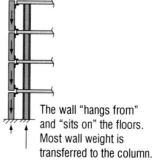

The wall "hangs from" and "sits on" the floors. Most wall weight is transferred to the column.

(b)

Demands

Column load effects from the exterior walls can be computed using tributary areas. Tributary areas are defined by drawing vertical lines between all of the columns. Horizontal lines are drawn through the middle of each story, since the wall is assumed to "hang" from the level above and "sit" on the level below. Only the exterior columns will have load effects from the exterior wall weight. The example below illustrates how tributary areas are used to compute the load effects from the exterior walls.

Example 6.6 Calculating Load Effects from Exterior Walls

The exterior walls are supported at each level. If the exterior wall weight is 25 psf, what is the load effect in the column of interest at the first story?

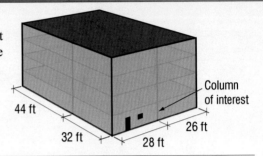

Step 1 - Identify the tributary area

The tributary areas are defined by vertical lines located halfway between the exterior columns and horizontal lines that run through the middle of each story. At the first story, the column of interest has tributary area from all the stories above and half of the first story (since the wall is assumed to hang from the floor above).

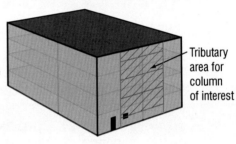

$$A_t = \left(\frac{28\text{ ft}}{2} + \frac{26\text{ ft}}{2}\right)\left(3\tfrac{1}{2}\text{ stories}\right)(15\text{ ft/story}) = 1418\text{ ft}^2$$

Step 2 - Calculate the load effect

The load effect in the column at the first story is equal to the wall weight multiplied by the tributary area. Since the wall weight is dead load, the load effect from the exterior wall is designated, $P_{D,wall}$.

$$P_{D,wall} = (25\text{ psf})(1418\text{ ft}^2) = \textbf{35.5 kips}$$

You Should Know

- When will columns have load effects from the exterior walls?
- Will interior columns ever have load effects from the exterior walls?
- In Example 6.6, why were 3.5 stories used when computing the tributary area, if only 3 stories are above the first story column?

when they are connected (walls supported by floors)

no

6.6 Factored Demands

With an understanding of tributary areas, live load reduction, and exterior wall loads, the load effects in any column at any story can be determined in four steps:

1. Compute the tributary floor area and tributary roof area (keep them separate).
2. Compute the tributary wall area (for exterior columns only).
3. Reduce the floor and roof live loads.
4. Compute and factor the load effects.

The following example shows how these steps are applied.

Example 6.7 Computing Column Demands

The building shown has eleven stories. The story height is 13 ft. Compute the demand in a corner column at the third story given the following loads.

Floor Dead: 80 psf
Floor Live: 50 psf
Roof Dead: 42 psf
Roof Live: 20 psf
Ext Wall: 22 psf

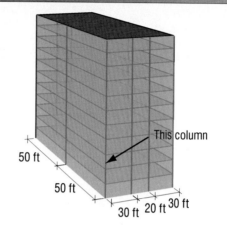

Step 1 - Calculate tributary floor and roof area

$$A_{t,level} = \left(\frac{50\ ft}{2}\right)\left(\frac{30\ ft}{2}\right)$$
$$= 375\ ft^2\ \text{per level}$$

$$A_{t,floors} = (375\ ft^2\ \text{per level})(8\ \text{floors})$$
$$= 3000\ ft^2$$

$$A_{t,roof} = (375\ ft^2\ \text{per level})(1\ \text{roof})$$
$$= 375\ ft^2$$

Step 2 - Calculate tributary wall area

$$A_{t,wall} = \left(\frac{50\ ft}{2} + \frac{30\ ft}{2}\right) \times$$
$$(8\tfrac{1}{2}\ \text{stories})(13\ ft/\text{story})$$
$$= 4420\ ft^2$$

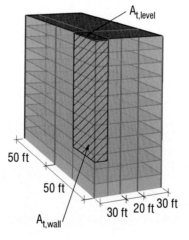

continued on next page

Step 3 - Calculate the reduced live loads

For the floor:

$$L = L_o\left(0.25 + \frac{15}{\sqrt{4A_t}}\right) = (50\text{ psf})\left(0.25 + \frac{15}{\sqrt{4(3000)}}\right) = (50\text{ psf})(0.387)$$

The formula indicates the reduced live load is 38.7 % of the unreduced live load. This is less than the 40 % lower limit so the lower limit governs:

$$L = (50\text{ psf})(0.40) = \mathbf{20}\text{ psf}$$

For the roof:

$$L_r = L_o R_1 R_2$$
$$R_1 = 1.2 - 0.001A_t = 1.2 - 0.001(375) = 0.825$$
$$R_2 = 1$$
$$L_r = L_o R_1 R_2 = (20\text{ psf})(0.825)(1) = 16.5\text{ psf}$$

The computed value is greater than 12 psf, so we use the computed value.

$$L_r = \mathbf{16.5}\text{ psf}$$

Step 4 - Calculate the load effects and factor them

The dead load effect is the sum of the effects from the floor dead loads, roof dead loads, and exterior wall loads:

$$P_D = (80\text{ psf})(3000\text{ ft}^2) + (42\text{ psf})(375\text{ ft}^2) + (22\text{ psf})(4420\text{ ft}^2)$$
$$P_D = 353.0\text{ kips}$$

The effects from live loads and roof live loads are:

$$P_L = (20\text{ psf})(3000\text{ ft}^2) = 60.0\text{ kips}$$
$$P_{Lr} = (16.5\text{ psf})(375\text{ ft}^2) = 6.19\text{ kips}$$

By inspection, load combination 2 governs (since the dead load is not more than eight times greater than the live):

$$P_U = 1.2(353.0\text{ kips}) + 1.6(60.0\text{ kips}) + 0.5(6.19\text{ kips}) = \mathbf{523}\text{ kips}$$

You Should Know

- How would Example 6.7 be different if we were calculating demands for the corner column at the tenth story?
- When do you need to include load effects from the exterior wall?

when floor is being supporting exterior walls

6.7 Buckling

The previous sections have discussed column demands. Now let's turn our attention to column capacities. The maximum load a column can carry is limited by buckling. Buckling can either be global or local. When a column experiences global buckling, it pops out of alignment and appears bowed (a). There is no deformation of any of the cross sections; they just rotate relative to each other. When a column experiences local buckling (b), it may crush like a soda can or have concentrated deformation at one section. Local buckling involves deformation at the cross-sectional level. Shapes that have very thin elements of the cross section are susceptible to local buckling.

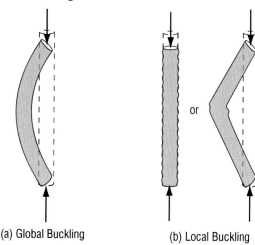

(a) Global Buckling   (b) Local Buckling

In the following sections global buckling will be addressed first. We will then come back to local buckling.

You Should Know

- What are the differences between global and local buckling?

6.8 Euler Buckling Capacity

In the mid 1700's the mathematician Leonhard Euler developed the column buckling theory that is the basis for column capacity equations. From Euler's theory, a column that is initially straight and pinned at each end (pinned-pinned) will experience *global* buckling when the axial load equals:

$$P_e = \frac{\pi^2 EI}{L^2}$$

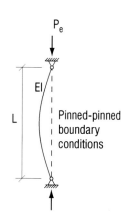

In the equation above, P_e is the *Euler buckling load* for a pinned-pinned column, E is the modulus of elasticity of the column material, I is the moment of inertia of the cross-section, and L is the unbraced length of the column. The derivation of the Euler buckling load can be found in most Mechanics of Materials textbooks. It is interesting to note that the Euler buckling load is not a function of the material strength (F_y).

Example 6.8 Calculating the Euler Buckling Load for a Column

What is the Euler buckling load for a pinned-pinned column that is a 30 ft long Pipe 8 Std.?

Step 1 - Get appropriate values

The Euler buckling load is a function of the modulus of elasticity, E, moment of inertia, I, and the length, L.

$E = 29,000$ ksi
$I = 68.1$ in.^{4} (see Table 1-14)
$L = 30$ ft $= 360$ in. (given)

Note: a common mistake in column calculations is to forget to convert the column length to inches.

Step 2 - Use the Euler buckling load equation

$$P_e = \frac{\pi^2 EI}{L^2} = \frac{(3.14^2)(29,000 \text{ ksi})(68.1 \text{ in.}^4)}{(360 \text{ in.})^2} = \mathbf{150} \text{ kips}$$

So the column would experience global buckling if an axial load of 150 kips were applied.

You Should Know

- If two pinned-pinned columns have the same cross-section, material, and boundary conditions, but one is twice as long as the other, what will be the difference in the Euler buckling load?
- What is the *only* material property that influences the Euler buckling load?

6.9 Boundary Conditions

The previous discussion was about columns with pinned-pinned boundary conditions. Columns with more or less constraint at the ends will have higher or lower buckling loads than the pinned-pinned case.

Consider the three columns shown below. The *Euler* buckling load has been derived for each case and is indicated next to each figure. The fixed-fixed column (center) has four times the buckling load as the pinned-pinned column (left); but the fixed-free (right) case has only one-fourth the buckling load as the pinned-pinned.

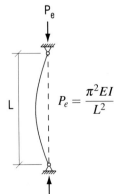

$$P_e = \frac{\pi^2 EI}{L^2}$$

$$P_e = \frac{4\pi^2 EI}{L^2}$$

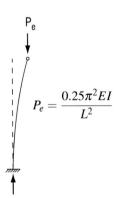

$$P_e = \frac{0.25\pi^2 EI}{L^2}$$

pinned-pinned
connection
L →unbraced
length of
column

We observe from the three cases just shown that the buckling load equations are the same except for one coefficient. It is convenient to write a general form of the Euler buckling that can be applied to columns with any boundary conditions. This is accomplished by introducing an *effective length factor*, K:

$$P_e = \frac{\pi^2 EI}{(KL)^2}$$

The *effective length factor* accounts for the influence of the boundary conditions. For the pinned-pinned case, $K=1$; but for the fixed-fixed case K would be equal to 0.5 (since K is squared in the denominator, this is equivalent to 4 in the numerator).

Study the Manual

In the Commentary to Appendix 7, there is a table that gives values for K for different situations. Turn to Table C-A-7.1 (page 16.1-511).

- Which case corresponds to fixed-fixed boundary conditions?

- What is the value for K when the column is fixed-fixed?

- What is the difference between case (a) and case (c)?

The table gives both the theoretical value for K, obtained directly from Euler buckling theory, and a recommended design value. Recommended design values should be used for design; they account for differences between actual and idealized boundary conditions.

Example 6.9 Calculating the Buckling Load for a Flagpole

What is the Euler buckling load for a 50 ft flag pole that is fixed at the base and made from Pipe 8 Std. Use the recommended design value for K.

Step 1 - Look up cross-sectional properties

The properties for Pipe 8 Std. can be looked up in Table 1-14:

$A = 7.85$ in.^{2}
$I = 68.1$ in.^{4}

Step 2 - Look up the effective length factor

From Table C-A-7.1, case (c) applies for a flag pole that is fixed at the base and free to sway at the top:

$K = 2.10$

We should use the recommended design K and not the theoretical K value.

Step 3 - Compute the buckling load

$$P_e = \frac{\pi^2 EI}{(KL)^2} = \frac{(3.14^2)(29,000 \text{ ksi})(68.1 \text{ in.}^4)}{[(2.10)(50 \times 12 \text{ in.})]^2} = \mathbf{12.3} \text{ kips}$$

6.10 Slenderness Ratio

The stress in a column when it buckles is called the buckling stress. The equation for the buckling stress is simply the buckling load divided by the cross-sectional area of the column.

$$F_e = \frac{P_e}{A} = \frac{\pi^2 EI}{A(KL)^2}$$

It is convenient to replace the terms I and A with a single term called the *radius of gyration*, r. You may recall from Mechanics that the radius of gyration is defined as:

$$r = \sqrt{\frac{I}{A}}$$

The equation for the buckling stress can now be written as:

$$F_e = \frac{P_e}{A} = \frac{\pi^2 E}{\left(\dfrac{KL}{r}\right)^2}$$

The term in the denominator, KL/r, is called the *slenderness ratio*. This is the only term in the buckling stress equation that will vary from column to column. In other words, the buckling stress of a steel column is only a function of the slenderness ratio.

Study the Manual

Turn to Chapter E in the Specification (page 16.1-31). This is the chapter that explains how to compute the capacity of compression members. Read Section E2.

- What is the preferred limit for KL/r for compression members?

Section E3 presents equations for column design. We are not ready to fully understand E3-1 through E3-3, but it is good to point out E3-4 right now.

- What is Equation E3-4?

Later on we will see how the Euler buckling stress is used to compute design strengths for columns.

Example 6.11 Understanding the Radius of Gyration

The radius of gyration, r, is an indicator of flexural stiffness. Consider two pipes with different cross-sections but the same cross-sectional area:

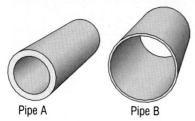

Pipe A   Pipe B

The radius of gyration for Pipe B is much larger than the radius of gyration for Pipe A because the material for Pipe B is farther from the centroid. If we were to try bending the two pipes, we would find that Pipe B is much stiffer. A higher radius of gyration gives a steel shape greater flexural stiffness.

Example 6.10 Calculating the Euler Buckling Stress for a Column

What is the slenderness ratio and Euler buckling stress for a pinned-pinned column that is a 30 ft long Pipe 8 Std.?

Step 1 - Get the necessary information

The values we'll need are:

$E = 29,000$ ksi
$r = 2.95$ in. (see Table 1-14)
$L = 30$ ft $= 360$ in. (given)
$K = 1$ (pinned-pinned column)

Step 2 - Compute the slenderness ratio

$$\frac{KL}{r} = \frac{(1)(360 \text{ in.})}{2.95 \text{ in.}} = \textbf{122.0}$$

A common mistake is to forget to convert L to inches when computing the slenderness ratio. Note that the slenderness ratio ends up unitless.

Step 3 - Use the Euler buckling stress equation

$$F_e = \frac{\pi^2 E}{\left(\frac{KL}{r}\right)^2} = \frac{(3.14^2)(29,000 \text{ ksi})}{122.0^2} = \textbf{19.2} \text{ ksi}$$

6.11 Governing Slenderness Ratio

From the preceding discussion, we see that it is easy to calculate the Euler buckling stress, once the slenderness ratio (KL/r) is known. However, most columns will have multiple values for r, K, and L and some work is required to determine what KL/r ratio is appropriate. In this subsection we will consider how one column may have multiple values for r, K, and L.

The radius of gyration, r, is calculated with respect to an axis that passes through the centroid of a cross-section. For a circular cross-section, r will be the same for any axis that passes through the centroid (below-left). This characteristic makes pipes and round HSS shapes efficient for columns.

 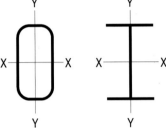

Rectangular tubes and wide-flange shapes are often used for columns, but they have different values for r for different axes that pass through the centroid. The Manual reports values of r corresponding to the axes that give the greatest and smallest r. The axis that gives the greatest r is designated the X-X axis and is often referred to as the "strong axis." The axis that gives the lowest r is designated the Y-Y axis and is often referred to as the "weak axis." (above-right).

Study the Manual

Turn to Table 1-13 and look at the HSS7.50×0.500.

- What is the value for r? (notice that there is only one)

Now Turn to Table 1-1. Notice that in the figure on the upper-left corner of the left-hand pages there is a key indicating the X-X and Y-Y axes.

- For a W14×132, what is r for the X-X axis?

- For a W14×132, what is r for the Y-Y axis?

For comparison consider a W30×132 which has the same weight (same cross-sectional area) but a much different shape.

- For a W30×132, what is r for the X-X axis?

- For a W30×132, what is r for the Y-Y axis?

In comparing the two, you'll notice that the W14×132 has more balanced values between the r for the strong and weak axes.

Just as the same shape can have multiple values of r, the same column could have multiple values of K. For example, consider the column illustrated below with idealized boundary conditions; about the x-axis the ends are free to rotate, whereas the ends are fixed against rotation about the y-axis. We might envision two ways in which the column might buckle. If it were to buckle about the x-axis (left) the ends would rotate, and we would consider K equal to 1.0 when computing the buckling load. Alternately, if it were to buckle about the y-axis (right) the ends would not rotate and we would consider K equal to 0.5 when computing the buckling load.

Strong Axis (x-axis)
Flexural Buckling

Since the end is free to rotatate in this direction, $K=1.0$ for strong axis (x-axis) buckling.

Weak Axis (y-axis)
Flexural Buckling

Since the end is NOT free to rotatate in this direction, $K=0.5$ for weak axis (y-axis) buckling.

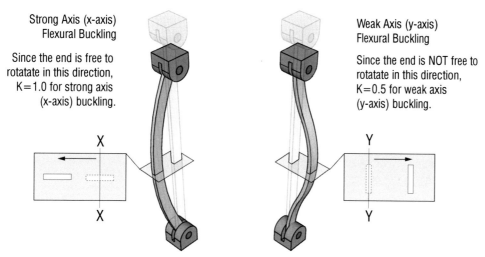

We have demonstrated how a column might have multiple values of K and r depending on what direction or axis we are considering. We will close this section by considering how we might have multiple values of L for the same column. Consider the case illustrated below of a column that has two restraining beams framing in one side and one restraining beam framing in the other. If the column were to buckle about its strong axis as shown on the left, the unbraced length is two times greater than if the column were to buckle about its weak axis as shown on the right.

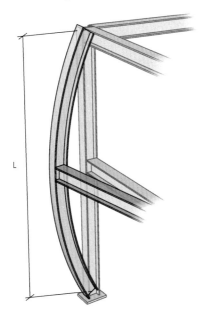

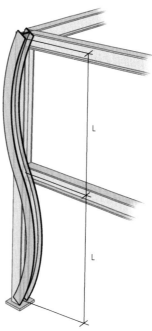

You Should Know

- How can there be different values of K and L for a single column?

depends on what axis is being looked at

When a column has multiple values of K, L, or r, we need to consider KL/r for all the directions in which the column *might* buckle. The KL/r that is the highest indicates how the column *will* buckle and is the KL/r that should be used in the buckling stress equation.

Example 6.12 Determining the Critical Value for KL/r

A steel column is 3 feet tall with the idealized boundary conditions and cross-section shown. Compute the slenderness ratio, KL/r, corresponding to buckling about the X-X axis and Y-Y axis. Which buckling would occur?

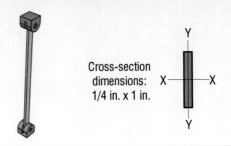

Cross-section dimensions: 1/4 in. x 1 in.

Step 1 - Calculate r_x and r_y

The radius of gyration for an area with respect to some axis is: $r = \sqrt{I/A}$. For the given cross-section:

$$A = (0.25 \text{ in.})(1.0 \text{ in.}) = 0.25 \text{ in.}^2$$

$$I_x = \frac{(0.25 \text{ in.})(1.0 \text{ in.})^3}{12} = 0.0208 \text{ in.}^4 \qquad r_x = \sqrt{\frac{0.0208 \text{ in.}^4}{0.25 \text{ in.}^2}} = 0.288 \text{ in.}$$

$$I_y = \frac{(1.0 \text{ in.})(0.25 \text{ in.})^3}{12} = 0.0013 \text{ in.}^4 \qquad r_y = \sqrt{\frac{0.0013 \text{ in.}^4}{0.25 \text{ in.}^2}} = 0.072 \text{ in.}$$

Step 2 - Calculate KL/r for strong-axis buckling

For buckling about the strong (X-X) axis, K will be equal to 1.0 (see discussion on previous page) so:

$$(KL)_x = 1.0(3 \times 12 \text{ in.}) = 36 \text{ in.}$$

Since the buckling is with respect to the strong (X-X) axis, r_x should be used when computing KL/r

$$\frac{(KL)_x}{r_x} = \frac{36 \text{ in.}}{0.288 \text{ in.}} = \mathbf{125}$$

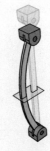

Step 3 - Calculate KL/r for weak-axis buckling

For buckling about the weak (Y-Y) axis, K will be equal to 0.5 (see discussion on previous page) so:

$$(KL)_y = 0.5(3 \times 12 \text{ in.}) = 18 \text{ in.}$$

Since the buckling is with respect to the weak (Y-Y) axis, r_y should be used when computing KL/r

$$\frac{(KL)_y}{r_y} = \frac{18 \text{ in.}}{0.072 \text{ in.}} = \mathbf{250}$$

Since this value of KL/r is the highest, weak-axis buckling will govern.

6.12 Effective Length for Typical Columns

The picture below shows a three-story building during erection. The columns are made from single pieces of steel that are 50 ft. long; however, in design it would *not* be appropriate to use L=50 ft. for the column buckling calculations.

The reason why we don't use L=50 ft for the columns is that they are restrained at each floor level. You'll notice from the picture that some of the bays are (or will be) braced. These braced bays inhibit lateral translations of the floors in either direction. Even though the columns are 50 ft. long, they are restrained against translation at each floor level so the *unbraced* length is the story height.

The preceding discussion was about L, but we also need to know an appropriate value for K. While the framing provides lateral restraint to the columns at each floor, it generally does not provide rotational restraint (unless there are welded moment connections between the beams and columns). Recall that the maximum value of K for a column that cannot translate at either end is K=1.0. For gravity columns (that *only* carry gravity loads) it is reasonable to use a value of K=1.0 for both directions (strong and weak-axis buckling).

For columns that are part of the lateral force resisting system (braced bays or moment-resisting bays) greater care must be taken in determining an appropriate value for K. The commentary for Appendix 7 discusses some accepted procedures for determining K for lateral force resisting columns. In the remaining examples in this section, K will either be assumed as 1.0 for both directions or will be given.

6.13 Inelastic Buckling

The equation for the Euler buckling stress is:

$$F_e = \frac{\pi^2 E}{\left(\dfrac{KL}{r}\right)^2}$$

The graph to the right shows the Euler buckling stress plotted versus the slenderness ratio. As the slenderness gets small (column becomes stout), the Euler buckling stress approaches infinity. However, we know that even stout steel columns are not infinitely strong. The maximum stress that can develop is F_y (indicated by the horizontal line on the plot). In other words, material yielding puts a "cap" on the buckling capacity of shorter columns.

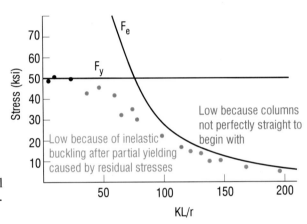

When experiments are conducted, columns buckle at stresses lower than those indicated by the lines in the graph above. All columns will fall a little below the lines because they are not perfectly straight to begin with, as assumed in Euler buckling theory, and it is challenging to load them precisely in the center. Wide flange columns with KL/r around 100 or less tend to yield early at the tips of the flanges because of residual stresses. When parts of the flanges yield, some stiffness is lost and the column then buckles. This mode of failure is called inelastic global buckling. When we get to design, you will begin to notice that most columns will end up having KL/r around 100 or less. This means that inelastic global buckling is most often what limits the capacity of columns.

> Residual stresses are stresses that get locked into a hot-rolled shape as it cools and shrinks. After a wide flange is rolled, the tips of the flanges cool at a faster rate than the rest of the shape. When the rest of the cross section cools and shrinks, it locks in compressive stresses in the already-cooled flanges. Thus, when a wide flange is subjected to compressive axial loads, the tips of the flanges will yield earlier than the rest of the cross section.

- Does the Euler buckling stress depend on the material strength?
- Why don't actual tall columns reach the Euler buckling stress when tested? *bc don't start out straight to begin w/*
- Which part of a wide flange cross section has residual compressive stresses? *tips*
- What type of failure governs the capacity of most columns? *inelastic global buckling*

6.14 Design Equations

Chapter E of the Specification begins with preliminary information about the design of compression members.

Turn to Chapter E of the Specification. Read Section E1 (page 16.1-31).

- What is the notation for designating the design compressive strength of a column?

- What is the value for the resistance factor?

E1 mentions three different kinds of buckling: flexural buckling (FB), torsional buckling (TB), and flexural-torsional buckling (FTB). The TABLE USER NOTE E1.1 (on page 16.1-32) indicates which limit states are pertinent to which cross sections.

Look at TABLE USER NOTE E1.1.

- Which limit states (kinds of buckling) pertain to wide flange columns?

- Which limit states (kinds of buckling) pertain to HSS or Pipe columns?

The discussion in this chapter thus far has been about flexural buckling (FB). Flexural buckling IS the global buckling that we've been discussing (Euler buckling). As indicated in the table, wide flange shapes may also be susceptible to torsional buckling (where the cross sections along the length twist rather than translate). Torsional buckling of wide flange shapes rarely governs; it will be addressed in the next chapter.

From TABLE USER NOTE E1.1.

- Which section of the Specification addresses flexural buckling?

- Which section of the Specification addresses torsional buckling?

You read E2 earlier when we were discussing KL/r. Quickly review it again before moving on.

Section E3 of the Manual gives the equations for computing the flexural buckling capacity of wide flange and tube columns that do not have local buckling issues. We will discuss local buckling separately.

Study the Manual

Look at equation E3-1 (page 16.1-33). The nominal compressive strength is determined by getting a critical stress and multiplying it by the gross area of the column.

There are two equations for getting the critical stress, E3-2 and E3-3. Which one you use depends on KL/r for the column you are checking.

- For what values of KL/r does E3-2 apply?

- For what values of KL/r does E3-3 apply?

It can be tedious to compute 4.71 times the square root of (E/F_y) every time you use the equations. It is helpful if you just compute it once and write it in the margin of the manual. When F_y is 50 ksi, it will be 113.

- What is 4.71 times the square root of (E/F_y) when F_y is 46 (rectangular HSS)?

- What is 4.71 times the square root of (E/F_y) when F_y is 42 (round HSS)?

- Have you written these values in the margin of your Manual?

The figure below shows what Equations E3-2 and E3-3 look like when they are graphed (for $F_y=50$ ksi). You can see that one or the other will apply, depending on what KL/r is for your column.

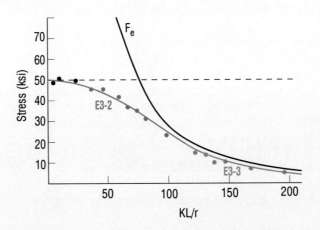

When KL/r is less than 4.71 times the square root of (E/F_y), it means that inelastic global buckling will limit the capacity and E3-2 is used to compute the critical stress. Otherwise, elastic global buckling is what limits capacity and equation E3-3 applies.

Example 6.13 Computing Column Capacity Using the Equations

Compute the factored capacity of a W12×96 column. $KL_x = KL_y = 16$ ft.

Step 1 - Look up cross sectional properties

From Table 1-1:

$$A_g = 28.2 \text{ in.}^2$$
$$r_y = 3.09 \text{ in.}$$

We only need to get r_y because we know that weak axis buckling will govern since KL is the same for both the strong and weak axis

Step 2 - Compute the slenderness and the Euler buckling stress

A common mistake is to mess-up units when computing the slenderness. Remember to convert your effective length into units of inches.

$$\frac{KL}{r} = \frac{(16 \times 12 \text{ in.})}{(3.09 \text{ in.})} = 62.1$$

$$F_e = \frac{\pi^2 E}{\left(\frac{KL}{r}\right)^2} = \frac{(3.14^2)(29,000 \text{ ksi})}{(62.1)^2} = 74.1 \text{ ksi}$$

Step 3 - Compute the critical stress

Since

$$\frac{KL}{r} < 4.71\sqrt{E/F_y} \qquad (62.1 < 113)$$

Equation E3-2 applies.

$$F_{cr} = \left[0.658^{\frac{F_y}{F_e}}\right] F_y = \left[0.658^{\left(\frac{50 \text{ ksi}}{74.1 \text{ ksi}}\right)}\right](50 \text{ ksi}) = 37.7 \text{ ksi}$$

Step 4 - Compute the factored capacity

Using Equation E3-1

$$P_n = F_{cr}A_g = (37.7 \text{ ksi})(28.2 \text{ in.}^2) = 1063 \text{ kips}$$

So the factored capacity is:

$$\phi_c P_n = (0.9)(1063 \text{ kips}) = \mathbf{957} \text{ kips}$$

You Should Know

- What part of the Specification discusses compression members? Ch E section E1
- Why are there two equations for the critical stress?
- How can you tell if the capacity of a column is limited by inelastic buckling?

6.15 Axial Capacity Tables

The Manual has several tables for determining column capacities. Tables 4-1 through 4-6 give capacities for wide flange and HSS shapes that are commonly used as columns. For all other cases, Table 4-22 can be used.

Study the Manual

Turn to the first page of Table 4-1.

On the left side of the table there are values for KL (with respect to the weak axis). This means that the Table is assuming that weak-axis buckling governs the capacity. This is usually the case, but not always.

There are columns in the table for the wide flange shapes that are typically used for columns (W14s, W12s, and W10s). For each shape the factored capacity, $\phi_c P_n$, is listed for various values of KL.

Example 6.14 Computing Column Capacity Using Table 4-1

Look up the factored capacity of a W12×96 column. $KL_x = KL_y = 16$ ft.

Step 1 - Verify that the weak axis governs

Since the effective length is the same for the strong and weak axis, weak axis buckling will govern.

Step 2 - Look up the factored capacity

$\phi_c P_n$ can be read directly from Table 4-1. For a W12×96 and KL of 16 ft:

$\phi_c P_n = $ **957** kips

Note that it is much faster to look up the capacity rather than use the equations.

Table 4-1 can be used to calculate the capacity when strong-axis buckling governs, but you need to use a special procedure since the table is designed for weak-axis buckling. The flow-chart below shows what the table is "doing" when you use it normally to get the capacity for weak-axis buckling.

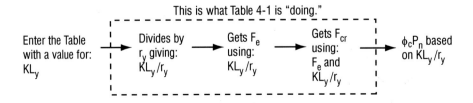

What would happen if you entered the table with KL_x instead of KL_y? The flowchart below shows that you would get a buckling capacity based on KL_x/r_y - which doesn't make any sense. What we really want is the strong-axis buckling capacity - the buckling capacity based on KL_x/r_x.

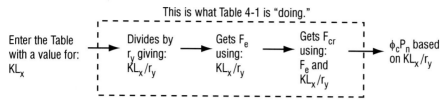

The way to get what we want, is to enter the table with the value $KL_x/(r_x/r_y)$. Watch what happens:

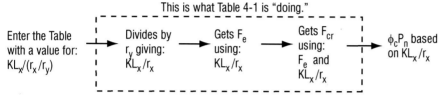

The expression $KL_x/(r_x/r_y)$ is called KL_y *equivalent*. The example below illustrates how to use Table 4-1 to compute the capacity for strong axis buckling by using KL_y *equivalent*.

Example 6.15 Computing Column Capacity Using Table 4-1

What is the factored capacity of a W12×96 column if $KL_x = 16$ ft and $KL_y = 8$ ft?

Step 1 - Compute KLy equivalent

To compute KL_y equivalent we need to get $\frac{r_x}{r_y}$. We can look up values for r_x and r_y in Table 1-1 and compute $\frac{r_x}{r_y}$, but there is a faster way. In Table 4-1, values for $\frac{r_x}{r_y}$ are given at the bottom of each page. For a W12×96, $\frac{r_x}{r_y} = 1.76$.

$$KL_{y,equiv} = \frac{KL_x}{\frac{r_x}{r_y}} = \frac{16 \text{ ft}}{1.76} = 9.09 \text{ ft}$$

Step 2 - Compute the capacity for weak and strong-axis buckling

The capacity for weak-axis buckling is looked up directly in Table 4-1, using KL_y (8 ft):

$\phi_c P_n = 1180$ kips

The capacity for strong-axis buckling is looked up, using $KL_{y,equiv} = 9.09$ ft. Since there isn't a row for 9.09 ft, values are looked up for 9 and 10 ft, and then a value is interpolated for 9.09 ft.

$\phi_c P_n = 1158$ kips (for 9.09 ft)

Step 3 - Summarize capacity

The capacity is less for strong-axis buckling so it governs:

$\phi_c P_n = \mathbf{1158}$ kips

Tables 4-1 through 4-6 give capacities for the shapes that are most frequently used as columns. For all other situations, Table 4-22 can be used.

Study the Manual

Turn to the first page of Table 4-22.

On each page of Table 4-22, there are columns for different values of F_y. For each value of F_y, the factored critical stress is given for a variety of values of KL/r.

- What is the factored critical stress for a column with $F_y=46$ ksi and $KL/r=115$?

The following example illustrates how Table 4-22 can be used to determine factored capacities.

Example 6.16 Computing Column Capacity Using Table 4-22

What is the factored capacity of a W12×96 made from A36 steel with $KL_x=KL_y=20$ ft.

Step 1 - Recognize that Table 4-1 does not apply

At first glance, we may think that we can use Table 4-1 since it has information for W12×96 columns. But we must remember that Tables 4-1 through 4-6 assume the preferred material for the shapes. For the case of wide flange sections, Table 4-1 assumes $F_y = 50$ ksi. Since the question at hand is about a W12×96 made from A36 steel, Table 4-1 will not apply.

Step 2 - Compute the slenderness

Since KL is the same for both axes, the weak axis will govern:

$r_y = 3.09$ in. (Table 1-1)

$$\frac{KL}{r} = \frac{KL_y}{r_y} = \frac{20 \times 12 \text{ in.}}{3.09 \text{ in.}} = 78$$

It is a common error to forget to convert KL into units of inches. If you ever compute a value for $\frac{KL}{r}$ that is less than 20, you probably have made this mistake.

Step 3 - Look up the critical stress in Table 4-22

For $F_y = 36$ ksi and $\frac{KL}{r} = 78$:

$\phi_c F_{cr} = 23.5$ ksi

Step 4 - Calculate the factored capacity

$\phi_c P_n = (\phi_c F_{cr})(A_g)$
$A_g = 28.2 \text{ in.}^2$ (Table 1-1)
$\phi_c P_n = (23.5 \text{ ksi})(28.2 \text{ in.}^2) = \textbf{663}$ kips

- Which tables in the Manual list the capacities of common columns?
- What is the factored capacity for an HSS8x8x1/2 column with $KL_x = KL_y = 30$ ft?
- When should you use Table 4-22?
- What is a common mistake when using Table 4-22? How can you tell if you have made the mistake?

6.16 Local Buckling

In Section 6.7, two different kinds of buckling were introduced: global buckling and local buckling. The previous sections have discussed global buckling, which will limit the capacity of most columns. This section will discuss local buckling and how to compute column capacities in the few situations where it governs.

Consider the soda can shown on the right. What will happen to it when an increasing axial load is applied? Experience tells us that it will crumple and crush down rather than bow out. It will experience local, rather than global, buckling. The reason why a soda can experiences local buckling is that the thickness of the can is small relative to the diameter.

> A 12 oz. soda can has a diameter of 2.62 in. and a thickness of 0.0047 in. The ratio of the diameter to the thickness is 560!

The relative thickness of the elements of a cross section is what determines if a shape is susceptible to local buckling. The symbol λ is used to designate a relative thickness or width-thickness ratio. The Manual classifies an element as compact, non-compact, or slender, based on the width-thickness ratio of the element, λ, and two limit values, λ_p and λ_r. If λ for an element is greater than λ_r, then the element is called "slender."

When a cross section has one or more elements that are "slender," local buckling may limit the capacity. Otherwise, local buckling is not an issue and the capacity can be computed as shown in the previous sections.

Study the Manual

Read §B4.1 of the Manual (page 16.1-14).

- What are the three classifications for sections?

- What is the definition of a "slender-element"? (see the last line of the paragraph)

Study the Manual

Turn to Table B4.1a. This table is designed to help you determine if your column has slender elements. The left-most column says either "unstiffened elements" or "stiffened elements." These terms are defined in the text preceding the table, but basically unstiffened elements of a cross section have a free edge while stiffened elements do not.

- Are the flanges of I-shaped members "stiffened" or "unstiffened" elements?

The next two columns indicate the "case" and a description of the element being considered.

- Which case would apply if you are checking local buckling for the web of a W12×96?

After the description of the element, there is a column for the width-thickness ratio. This column defines how the width-thickness ratio, λ, is calculated for the particular element.

- For Case 1, how is λ calculated?

Be careful when computing λ for the flanges of I-shaped sections. The b in the formula for λ is defined as 1/2 of the flange width (see the picture in Table B4.1a) and not the whole flange width, b_f.

- Compute λ for the flange of a W12×96. What is it?

An element is "slender" if the value of λ is greater than the limiting value λ_r. The formula for λ_r, for each case, is listed in another column of Table B4.1.

- Compute λ_r for the flange of a W12×96. What is it?

- Is the flange of a W12×96 a "slender" element. Why or why not?

Example 6.17 Checking for Local Buckling Issues

Will local buckling impact the capacity of a W10×15 column?

Step 1 - Check the flanges

We first need to check to see if the flanges are slender elements. Since this is a column (uniform compression) and the W10×15 is a rolled shape, Case 1 in Table B4.1a applies for the flanges.

$$\lambda = \frac{b}{t} = \frac{\frac{b_f}{2}}{t_f} = \frac{\frac{4.0 \text{ in.}}{2}}{0.27 \text{ in.}} = 7.41$$

Note that this value is actually listed in Table 1-1 under the column **Compact Section Criteria**. You don't need to recalculate it every time.

$$\lambda_r = 0.56\sqrt{\frac{E}{F_y}} = 0.56\sqrt{\frac{29000 \text{ ksi}}{50 \text{ ksi}}} = 13.5 \text{ (Table B4.1a, Case 1)}$$

Since $\lambda < \lambda_r$ the flanges are not slender.

Helpful hint: whenever you calculate a value for λ_r for a particular Case and value of F_y, write it into Table B4.1a so you won't have to calculate it again.

Step 2 - Check the web

We also need to check the web to see if it is a slender element. Since this is a column (compression element) and the W10×15 is I-shaped, Case 5 in Table B4.1a applies for the web.

$$\lambda = \frac{h}{t_w} = 38.5$$

A value for the dimension h isn't given in Table 1-1, so we didn't calculate λ above. We simply looked at the value listed under the column **Compact Section Criteria** in Table 1-1.

$$\lambda_r = 1.49\sqrt{\frac{E}{F_y}} = 1.49\sqrt{\frac{29000 \text{ ksi}}{50 \text{ ksi}}} = 35.9 \text{ (Table B4.1a, Case 5)}$$

Since $\lambda > \lambda_r$ the web IS slender.

Since the W10×15 has a slender element (the web), **local buckling may impact the capacity.**

The calculations shown in Example 6.17 have already been done for all the standard shapes. It turns out that only a few of the standard shapes have slender elements. These shapes are "flagged" in Table 1-1 with the footnote c.

For shapes with slender elements, the regular equations for capacity from Section E3 do not apply.

Tables 4-1 through 4-6 account for the effects of local buckling. The capacities for shapes that have slender elements were determined using the equations in Section E7.

Example 6.18 Capacity of a Column With Slender Elements

Does an HSS12×6×3/16 have slender elements? What is the capacity of an HSS12×6×3/16 column with $KL_x=KL_y=10$ ft?

Step 1 - Check for slenderness

Table 4-3 has all the information needed for both parts of the problem. In Table 4-3 there is a footnote "c" for HSS12×6×3/16 so the shape does have slender elements (when $F_y = 46$ ksi).

Step 2 - Look up capacity

The tabulated capacities account for the effects of local buckling. For $KL_y = 10$ ft:

$$\phi_c P_n = \textbf{173} \text{ kips}$$

one or more elements are slender

6.17 Practical Considerations

Most of the columns in buildings will be significantly stronger than they need to be to carry the loads. This may seem inefficient because extra steel is being used where strength does not require it. But good engineers will use extra steel when it decreases labor costs enough to offset the increase in material costs.

Imagine for a moment a building with columns that have been designed to minimize the amount of steel, without regard for practical considerations and labor costs. In this building, the column sizes would change at every story because the demands are different at every story. At a given story, column sizes would be different throughout the building because the tributary areas may be different for each column. A great variety of shapes would be used (W14s, W12s, W10s, W8s, and HSS sections) so that the strength of each column would be just slightly greater than the demand.

Such a design would be terribly expensive to build. The steel fabricator would have to order dozens of different shapes. There would be little or no repetition in the fabrication. The columns would need to be spliced at every story requiring significant labor in the shop and in the field. Splice details would be complicated, as shown in the example below.

The most economical designs tend to follow these four practical recommendations:
1. Minimize the number of column splices.
2. Use the same column depth throughout the building. For example, all of the columns in a building may be W12s or W14s.
3. Pick a few sizes at critical locations and repeat them elsewhere.
4. Don't use W8 columns. They make connections difficult.

Example 6.19 Why Same-Series Shapes Should Be Used

Why is it good to use same-series shapes throughout a project?

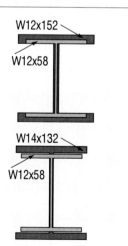

The figure to the right shows two W12s stacked on top of each other. The geometries of the various W12s are purposely coordinated to facilitate splicing. The same is true for W10s and W14s.

The other figure shows a W12×58 on top of a W14×132. The column splice connection would be much more complicated than for the case illustrated above. To fix the problem, both columns should be W14s or both should be W12s.

You Should Know

* Why do most of the columns in a building end up being stronger than they need to be?

6.18 Design

Once you know how to compute column demands and are comfortable with the column capacity tables, design is fairly straightforward. The general steps of member design, as outlined in section 3.9, apply:

1. Compute demands.
2. Pick a shape to try.
3. Compute the capacity of the shape and compare with demands.
4. Finalize the design or iterate to find a better design.

Step 1 will usually take the most time. Steps 2 through 4 are performed simultaneously by using Tables 4-1 through 4-6 of the Manual. When picking shapes, keep in mind the practical considerations discussed in the previous section.

Examples 6.20 and 6.21 demonstrate how to size columns after the demands are known.

Example 6.20 Column Design After Demands Are Known

What is the lightest W12× that will work for a column that has $KL_x=KL_y=30$ ft and a demand, P_u, of 500 kips?

Step 1 - Determine which axis governs

Since $KL_x = KL_y$ the y axis will govern. We will enter Table 4-1 with $KL_y=30$ ft.

Step 2 - Find the lightest W12

Turn to the pages of Table 4-1 with W12 shapes. Enter the table on the left side with $KL_y=30$ ft. Read across until you find the lightest shape with a capacity greater than 500 kips. It looks like it is:

W12×106 with $\phi_c P_n = 526$ kips

Example 6.21 Column Design with Different KLs

What is the lightest W14× that will work for a column that has $KL_x= 40$ ft and $KL_y= 20$ ft and a demand, P_u, of 1000 kips?

Step 1 - Determine which axis governs

Since $KL_x > KL_y$ it is possible that x-axis buckling may govern. In order to know, we have to compute $KL_{y,equiv}$ and compare with KL_y.

$$KL_{y,equiv} = \frac{KL_x}{\frac{r_x}{r_y}}$$

Fortunately, $\frac{r_x}{r_y}$ is similar for most of the heavy W14x shapes that we are trying to pick from. Turn to Table 4-1 and look at $\frac{r_x}{r_y}$ for the heavy W14x shapes. They all have $\frac{r_x}{r_y}$ around 1.6 or 1.7.

$$KL_{y,equiv} \approx \frac{40 \text{ ft}}{1.6}=25 \text{ ft}$$

Since $KL_{y,equiv} > KL_y$, x-axis buckling will govern and we should enter Table 4-1 using $KL_{y,equiv}$

Step 2 - Find the lightest W14

Turn to the pages of Table 4-1 with W14 shapes. Enter the table on the left side with $KL_{y,equiv}=25$ ft (Look between 24 and 26 and interpolate in your head.) Read across until you find the lightest shape with a capacity greater than 1000 kips. It looks like the lightest shape will either be W14×120 or W14×132. Now $KL_{y,equiv}$ can be computed precisely since both shapes have the same value for $\frac{r_x}{r_y}$:

$$KL_{y,equiv} = \frac{40 \text{ ft}}{1.67}=24 \text{ ft}$$

This is convenient since values are listed for 24 ft. The lightest shape is:

W14×120 with $\phi_c P_n = 1030$ kips

The procedure for designing HSS columns is similar, but you will be using Tables 4-3 through 4-5 rather than Table 4-1.

The final example of this chapter will go through the entire process of column design beginning with calculating the demands. You will notice that most of the effort in column design is in computing demands; this is also where most mistakes are made.

Design the columns at grid-point B-1 for the four-story building shown in plan and elevation below. The maximum length member that can be delivered to the site is 50 ft. Sketch the elevation of the columns indicating the member sizes. The loads are: Floor Dead: 85 psf; Floor Live: 50 psf; Roof Dead: 40 psf; Roof Live: 20 psf; and Ext. Wall: 20 psf.

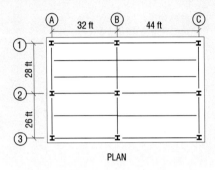

PLAN

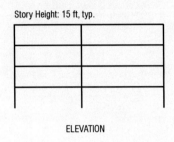

Story Height: 15 ft, typ.

ELEVATION

Step 1 - Envision the building and decide where to splice

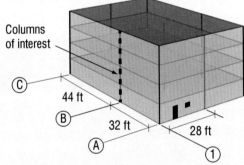

The figure to the right shows the building and the column we are designing. Since the building is 60 ft tall, and the maximum length of a piece is 50 ft, at least one splice will be required. The loads will be increasing at each story moving down the building. We could splice either at the second story, third story, or fourth story. Splicing (and changing column size) at the third story will keep column pieces about the same length and will probably result in the lowest steel weight.

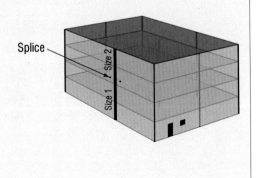

Our objective now is to pick sizes for the column. We will pick one size for the first two stories, and another size for the upper two stories. The size for the first two stories will be based on the demands at the first story and will be over-strong for the second story. The size for the upper two stories will be based on the demands at the third story and will be over-strong for the top story.

Example Continued

Step 2 - Compute demands

2a - Compute tributary floor and roof areas for the first-story column

$$A_{t,level} = \left(\frac{44\text{ ft}}{2} + \frac{32\text{ ft}}{2}\right)\left(\frac{28\text{ ft}}{2}\right) = 532\text{ ft}^2 \text{ per level}$$

$$A_{t,floors} = (532\text{ ft}^2 \text{ per level})(3\text{ floors}) = 1596\text{ ft}^2$$

$$A_{t,roof} = (532\text{ ft}^2 \text{ per level})(1\text{ roof}) = 532\text{ ft}^2$$

2b - Compute tributary exterior wall area for the first-story column

$$A_{t,wall} = \left(\frac{44\text{ ft}}{2} + \frac{32\text{ ft}}{2}\right) \times$$
$$\left(3\tfrac{1}{2}\text{ stories}\right)(15\text{ ft/story})$$
$$= 1995\text{ ft}^2$$

2c - Calculate reduced live loads for first-story column

For the floor:

$$L = (50\text{ psf})\left(0.25 + \frac{15}{\sqrt{4(1596)}}\right) = (50\text{ psf})(0.438)$$

The formula indicates the reduced live load is 43.8 % of the unreduced live load. This is greater than the 40 % lower limit for columns supporting multiple floors, so we use the computed value:

$$L = (50\text{ psf})(0.438) = 21.9\text{ psf}$$

For the roof:

$$L_r = L_o R_1 R_2$$
$$R_1 = 1.2 - 0.001A_t = 1.2 - 0.001(532) = 0.668$$
$$R_2 = 1$$
$$L_r = L_o R_1 R_2 = (20\text{ psf})(0.668)(1) = 13.4\text{ psf}$$

The computed value is greater than 12 psf, so we use the computed value.

$$L_r = 13.4\text{ psf}$$

2d - Calculate and factor load effects for the first-story column

The dead load effect is the sum of the effects from the floor dead loads, roof dead loads, and exterior wall loads:

$$P_D = (85\text{ psf})(1596\text{ ft}^2) + (40\text{ psf})(532\text{ ft}^2) + (20\text{ psf})(1995\text{ ft}^2)$$
$$P_D = 196.8\text{ kips}$$

The effects from live loads and roof live loads are:

$$P_L = (21.9\text{ psf})(1596\text{ ft}^2) = 35.0\text{ kips}$$
$$P_{Lr} = (13.4\text{ psf})(532\text{ ft}^2) = 7.13\text{ kips}$$

By inspection, load combination 2 governs (since the dead load is not more than eight times greater than the live):

$$P_U = 1.2(196.8\text{ kips}) + 1.6(35.0\text{ kips}) + 0.5(7.13\text{ kips}) = \mathbf{296}\text{ kips}$$

continued on next page

Example Continued

2e - Repeat the previous steps for the third-story column

A lot of the numbers from the previous steps can be reused, but we must recalculate the reduced floor live load since the third-story column has a smaller tributary floor area.

$$A_{t,floors} = (532 \text{ ft}^2 \text{ per level})(1 \text{ floors}) = 532 \text{ ft}^2$$
$$A_{t,roof} = 532 \text{ ft}^2 \text{ (same as before)}$$
$$A_{t,wall} = \left(\tfrac{44 \text{ ft}}{2} + \tfrac{32 \text{ ft}}{2}\right)(1\tfrac{1}{2} \text{ stories})(15 \text{ ft/story}) = 855 \text{ ft}^2$$
$$L = (50 \text{ psf})\left(0.25 + \frac{15}{\sqrt{4(532)}}\right) = (50 \text{ psf})(0.575) = 28.8 \text{ psf}$$
$$L_r = 13.4 \text{ psf (same as before)}$$
$$P_D = (85 \text{ psf})(532 \text{ ft}^2) + (40 \text{ psf})(532 \text{ ft}^2) + (20 \text{ psf})(855 \text{ ft}^2)$$
$$P_D = 83.6 \text{ kips}$$
$$P_L = (28.8 \text{ psf})(532 \text{ ft}^2) = 15.3 \text{ kips}$$
$$P_{Lr} = (13.4 \text{ psf})(532 \text{ ft}^2) = 7.13 \text{ kips (same as before)}$$
$$P_U = 1.2(83.6 \text{ kips}) + 1.6(15.3 \text{ kips}) + 0.5(7.13 \text{ kips}) = \mathbf{128} \text{ kips}$$

Note that computing demands is typically the most time-consuming part of column design. You will notice that the rest is quite fast.

Step 3 - Pick shapes, get capacities, and finalize designs

3a - Pick the first-story column

For gravity columns, K can conservatively be taken as 1.0. Since beams frame into the column from both directions at each story, $KL_x = KL_y = 15$ ft (the story height). Weak-axis buckling will govern, so Table 4-1 can be used directly.

We enter Table 4-1 from the left with $KL_y = 15$ and identify columns that have a factored capacity slightly greater than the demand of 296 kips.

W14×48 with $\phi_c P_n = 332$
W12×45 with $\phi_c P_n = 317$
W10×45 with $\phi_c P_n = 332$

All of these are acceptable and which is best may depend on the other columns in the building (which we are not considering in this problem). The W10×45 is probably the best because it takes up the least space (in plan) and it will accommodate a lighter column above the splice.

Use **W10×45** with $\phi_c P_n = 332$

3b - Pick the third-story column

Since we picked a W10× for the first story, we are constrained to use a W10× for the third story. The lightest W10× with capacity greater than 128 kips (for $KL_y = 15$ ft) is:

W10×33 with $\phi_c P_n = 233$

The capacity is much greater than the demand. This will often be the case for columns in the upper stories because of the practical constraints that have been previously discussed.

Use **W10×33** with $\phi_c P_n = 233$

Example Continued

Step 4 - Sketch the column elevation

Column @ B

Remember This

- Wide flange and HSS shapes are typically used for columns in buildings.
- When uniform loads are assumed, tributary areas can be used to compute the load effects from dead and live loads.
- Live load reduction accounts for the fact that heavy live loading is not usually present over large areas at the same time. Floor live load reduction is a function of the area of influence (four times the tributary area).
- Exterior walls cause load effects in exterior columns.
- There are four steps for computing column demands: 1) get tributary floor and roof areas, 2) get tributary wall areas, 3) reduce live loads, and 4) compute and factor load effects.
- The capacity of most columns is limited by global buckling. Euler buckling theory is the basis for our global buckling equations.
- The effective length factor, K, accounts for boundary conditions. K can be conservatively taken as 1.0 for columns in a building that resist only gravity loads.
- The Euler buckling stress depends on the slenderness ratio KL/r. The greatest KL/r for a column will govern.
- Inelastic buckling occurs when part of the cross section yields (due to residual stresses).
- The equations for column capacity are found in Section E of the Specification, but the tables in Part 4 are much faster for determining column capacity.
- Local buckling may limit column capacity if one or more elements of the cross section is slender.
- Because of practical considerations, most columns in a building will have capacities significantly greater than the demands.

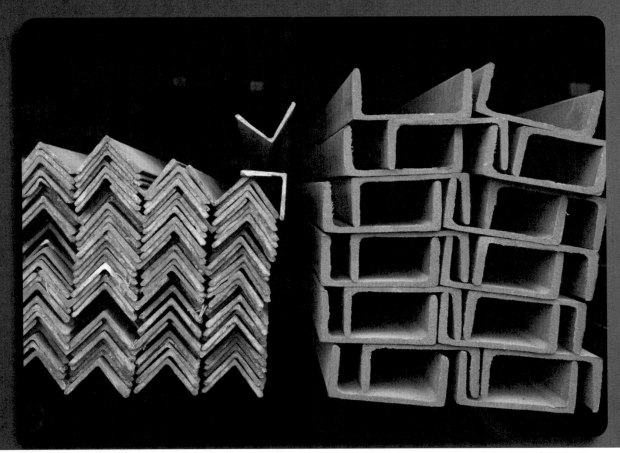

These angles and channels are stockpiled for later use. While these shapes are less efficient for compression members than tubes, they are often used because their geometry facilitates easy connections.

Angles (single and double) are regularly used for compression members.

7. Other Compression Members

7.1 Different Types

The previous chapter focused on wide flange and HSS columns, but these columns are only a subset of steel compression members. Most structures will have other kinds of compression members, including truss members and braces. The limit states discussed for columns (flexural buckling and local buckling) will apply to truss members and braces, but there are additional limit states to consider.

Shapes other than wide flanges and tubes are frequently used for truss members and braces. Angles, double angles, tees, and channels may be used for truss members because their geometries facilitate relatively simple connections, as illustrated in the next example.

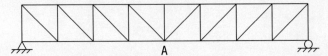

Example 7.1 Truss Connections

Consider a truss with the geometry shown. What will the connections look like if the members are wide-flanges? What will the connections look like if the members are tees and angles?

If all the members were wide flange shapes, the connection at A might look something like the detail on the left. This connection requires additional plates to join the members. In contrast, if the members were tees and angles, the connection at A might look something like the detail on the right.

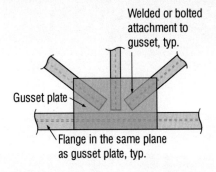

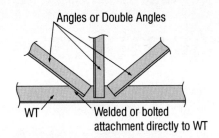

Notice that on the connection on the right, no additional gusset plates are required. The angles have flat "backs" that are easily connected to the flat stem of the tee. So, **the connections will probably be easier to make if the members are tees and angles**. Wide flange shapes will be used if the loads are too great for tees and angles.

The procedures for computing the demands in truss tension members were discussed in Chapter 4. The same principles and procedures apply when computing the demands in truss compression members. This chapter will not go over any additional information on computing demands.

The focus of this chapter is on computing the capacity of compression members made from angles, tees, and channels. All of the information on column capacity from Chapter 6 will apply (Euler buckling theory, effective length, global buckling, local buckling, elastic and inelastic buckling). The new material for this chapter centers on a failure mode called *flexural torsional buckling*.

You Should Know

- Why are angles and tees commonly used for truss compression members?
- Why aren't demands discussed in this chapter?
- What is the new compression limit state that will be discussed in this chapter?

7.2 Flexural-Torsional Buckling

In the previous chapter, the capacities of wide flange and HSS shapes without slender elements were calculated by considering *flexural buckling* (elastic or inelastic, strong-axis or weak axis). In flexural buckling, the member bends such that at any point along the member the cross-section has translated perpendicular to the axis of buckling. The figures below illustrate flexural buckling of a wide flange shape about the x- or y-axis.

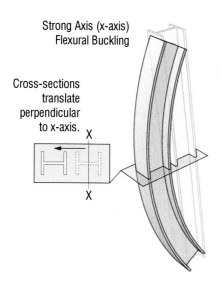

Strong Axis (x-axis) Flexural Buckling

Cross-sections translate perpendicular to x-axis.

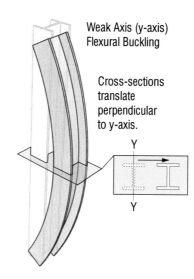

Weak Axis (y-axis) Flexural Buckling

Cross-sections translate perpendicular to y-axis.

Another mode of buckling, called *flexural-torsional buckling*, may occur in some shapes. As the name implies, flexural-torsional buckling means that the cross-sections both translate and twist. Tees, double angles, and channels are susceptible to flexural-torsional buckling about their axis of symmetry because the *shear center* of the cross-section is not located at the centroid of the cross section. The concept of shear center is explained in most Mechanics textbooks.

The derivation of the formulas for flexural-torsional buckling are beyond the scope of typical undergraduate courses in design or analysis. In the rest of this section we will look at what the equations are and see how they are applied. You will need to refer elsewhere for details on how the equations were developed.

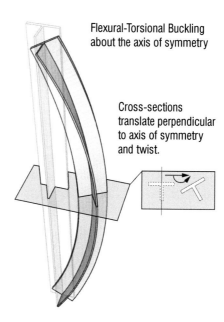

Flexural-Torsional Buckling about the axis of symmetry

Cross-sections translate perpendicular to axis of symmetry and twist.

Turn to TABLE USER NOTE E1.1 in the Specification (page 16.1-32).

- What are the pertinent limit states for channels without slender elements?

- Which Sections in Chapter E correspond to the pertinent limit states?

- What are the pertinent limit states for double angles, and tees without slender elements?

- Which Sections in Chapter E correspond to the pertinent limit states?

Also note that torsional buckling (TB) is indicated as a pertinent limit state for wide flange shapes. This was not discussed in the previous chapter, because it rarely governs design. Torsional buckling of wide flange shapes will be discussed briefly when we explore §E4. of the Specification.

When checking *flexural buckling* modes for tees, double angles, and channels we use the equations in §E3. of the Specification, just as was done previously for wide flange and HSS columns. When checking *flexural-torsional buckling* modes for tees, double angles, and channels we need to refer to §E4.

Read the first three paragraphs of §E4. of the Specification (page 16.1-34).

- From the first paragraph, when does this section apply to double symmetric members without slender elements?

Wide flange shapes are doubly symmetric and may experience torsional buckling IF the torsional unbraced length exceeds the lateral unbraced length. This is rarely the case, which is why our previous discussion on wide flange columns only addressed the limit states of flexural buckling and local buckling.

Eqn. E4-1 is used for calculating the nominal compressive strength for flexural-torsional buckling which will apply to some buckling modes for tees, double angles, and channels.

- How does Eqn. E4-1 compare with Eqn. E3-1?

- How is F_{cr} computed for double angles and tees?

Read the commentary for §E4.

- Where is Eqn. E4-2 derived?

There are several terms in Eqn. E4-2 which are defined in the text and equations that follow. The next example demonstrates how Eqn. E4-2 is applied to compute the capacity for flexural-torsional buckling of a WT.

Eqn. E4-2 is specifically for computing the critical stress for flexural-torsional buckling of tees and double angles about the axis of symmetry (y-axis). When checking the capacity for these shapes we should also consider plain flexural buckling about the axis of no symmetry (x- axis). The procedure is illustrated in the following example.

Example 7.2 Calculating the Buckling Capacity Load for a WT

Determine the compression capacity, $\phi_c P_n$, of a WT5×16.5 with $KL_x = KL_y = 8$ ft.

Step 1 - Identify the limit states

The figures below illustrate the two limit states that we will consider: flexural buckling about the x-axis, and flexural-torsional buckling about the y-axis.

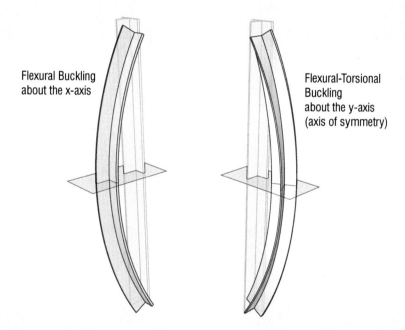

Flexural Buckling about the x-axis

Flexural-Torsional Buckling about the y-axis (axis of symmetry)

In order to determine which governs, we will need to compute the nominal capacity, P_n, for both limits, and then see which is least.

Step 2 - Compute the capacity for flexural buckling about the x-axis

The work in this step follows the same procedures as used in Chapter 6 since we are checking a flexural buckling mode.

2a - Look up cross sectional properties

From Table 1-8:

$A_g = 4.85$ in.^{2}
$r_x = 1.26$ in.

2b - Compute the slenderness and the Euler buckling stress

$$\frac{KL}{r} = \frac{(8 \times 12 \text{ in.})}{(1.26 \text{ in.})} = 76.2$$

$$F_e = \frac{\pi^2 E}{\left(\frac{KL}{r}\right)^2} = \frac{(3.14^2)(29,000 \text{ ksi})}{(76.2)^2} = 49.3 \text{ ksi}$$

continued on next page

Example Continued

2c - Compute the critical stress

$$4.71\sqrt{E/F_y} = 113.4 \text{ for } F_y = 50 \text{ ksi, which is the preferred material for WTs.}$$

Since

$$\frac{KL}{r} < 4.71\sqrt{E/F_y} \qquad (76.2 < 113)$$

Equation E3-2 applies.

$$F_{cr} = \left[0.658^{\frac{F_y}{F_e}}\right]F_y = \left[0.658^{\left(\frac{50 \text{ ksi}}{49.3 \text{ ksi}}\right)}\right](50 \text{ ksi}) = 32.7 \text{ ksi}$$

2d - Compute the nominal capacity

Using Equation E3-1

$$P_n = F_{cr}A_g = (32.7 \text{ ksi})(4.85 \text{ in.}^2) = 158.6 \text{ kips}$$

So

$$\phi_c P_n = (0.9)(158.6 \text{ kips}) = \mathbf{143} \text{ kips}$$

Step 3 - Compute the capacity for flexural-torsional buckling about the y-axis

To get the capacity for flexural-torsional buckling about the y-axis, we will use equation E4-2. This equation computes the critical stress for flexural-torsional buckling, F_{cr}, by using the critical stress for flexural buckling about the y-axis, F_{cry}, and the critical stress for torsional buckling, F_{crz}.

3a - Look up and calculate cross-sectional properties

We need to look up several values in order to compute the parameters that show up in equation E4-2. From Table 1-8:

$A_g = 4.85 \text{ in.}^2$
$t_f = 0.435 \text{ in.}$
$I_x = 7.71 \text{ in.}^4$
$\bar{y} = 0.869 \text{ in.}$
$I_y = 18.3 \text{ in.}^4$
$r_y = 1.94 \text{ in.}$
$J = 0.291 \text{ in.}^4$ (polar moment of inertia)

We will need some other values that are not given in Table 1-8. The formulas for these are developed in Mechanics textbooks and many are summarized in Section E4:

$x_o = 0 \text{ in}$ (distance from the centroid to the shear center in x-dir)

$$y_o = \bar{y} - \frac{t_f}{2} = 0.869 \text{ in.} - \frac{0.435 \text{ in.}}{2} = 0.652 \text{ in}$$

(y_o is the distance from the centroid to the shear center in y-dir)

$G = 11200 \text{ ksi}$ (shear modulus of elasticity for steel)

$$\bar{r}_o^2 = x_0^2 + y_o^2 + \frac{I_x + I_y}{A_g}$$ (polar radius of gyration about the shear center)

$$\bar{r}_o^2 = (0)^2 + (0.652 \text{ in.})^2 + \frac{7.71 \text{ in.}^4 + 18.3 \text{ in.}^4}{4.85 \text{ in.}^2} = 5.79 \text{ in.}^2$$

Example Continued

3b - Calculate the critical stress for flexural buckling about the Y-Y axis

Since F_{cry} is a stress associated with flexural buckling only, it is computed using the exact same process as step 2.

$$\frac{KL_y}{r_y} = \frac{(8 \times 12 \text{ in.})}{(1.94 \text{ in.})} = 49.5$$

$$F_e = \frac{\pi^2 E}{\left(\frac{KL}{r}\right)^2} = \frac{(3.14^2)(29,000 \text{ ksi})}{(49.5)^2} = 116.8 \text{ ksi}$$

Since

$$\frac{KL}{r} < 4.71\sqrt{E/F_y} \qquad (49.5 < 113)$$

Equation E3-2 applies.

$$F_{cr} = \left[0.658^{\frac{F_y}{F_e}}\right]F_y = \left[0.658^{\left(\frac{50 \text{ ksi}}{116.8 \text{ ksi}}\right)}\right](50 \text{ ksi}) = 41.8 \text{ ksi}$$

$$F_{cry} = F_{cr} = 41.8 \text{ ksi}$$

3c - Calculate the critical stress for torsional buckling

The critical stress for torsional buckling, F_{crz}, is calculated using Equation E4-3:

$$F_{crz} = \frac{GJ}{A_g \bar{r}_o^2} = \frac{(11200 \text{ ksi})(0.291 \text{ in.}^4)}{(4.85 \text{ in.}^2)(5.79 \text{ in.}^2)} = 116.11 \text{ ksi}$$

3d - Calculate H

H is calculated using Equation E4-10:

$$H = 1 - \frac{x_o^2 + y_o^2}{\bar{r}_o^2} = 1 - \frac{(0)^2 + (0.652 \text{ in.})^2}{(5.79 \text{ in.}^2)} = 0.927$$

3e - Calculate the flexural-torsional buckling capacity

F_{cr} can now be calculated using Equation E4-2:

$$F_{cr} = \left(\frac{F_{cry} + F_{crz}}{2H}\right)\left[1 - \sqrt{1 - \frac{4F_{cry}F_{crz}H}{(F_{cry} + F_{crz})^2}}\right]$$

$$= \left(\frac{41.8 \text{ ksi} + 116.11 \text{ ksi}}{2(0.927)}\right)\left[1 - \sqrt{1 - \frac{4(41.8 \text{ ksi})(116.11 \text{ ksi})(0.927)}{(41.8 \text{ ksi} + 116.11 \text{ ksi})^2}}\right]$$

$$F_{cr} = 40.2 \text{ ksi}$$

Finally, using Equation E4-1

$$P_n = F_{cr}A_g = (40.2 \text{ ksi})(4.85 \text{ in.}^2) = 195.0 \text{ kips}$$

So

$$\phi_c P_n = (0.9)(195.0 \text{ kips}) = \mathbf{176} \text{ kips}$$

continued on next page

Example Continued

Step 4 - Identify the governing mode and compute the factored capacity

The factored capacity for x-axis flexural buckling is 143 kips, and the factored capacity for flexural-torsional buckling is 176 kips. Therefore, x-axis flexural buckling governs and the factored capacity is:

$$\phi_c P_n = \mathbf{143} \text{ kips}$$

Note: It is a little disappointing that we went to all the effort of computing the flexural-torsional buckling capacity and it didn't end up governing. There are some quick checks that could have been done before step 3, to determine if flexural-torsional buckling would govern. For rolled tees with a (flange width)/(depth) ratio greater than 0.5 and a (flange thickness)/(stem thickness) greater than 1.10, flexural buckling generally governs. In this example the WT5×16.5 had a (flange width)/(depth) ratio of (7.96 in./4.87 in.) which is greater than 0.50 and a (flange thickness)/(stem thickness) ratio of (0.435 in./0.290 in.) which is greater than 1.10. If we had done these checks beforehand we might have guessed that flexural buckling about the x-axis would govern.

You Should Know

- Which part of Chapter E in the specification applies to flexural-torsional buckling?
- What is the most time-consuming step in computing the compression capacity of a tee shape?
- How can you tell if flexural-torsional buckling will govern without actually doing the calculations?

7.3 Tees

In the previous section we practiced calculating the capacity of a tee in compression. The Manual has a table that lists the compression capacities for tees to facilitate rapid checks and design.

Study the Manual

Turn to Table 4-7 in the Manual (page 4-89). Notice how the layout is similar, in some respects, to Table 4-1. On the left of the table we have effective length, *KL*, with respect to an axis. There are some important differences though.

- Notice the double line that passed roughly through the center of the table. What is the difference between the values above and below the double line?

The table permits you to check the buckling capacity about both the x- and y-axis. This is demonstrated in the following example.

Example 7.3 Determining Buckling Capacity for a WT

Determine the compression capacity, $\phi_c P_n$, of a WT5×16.5 with $KL_x = KL_y = 8$ ft. Use Table 4-7.

Step 1 - Look up the factored capacity for flexural buckling about the x-axis

Table 4-7 in the Manual gives values for the buckling capacity for different combinations of shape and effective length. For the WT5×16.5 with $KL = 8$ ft:

$$\phi_c P_n = 143 \text{ kips}$$

Step 2 - Look up the factored capacity for flexural-torsional buckling about the y-axis

From the bottom part of the page in Table 4-7:

$$\phi_c P_n = 176 \text{ kips}$$

Step 3 - Identify the governing limit state and the factored capacity

Flexural buckling about the x-axis governs:

$$\phi_c P_n = \mathbf{143} \text{ kips}$$

Note: These values are the same as those computed in the previous example. It is much easier to look up these values than compute them. Use the tables for design.

You Should Know

- For a given tee shape, how can you determine whether flexural or flexural-torsional buckling will govern using Table 4-7?
- What is an example of a tee (shape and length) with a capacity that is governed by flexural-torsional buckling?

7.4 Double Angles

Double angles are similar to tees and need to be checked for the same modes of failure: flexural buckling about the x-axis and flexural-torsional buckling about the y-axis. However, since double angles are built-up members there are two additional things that must be considered: 1) decreased flexural-torsional buckling capacity because of shearing of the connectors, and 2) buckling of the angles individually between connectors.

The procedures for addressing both of these issues are given in §E6. The shearing of connectors is accounted for by using a modified KL/r_y when computing F_{cry} for Eqn 4-2. Individual buckling is prevented by providing intermediate connectors at intervals, a, such that Ka/r_i

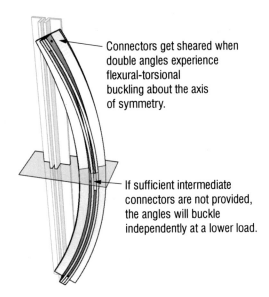

Connectors get sheared when double angles experience flexural-torsional buckling about the axis of symmetry.

If sufficient intermediate connectors are not provided, the angles will buckle independently at a lower load.

for the individual components does not exceed three-fourths times the governing KL/r for the built-up section. The tables for double angle compression members incorporate the requirements of §E6.

Study the Manual

Turn to Table 4-8 in the Manual (page 4-122). Notice how the table layout is similar to Table 4-7 that we used for tees. The top half of each page gives values of $\phi_c P_n$ based on flexural buckling about the x-axis. The bottom half of each page gives values of $\phi_c P_n$ based on flexural-torsional buckling about the y-axis (incorporating requirements of §E6.)

You will notice, in Table 4-8, there are columns that indicate the number of connectors. Footnote b refers us to the discussion of Table 4-8.

Turn to the discussion of Table 4-8 on page 4-7 and read it.

- What separation between the angles is assumed in Table 4-8?

- What should you do if your separation is different?

- Is buckling about the x-axis affected by the number of intermediate connectors?

- What do the dashed lines in Table 4-8 indicate?

Tables 4-9 and 4-10 are similar to Table 4-8, but provide values for double angles with unequal legs.

Example 7.4 Determining Buckling Capacity for a Double Angle

Determine the compression capacity, $\phi_c P_n$, of a 2L5×3×1/2 with $KL_x = KL_y = 16$ ft and specify the number of intermediate connectors required. Use Table 4-9.

Step 1 - Look up the factored capacity for flexural buckling about the x-axis

Table 4-9 in the Manual gives values for the buckling capacity for double angles. Values for 2L5×3×1/2 are given on page 4-138. The top half of the table pertains to flexural buckling about the x-axis. For $KL = 16$ ft the table indicates:

$$\phi_c P_n = 112 \text{ kips}$$

Step 2 - Look up the factored capacity for flexural-torsional buckling about the y-axis

Next, we look at the bottom of the Table to determine the capacity for flexural-torsional buckling about the y-axis. For $KL = 16$ ft the table indicates:

$$\phi_c P_n = 62.6 \text{ kips}$$

Step 3 - Determine the governing limit state and number of intermediate connectors

Comparing the results from Steps 1 and 2 we see that flexural-torsional buckling about the y-axis governs. The column on the right side of page 4-138 (bottom half) indicates that two intermediate connectors are required in order to achieve the indicated capacities.

In summary:

$\phi_c P_n = $ **63** kips (flexural-torsional buckling about y-axis governs)
Provide **(2)** intermediate connectors

You Should Know

- With regards to compression capacity, in what ways are double angles different than tee shapes?
- How is independent buckling of the two angles of a double angle prevented?
- What is an example of a double angle (find a shape and length) that has a capacity limited by flexural buckling about the x-axis?

7.5 Single Angles

Single angles are less commonly used than double, but the Specification provides guidance for computing single angle capacities and tables are provided for design.

Study the Manual

Turn to TABLE USER NOTE E1.1 on page 16.1-32 of the Specification.

• Which Section of Chapter E pertains to single angles?

Turn to the pertinent section and read the opening paragraph. It basically says that single angles will be designed using the same formulas as we have used previously.

Single angles connected by only one leg will be eccentrically loaded. In many cases this eccentricity can be accounted for with an effective value of KL/r. Equations E5-1 through E5-4 provide effective values for KL/r that account for various cases of eccentric loading. For cases other than those listed in E5(a) or (b), a more rigorous approach (Chapter H) is required.

Turn to Table 4-11.

• What kind of loading is assumed in this Table?

Turn to the discussion of Table 4-11 on page 4-8 and read it.

• When can Table 4-11 be used for angles with only one leg connected?

You Should Know

• Which sections of the Specification and which Tables in the Manual pertain to single angle compression members?

7.6 Channels

Channels may be used as compression members, either singly or as part of built-up cross sections. When used singly, the capacity of a channel is determined using the equations in §E3 and §E4. If the channels are part of a built-up member, a modified KL/r should be computed following the procedures in §E6.

Example 7.5 Using Channels as Compression Members

This picture shows a truss joint in a stadium roof. The "web" members of the truss are channels, some of which are functioning as compression members. Although the channels are used in pairs, they are not sufficiently connected to each other to be built-up shapes, and the capacity of each would be determined separately by considering flexural buckling about the y-axis and flexural-torsional buckling about the x-axis.

Example 7.6 Using Channels for Compression Members

What is the compression capacity of a C9×20 with $KL_x = KL_y = 9$ ft?

Step 1 - Identify the limit states

The figures below illustrate the two limit states that we will consider: flexural buckling about the y-axis (axis with no symmetry), and flexural-torsional buckling about the x-axis.

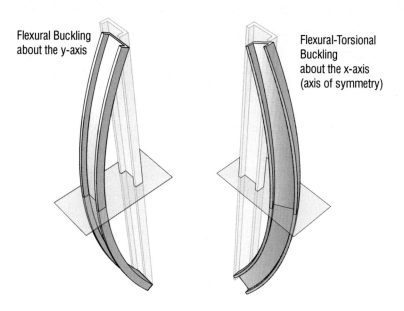

Flexural Buckling
about the y-axis

Flexural-Torsional
Buckling
about the x-axis
(axis of symmetry)

In order to determine which governs, we will need to compute the nominal capacity, P_n, for both limits, and then see which is least.

Step 2 - Compute the capacity for flexural buckling about the y-axis

The work in this step follows the same procedures as used in Chapter 6 since we are checking a flexural buckling mode.

2a - Look up cross sectional properties

From Table 1-5 (pages 1-36, 37):

$$A_g = 5.87 \text{ in.}^2$$
$$r_y = 0.64 \text{ in.}$$

2b - Compute the slenderness

$$\frac{KL_y}{r_y} = \frac{(9 \times 12 \text{ in.})}{(0.64 \text{ in.})} = 168.8$$

2c - Determine the critical stress

The critical stress for flexural buckling could be determined using the Equations in E, or by using Table 4-22. From Table 4-22, with $KL/r = 169$ and $F_y = 36$ ksi (preferred material for channels is A36):

$$\phi_c F_{cr} = 7.89 \text{ ksi}$$

continued on next page

Example Continued

2d - Compute the nominal capacity

The factored capacity for y-axis buckling is:

$$\phi_c P_n = (\phi_c F_{cr})(A_g) = (7.89 \text{ ksi})(5.87 \text{ in.}^2) = \mathbf{46} \text{ kips}$$

Step 3 - Compute the capacity for flexural-torsional buckling about the x-axis

To get the capacity for flexural-torsional buckling about the x-axis, we will turn to part E4 of the specification. Since the channel is not a double angle or tee, and is singly symmetric, equation E4-5 applies. Note that the notation for this equation assumes the axis of symmetry is the y-axis. For the case of a channel, the axis of symmetery is the x-axis, so we will use KL_x/r_x when computing "F_{ey}."

In Eqn. 4-5 the Euler stress for flexural-torsional buckling is computed based on a flexural buckling stress and a torsional buckling stress.

3a - Look up and calculate cross-sectional properties

We need to look up several values in order to compute the parameters that show up in equation E4-5. From Table 1-5:

$A_g = 5.87 \text{ in.}^2$
$r_x = 3.22 \text{ in.}$
$J = 0.427 \text{ in.}^4$ (polar moment of inertia)
$C_w = 39.4 \text{ in.}^6$
$\bar{r}_o = 3.46 \text{ in.}$
$H = 0.899$

3b - Calculate the Euler stress for flexural buckling about the x-axis

We will calculate the Euler buckling stress for flexural buckling about the x-axis, but call it F_{ey} since this is what we will substitute into Eqn. E4-5.

$$\frac{KL_x}{r_x} = \frac{(9 \times 12 \text{ in.})}{(3.22 \text{ in.})} = 33.54$$

$$F_{ey} = \frac{\pi^2 E}{\left(\frac{KL_x}{r_x}\right)^2} = \frac{(3.14^2)(29,000 \text{ ksi})}{(33.54)^2} = 254.2 \text{ ksi}$$

3c - Calculate the Euler stress for torsional buckling

The critical stress for torsional buckling, F_{ez}, is calculated using Equation E4-9:

$$F_{ez} = \left(\frac{\pi^2 E C_w}{(K_z L)^2} + GJ\right)\frac{1}{A_g \bar{r}_o^2}$$

$$F_{ez} = \left(\frac{3.14^2(29000 \text{ ksi})(39.4 \text{ in.}^6)}{(9 \times 12 \text{ in.})^2} + (11200 \text{ ksi})(0.427 \text{ in.}^4)\right) \times$$

$$\left(\frac{1}{(5.87 \text{ in.}^2)(3.46 \text{ in.})^2}\right)$$

$$F_{ez} = 81.8 \text{ksi}$$

Example Continued

3d - Calculate the Euler stress for combined flexural torsional buckling

F_e can now be calculated using Equation E4-5:

$$F_e = \left(\frac{F_{ey} + F_{ez}}{2H}\right)\left[1 - \sqrt{1 - \frac{4F_{ey}F_{ez}H}{(F_{ey} + F_{ez})^2}}\right]$$

$$= \left(\frac{254.2\text{ ksi} + 81.8\text{ ksi}}{2(0.899)}\right)\left[1 - \sqrt{1 - \frac{4(254.2\text{ ksi})(81.8\text{ ksi})(0.899)}{(254.2\text{ ksi} + 81.8\text{ ksi})^2}}\right]$$

$$F_e = 78.28\text{ ksi}$$

3e - Calculate the critical stress and nominal capacity

We use the Euler stress from Step 3d in the equations of section E3 to compute the critical stress. Since $F_y/F_e = 78.28/36 = 2.17 \leq 2.25$, Eqn. E3-2 is appropriate for determining F_{cr}

$$F_{cr} = \left[0.658^{\frac{F_y}{F_e}}\right]F_y = \left[0.658^{\frac{(36\text{ ksi})}{(78.28\text{ ksi})}}\right](36\text{ ksi}) = 29.7\text{ ksi}$$

So the nominal flexural-torsional buckling capacity is:

$$P_n = F_{cr}A_g = (29.7\text{ ksi})(5.87\text{ in.}^2) = 174\text{ kips}$$

and the factored capacity for flexural-torsional buckling about the x-axis:

$$\phi_c P_n = \phi_c F_{cr}A_g = 0.9(29.7\text{ ksi})(5.87\text{ in.}^2) = 157\text{ kips}$$

Step 4 - Identify the governing mode and compute the factored capacity

The factored capacity for y-axis flexural buckling is 46 kips (from Step 2), and the factored capacity for flexural-torsional buckling is 157 kips (from Step 3). Therefore, y-axis flexural buckling governs and the factored capacity is:

$$\phi_c P_n = \textbf{46 kips}$$

There are no Tables in the Manual that provide compression capacity for channels. Such Tables could be designed and generated by engineers who frequently use channels as compression members, using the equations in §E3. and §E4.

You Should Know

- How is computing the compression capacity of a channel similar to computing the compression capacity of a tee?
- How is computing the compression capacity of a channel different than computing the compression capacity of a tee?

7.7 Design

Now that you understand how to determine the capacity of compression members made from tees, angles, and channels, you are ready to do design. Recall from previous chapters that the basic steps in design are:

1. Compute demands.
2. Pick a shape to try.
3. Compute the capacity of the shape and compare with demands.
4. Finalize the design or iterate to find a better design.

In practice, steps 2 through 4 will be performed rapidly as you use the tables to evaluate different options.

Example 7.7 Design of a Truss Compression Member

A truss is 40 ft. long and 10 ft. deep with equally spaced nodes. Pick an appropriate WT shape for the top chord.

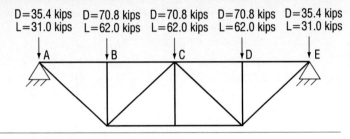

Step 1 - Get the factored demands for the critical member

By inspection, the critical segments for the top chord of the truss will be BC and CD. If the critical segment were not obvious, we would need to compute the load effects for all the top chord members.

1a - Compute dead load effects for BC

Considering only the dead loads, the vertical support reaction at point A would be:

$$R_y = \tfrac{1}{2}(35.4 \text{ kips} + 70.8 \text{ kips} + 70.8 \text{ kips} + 70.8 \text{ kips} + 35.4 \text{ kips})$$
$$R_y = 141.6 \text{ kips}$$

Using the method of sections, the axial load effect in BC can be computed with one equilibrium equation.

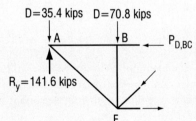

Summing the moments at F:

$$P_{D,BC}(10 \text{ ft}) + (35.4 \text{ kips})(10 \text{ ft}) - (141.6 \text{ kips})(10 \text{ ft}) = 0$$

so

$$P_{D,BC} = 106.2 \text{ kips}$$

1b - Compute live load effects for BC

Since the point live loads are all 87.5% of the point dead loads

$$P_{L,BC} = 0.875 P_{D,BC} = (0.875)(106.2 \text{ kips}) = 92.93 \text{ kips}$$

1c - Factor the load effects to get the ultimate demand

By inspection, load combination 2 will govern.

$$P_{U,BC} = 1.2 P_D + 1.6 P_L$$
$$P_{U,BC} = 1.2(106.2 \text{ kips}) + 1.6(92.6 \text{ kips}) = \mathbf{276 \text{ kips}}$$

Example Continued

Step 2 - Pick a shape to try

2a - Determine the effective lengths

We will use Table 4-7 to pick shapes, but we need to know the effective lengths of the member prior to entering the table. From the given information, the truss nodes are spaced 10 ft apart. Assuming out-of-plane restraint at the nodes, the unbraced length is 10 ft for both x- and y-axis buckling. While there may be some rotational restraint at the nodes, it can be conservatively neglected by letting $K=1.0$.

So $KL_x = KL_y = 10$ ft.

2b - Pick a shape from Table 4-7

To find possible shapes, we scan through Table 4-7, looking at x-axis buckling capacities (for $KL = 10$) that are greater than our factored demand (276 kips).

Based on the x-axis capacity from Table 4-7 the following WTs seem like good possibilities:

WT12×42 with x-axis $\phi_c P_n = 323$ kips
WT10.5×34 with x-axis $\phi_c P_n = 276$ kips
WT9×30 with x-axis $\phi_c P_n = 281$ kips
WT8×28.5 with x-axis $\phi_c P_n = 299$ kips
WT7×30.5 with x-axis $\phi_c P_n = 286$ kips

Of the shapes above, the WT8×28.5 is the lightest and has a reasonably long stem for making connections.

Try WT8×28.5

Step 3 - Check the capacity of the trial shape

We already checked the capacity for x-axis buckling during the selection process. The only other thing to check is the y-axis buckling capacity. From Table 4-7, $\phi_c P_n$ for y-axis bucking for a WT8×28.5 with $KL_y = 10$ ft is:

$\phi_c P_n = 230$ kips (<276 kips, No Good)

Step 4 - Iterate to find an acceptable design

It is easy to scan through Table 4-7 and check some of the other possibilities listed above. The WT7×30.5 has a y-axis buckling capacity of 318 kips. Unlike the WT8×28.5, the capacity of the WT7×30.5 is limited by x-axis buckling.

Use WT7×30.5
$\phi_c P_n = 286$ kips (>276 kips)

Note: In practice, Steps 2-4 above are integrated and performed simultaneously. As you scan the table looking for shapes, you will want to check both x- and y-axis buckling at the same time.

Design

The same principles of design apply for double angle and channel members. The procedure for designing double angle compression members is similar to that just illustrated for WTs in the previous example. Designing channel compression members is somewhat less straightforward because the Manual does not provide tables specific for channels. The best approach is to check channels based on flexural buckling about the y-axis, and only do the flexural-torsional buckling checks after a final shape has been selected.

You Should Know

- What two things should you know before you try to enter Table 4-7 (or Tables 4-8 through 4-10)?
- How do you design channels since tables are not provided in the Manual?

Remember This

- Double angles, tees, and channels may be used for light trusses or bracing because their geometry facilitates simpler connections.
- Flexural-torsional buckling may occur in shapes where the shear center is not at the same location of the centroid of the cross-section?
- The critical stress for flexural-torsional buckling is a combination of a flexural buckling stress and a torsional buckling stress.
- Double angles and tees should be checked for flexural buckling about the x-axis, and flexural-torsional buckling about the y-axis.
- Tables are provided that list compression capacities for tees, double angles, and single angles.
- Since double angles are built-up shapes, care must be taken to provide enough intermediate connectors so that the angles will not buckle independently.
- The tables in the Manual can be used to quickly design compression members.

This page blank.

The interior steel beams in this office building are around forty feet long and will support the floor above. In commercial office buildings, it is desirable to have large column-free areas so that tenants have maximum flexibility in using the space.

In most steel buildings the floors and roof are supported by a grid of beams.

8. Beams

8.1 Different Types

The word *beam* is used to describe a structural element that transmits vertical loads horizontally to a support or supports. Consider the two systems shown below. On the left, each vertical load is transferred to the ground via *axial* load effects in a column. This works, but it requires a lot of columns and the space below is less usable. On the right, a beam is used to transfer the vertical loads horizontally, via *shear forces and bending moments*, to two columns which then transmit the load to the ground. This approach will use less steel and will result in more column-free space.

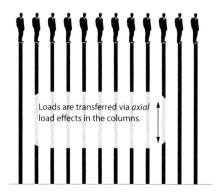

Loads are transferred via *axial* load effects in the columns.

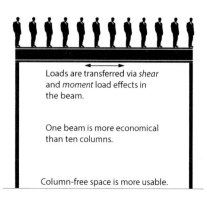

Loads are transferred via *shear* and *moment* load effects in the beam.

One beam is more economical than ten columns.

Column-free space is more usable.

Relatively deep beams are often referred to as *girders*. Two examples are given below.

Example 8.1 Bridge Girders

Steel beams are often used for highway bridges. These beams have long spans and carry heavy loads and, as a result, need to be several feet deep.

Since they are deep, they are referred to as *girders*. When girders are fabricated by welding plates together, they are called *plate girders*.

Example 8.2 Floor Beams and Girders in Buildings

In steel buildings, floor beams are often used to support the slab on metal deck; then, other beams are used to support the floor beams. The beams that support the floor beams must be deeper and/or heavier. So, in the context of buildings, the term girder is used to describe beams that support other beams.

The figure below shows the plan view of two steel buildings with the same overall dimensions. The plan on the left has fewer columns , but will have heavier beams because the spans are greater. The plan on the right has more columns, but would have lighter beams. The relative economy of the systems depends on a variety of things including: price of steel, price of fabrication/erection labor, and the magnitude of the loads. Bay areas of around 1000 ft² are commonly used. A common spacing is 30 ft × 30 ft and results in 900 ft² bay area.

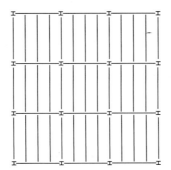
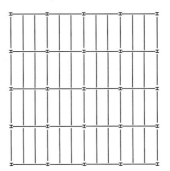

Spandrel beams (and girders) are those that are located around the perimeter of a building. The figure to the right identifies the various types of beams that have been discussed.

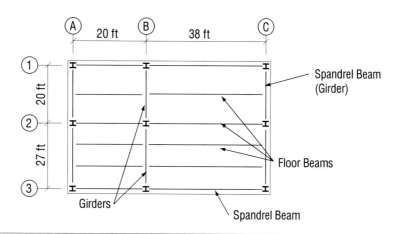

It is desirable to have the top of the floor beams and girders at the same elevation so that the floor deck can sit flush on both. One way to accomplish this is by cutting out the corners of the floor beams. This procedure is called coping. You can see from the connection that the floor beam is still "sitting" on the girder, even though the top flanges are at the same elevations.

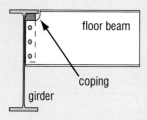

You Should Know

* What are the load effects in beams? *axial, shear, moment*
* What is the difference between a beam and girder? *beam→ transmits vertical loads horizontally to supports, girders→ longer spans & carry heavy loads*
* Where do you find spandrel beams? *→around perimeter of building*
* What is coping? *same elevation of floor beams & girders so flush, cutting out corners of floor beams*

8.2 Support Conditions

As discussed in Chapter 5, bolts are generally the most economical way to connect steel pieces in the field. Beams are often connected to each other, and to columns, via bolts through the beam web.

In structural analysis, the moment diagram for a beam depends on the stiffness of the connection, relative to the flexural stiffness of the beams. While bolted web connections do transmit some moment, the stiffness of such connections is minimal relative to the flexural stiffness of the beam. Thus, bolted-

web connections are considered pinned connections for structural analysis. When rotational stiffness at a beam connection is desired, the beam flanges must be fully connected, either through welding or rigorous bolting.

You Should Know

* Why are bolted-web connections considered pinned, even if they transmit moments? *→ stiffness of connections is minimal relative to flexural stiffness of beam*
* What is required to get a "fixed" boundary condition at the end of a beam?

145

8.3 Computing Demands with Tributary Widths

In order to understand how to calculate the demands on floor beams, you need to think about how corrugated metal deck works. Metal deck has flutes running in one direction. This makes the deck much stronger and stiffer in that direction.

Example 8.3 Load Paths in Corrugated Paper

How does a piece of corrugated paper transfer loads if it is supported all the way around?

If the corrugated paper is supported so that it is spanning in its strong direction, the paper can transmit loads to the supports (Case A below). If the supports are moved such that the paper is spanning in its weak direction, the deck cannot transmit significant loads to the supports (Case B).

Case A

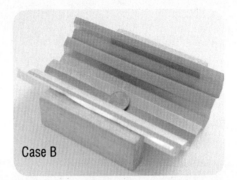

Case B

When supports are provided all the way around (Case C) the loads will "ignore" the supports in the weak direction, since the deck has no stiffness in that direction. The system is no stronger than Case A, and the weak direction supports will not see any significant part of the load.

Case C

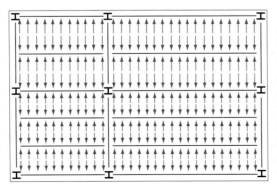

In a building, once the concrete floor slab cures, it strengthens the floor in both directions. But the weak direction will still be much softer than the strong direction. This means that essentially all of the loads will flow in the direction of the deck flutes to the floor beams. This is illustrated in the figure to the left for a floor subjected to a uniform load. Recall that the flutes will run perpendicular to the floor beams.

The tributary area for a floor beam can be determined by drawing lines between all of the floor beams. The width of the tributary area (always measured perpendicular from the floor beam) is especially useful for determining the load effects in the beam. This width is called the *tributary width*.

Example 8.4 Tributary Area and Tributary Width for Floor Beams

Determine the tributary width and tributary area for the floor beam running along Gridline 2 between Gridlines B and C.

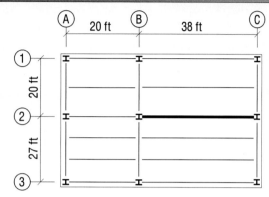

Step 1 - Draw lines between neighboring beams

The floor beam of interest is on Gridline 2 between Gridlines B and C. Unless otherwise stated, floor beams are assumed to be spaced evenly between dimensioned beams. This means that the floor beams in the upper-right quadrant are 10 ft apart, and the floor beams in the lower-right quadrant are 9 ft apart.

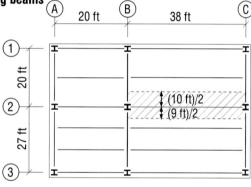

Step 2 - Calculate the tributary width

The tributary width is equal to the sum of half the spacing to each of the neighboring beams:

$$W_t = \frac{10 \text{ ft}}{2} + \frac{9 \text{ ft}}{2} = \textbf{9.5 ft}$$

Step 3 - Calculate the tributary area

The tributary area is equal to the tributary width multiplied by the length of the beam.

$$A_T = (9.5 \text{ ft})(38 \text{ ft}) = \textbf{361 ft}^2$$

The tributary area of a floor beam is useful for computing the reduced live load, but is not good for anything else. It is the tributary width that is used to compute the load effects, as will be demonstrated next.

When floor beams run parallel to each other, the tributary width is constant along the length of the beam. If a uniform load is applied to the floor area, the floor beam will have a uniform distributed load along the length of the beam. The uniform distributed load will be equal to the uniform area load multiplied by the tributary width.

Example 8.5 Computing Beam Loads

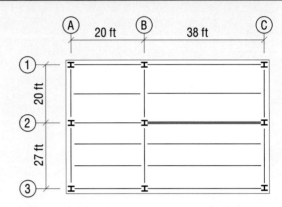

If a the floor has a uniform dead load of 90 psf, what is the uniform distributed load on the highlighted beam (in k/ft)? Indicate the load on a sketch of the beam.

Step 1 - Get the tributary width of the beam

This was done in Example 8.3.

$$W_t = \frac{10\text{ ft}}{2} + \frac{9\text{ ft}}{2} = \mathbf{9.5}\text{ ft}$$

Step 2 - Multiply the uniform area load by the tributary width

The usual notation for a distributed load is, w:

$$w = (9.5\text{ ft})(90\text{ psf}) = \mathbf{0.855}\text{ k/ft}$$

Note: It is customary to perform the units conversion without being explicit.

Step 3 - Sketch the beam

It is generally safe to assume that floor beams are connected at the ends through web bolts, and the beam can be considered simply supported.

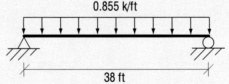

Note: Now this beam looks like something you've encountered before in Statics.

You Should Know

- Why are floor loads transmitted in the direction of the metal deck flutes? → stronger direction
- How do you calculate the tributary width for a beam? ⊥ to floor beam
- How do you calculate the distributed load on a floor beam?

8.4 Floor Beam Demands

Once the distributed load on a floor beam has been determined, the load effects can be calculated. The load effects in a beam are the shear forces and bending moments. Since the values of the shear forces and bending moments vary along the member, the load effects are presented in the form of shear and bending moment diagrams. The procedures for computing shear and bending moment diagrams are given in Statics textbooks. For common situations, there is a table in the Manual that will help you to quickly draw the diagrams and determine maximum load effects.

Study the Manual

Turn to Table 3-23 in the Manual (page 3-213). This table gives support reactions, shear diagrams, moments diagrams, and deflection formulas for beams that are commonly encountered in design. Look through the table and notice the different cases.

- How many different "Cases" are given in Table 3-23?

- Which case is pertinent for the beam of Example 8.5?

Using Table 3-23, determine the following:

- Where is the maximum moment for the beam of Example 8.5?

- Where is the maximum shear for the beam of Example 8.5?

- What is the value of the maximum moment for the beam of Example 8.5?

- What is the value of the moment at a location 5 ft from either support?

Example 8.6 Computing Beam Demands

A floor system has floor beams spaced at 10 ft on center. Draw the shear and bending moment diagrams for a floor beam if there is a uniform dead load of 90 psf.

Step 1 - Get the tributary width of the beam
$$W_t = \frac{10 \text{ ft}}{2} + \frac{10 \text{ ft}}{2} = \mathbf{10} \text{ ft}$$

Step 2 - Calculate the distributed dead load
$$w_D = (10 \text{ ft})(90 \text{ psf}) = \mathbf{0.90} \text{ k/ft}$$

Step 3 - Use Table 3-23
This floor beam is a simply supported beam with a uniform dead load. Case 1 of Table 3-23 can be used to draw the shear and bending moment diagrams.

$$V_{max} = \frac{wl}{2} = \frac{(0.90 \text{ k/ft})(20 \text{ ft})}{2} = \mathbf{9} \text{ kips}$$

$$M_{max} = \frac{wl^2}{8} = \frac{(0.90 \text{ k/ft})(20 \text{ ft})^2}{8} = \mathbf{45} \text{ k-ft}$$

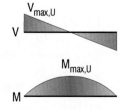

• What Case in Table 3-23 is a simply supported beam with a linearly-varying load?

8.5 Live Load Reduction

Floor beams will carry both live and dead loads. Floor and roof live loads are reduced for floor beams in a similar way as for columns, but there are two differences that should be noted. First is that the area of influence for a floor beam will be twice the tributary area, whereas it was four times the tributary area for columns. The formula for floor live load reduction for a beam is:

$$L = L_o \left(0.25 + \frac{15}{\sqrt{2A_t}} \right)$$

The other difference has to do with the limit on the reduction. Since floor beams only carry load from one level, the limit on live load reduction is always 50% of the unreduced load.

The *ultimate* load effects in floor beams can be calculated using similar steps as were used to compute the ultimate load effects in columns. Three basic steps are:

    1. Compute the tributary width.
    2. Reduce the live load (floor or roof live load; a beam is either in a floor or the roof).
    3. Compute and factor the load effects.

The following example shows how these steps are applied.

Example 8.7 Calculating Ultimate Demands (Load Effects)

Compute the ultimate demands on the indicated floor beam if the floor dead load is 80 psf and the floor live load is 50 psf.

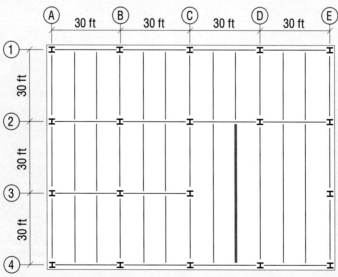

Step 1 - Get the tributary width and area
    $W_t = 10$ ft
    $A_t = (10 \text{ ft})(60 \text{ ft}) = 600 \text{ ft}^2$

Example Continued

Step 2 - Reduce the live load

The live load reduction for the beam is:

$$L = L_o \left(0.25 + \frac{15}{\sqrt{2A_t}} \right)$$

$$= (50 \text{ psf}) \left(0.25 + \frac{15}{\sqrt{2(600)}} \right) = (50 \text{ psf})(0.683)$$

The formula indicates that the reduced live load is 68.3% of the unreduced live load. This is greater than the 50% lower limit for beams, so we use the computed value:

$$L = (50 \text{ psf})(0.638) = 34.2 \text{ psf}$$

Step 3 - Compute and factor the load effects

The distributed loads are:

$$w_D = (90 \text{ psf})(10 \text{ ft}) = 0.90 \text{ k/ft}$$
$$w_L = (34.2 \text{ psf})(10 \text{ ft}) = 0.342 \text{ k/ft}$$

For beams it is convenient to apply the load combinations to these distributed loads to get an ultimated distributed load, w_U, from which the ultimate load effects are calcuated. We will get the same answer as if we computed the dead and live load effects separately and then used the combinations. By inspection, load combination 2 will govern:

$$w_U = 1.2w_D + 1.6w_L = 1.2(0.90 \text{ k/ft}) + 1.6(0.342 \text{ k/ft}) = 1.63 \text{ k/ft}$$

Case 1 of Table 3-23 applies:

$$V_{max,U} = \frac{w_U l}{2} = \frac{(1.63 \text{ k/ft})(60 \text{ ft})}{2} = \mathbf{48.9} \text{ kips}$$

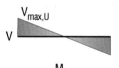

$$M_{max,U} = \frac{w_U l^2}{8} = \frac{(1.63 \text{ k/ft})(60 \text{ ft})^2}{8} = \mathbf{734} \text{ k-ft}$$

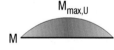

You Should Know

- What is the live load reduction limit for a floor beam? $2A_T \rightarrow$ LL reduction is 50% of unreduced load
- Why can't a beam have both L and L_r? beam is either in floor or roof

8.6 Girder Demands

Section 8.3 through 8.5 discussed how to compute ultimate demands in floor beams. The same principles apply to girders, but the application is a little different.

Girders will generally run parallel to the flutes of the metal deck, so essentially no load will be transmitted from the deck directly to the girder (except where the deck is actually sitting on the top flange of the girder). Rather, the loads will come into the girder at the points where the floor beams attach. These point loads on the girder will be equal to the support reactions for the floor beams. The example below illustrates two methods for computing these point loads.

Example 8.8 Computing Point Loads on a Girder

For a uniform dead load of 90 psf, compute the point load on the indicated girder. Indicate the load on a sketch of the idealized girder.

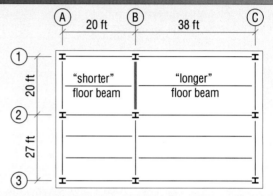

There are two methods that can be used to compute the point load.
The first method helps you to think about the load path. The second method uses tributary area to more quickly arrive at the same answer.

METHOD 1

Step 1 - Get the distributed loads on the floor beams that frame into the girder

$W_t = 10$ ft
$w_D = (10 \text{ ft})(90 \text{ psf}) = 0.9$ k/ft

Step 2 - Get the support reactions for beams that frame into the girder

For the longer floor beam, the support reactions are:

$$R = \frac{(0.9 \text{ k/ft})(38 \text{ ft})}{2} = 17.1 \text{ kips}$$

For the shorter floor beam, the support reactions are:

$$R = \frac{(0.9 \text{ k/ft})(20 \text{ ft})}{2} = 9 \text{ kips}$$

Step 3 - Sum the support reactions to get the point load on the girder

The support reactions for the floor beams are the point loads on the girder. Since both floor beams frame in at the same point, the point load is equal to the sum of the reactions:

$$P = 17.1 \text{ kips} + 9 \text{ kips} = \textbf{26.1 kips}$$

Example Continued

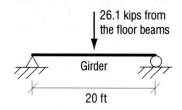

26.1 kips from
the floor beams

Girder

20 ft

METHOD 2

Step 1 - Identify the tributary area for the point load

By drawing lines between all the girders and beams we can define the tributary area for the point load. From the figure:

$$A_T = (\frac{20 \text{ ft}}{2} + \frac{38 \text{ ft}}{2})(10 \text{ ft})$$
$$= 290 \text{ ft}^2$$

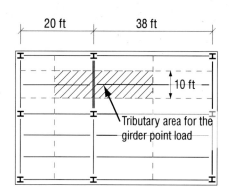

20 ft   38 ft

10 ft

Tributary area for the girder point load

Step 2 - Multiply the tributary area by the uniform load

The point load on the girder will be equal to the uniform load multiplied by the tributary area:

$$P = (90 \text{ psf})(290 \text{ ft}^2) = \mathbf{26.1} \text{ kips}$$

Note that this is the same answer obtained using Method 1.

Method 2 is generally more efficient because you need to compute tributary areas for the point loads anyway, in order to appropriately reduce the live load. The next example (next page) shows how to compute the ultimate demands on a girder.

Example 8.9 Calculating Ultimate Girder Demands

Compute the ultimate demands on the indicated girder if the floor dead load is 80 psf and the floor live load is 50 psf.

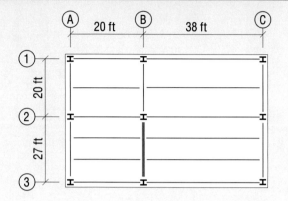

Step 1 - Identify the tributary area for the point loads

From the figure, the tributary area for one point load is:

$$A_{T,1} = (\frac{20 \text{ ft}}{2} + \frac{38 \text{ ft}}{2})(9 \text{ ft})$$
$$= 261 \text{ ft}^2$$

So the total tributary area for the girder is:

$$A_T = 2(261 \text{ ft}^2) = 522 \text{ ft}^2$$

Step 2 - Reduce the live load

$$L = L_o \left(0.25 + \frac{15}{\sqrt{2A_t}} \right)$$

$$= (50 \text{ psf}) \left(0.25 + \frac{15}{\sqrt{2(522)}} \right) = (50 \text{ psf})(0.714)$$

The formula indicates that the reduced live load is 71.4% of the unreduced live load. This is greater than the 50% lower limit for beams, so we use the computed value:

$$L = (50 \text{ psf})(0.714) = 35.7 \text{ psf}$$

Step 3 - Compute and factor the load effects

The point loads on the girder will be:

$$P_D = (80 \text{ psf})(261 \text{ ft}^2)$$
$$= 20.88 \text{ kips}$$
$$P_L = (35.7 \text{ psf})(261 \text{ ft}^2)$$
$$= 9.32 \text{ kips}$$

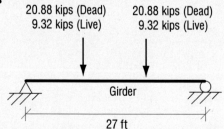

Example Continued

It is convenient to apply the load combinations to these point loads to get ultimate loads, P_U, from which the ultimate load effects are calculated. We will get the same answer as if we computed the dead and live load effects separately and then used the combinations. By inspection, load combination 2 will govern:

$$P_U = 1.2P_D + 1.6P_L = 1.2(20.88 \text{ kips}) + 1.6(9.32 \text{ kips}) = 40.0 \text{ kips}$$

Case 9 of Table 3-23 applies:

$$V_{max,U} = P_U = \textbf{40.0} \text{ kips}$$

$$M_{max,U} = P_U a = (40.0 \text{ kips})(9 \text{ ft}) = \textbf{360} \text{ k-ft}$$

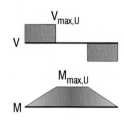

You Should Know

● In what ways is computing girder demands different from computing beam demands?

They run ⊥ to flutes, no load will be transmitted from the deck, loads come to girder as point loads

8.7 Spandrel Beam Demands

In order to understand how demands are computed for spandrel beams, it is helpful to understand what is going on around the edges of typical floors.

The picture to the right shows metal deck on top of a spandrel beam at the edge of a floor. There is a bent plate welded to the spandrel beam that will act as a pour stop when the concrete is placed on the metal deck. This bent plate extends the floor beyond the beam, typically by one or two feet. The weight of this part of the floor will be carried by the spandrel beam.

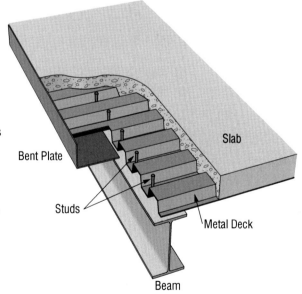

The detail to the right shows the cross section of an exterior wall. At the top and bottom of the detail you can see the spandrel beams. The exterior wall is connected to the spandrel beams at regular intervals, so the weight of the exterior wall can be represented as a uniform dead load. The spandrel beams (except at the roof) will support half-a-story's-worth of wall below and half-a-story's-worth of wall above since the exterior wall both hangs from and sits on the spandrel beams.

Note: exterior wall loads will also cause torsional load effects in most cases. Design for torsion is beyond the scope of this beginning book. The following two examples show how to compute ultimate shears and moments in spandrel beams and girders.

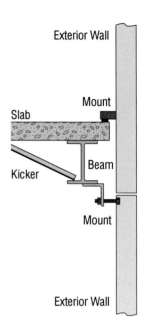

Example 8.10 Computing Ultimate Demands in Spandrel Beams

Compute the ultimate demands on the indicated spandrel beam if the floor dead load is 80 psf, the floor live load is 50 psf, and the exterior wall weight is 25 psf.

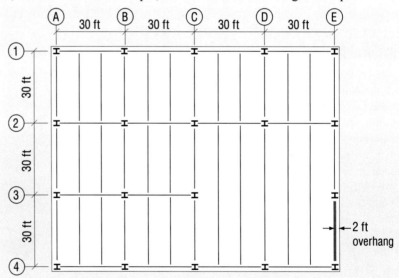

Step 1 - Get the tributary floor width and floor area for the beam

The tributary floor width for the beam is half of the distance to the beam on the left and the full overhang distance to the right:

$$W_t = \frac{10 \text{ ft}}{2} + 2 \text{ ft} = 7 \text{ ft}$$
$$A_t = (7 \text{ ft})(30 \text{ ft}) = 210 \text{ ft}^2$$

Example Continued

Step 2 - Reduce the live load

$$L = (50 \text{ psf})\left(0.25 + \frac{15}{\sqrt{2(210)}}\right) = (50 \text{ psf})(0.982)$$

This is above the lower limit so go ahead with:

$$L = (50 \text{ psf})(0.982) = 49.1 \text{ psf}$$

Step 3 - Calculate the wall load

Most spandrel beams will carry the weight of a story-heights-worth of wall (half-a-story above the beam and half-a-story below). So the tributary width of wall area is equal to the story height.

$$W_{t,wall} = 15 \text{ ft}$$

The wall load on the spandrel beam is a dead load and is equal to the tributary wall width multiplied by the wall weight in psf.

$$w_{D,wall} = (15 \text{ ft})(25 \text{ psf}) = 0.375 \text{ k/ft}$$

Step 4 - Compute and factor the load effects

The distributed floor loads are:

$$w_{D,floor} = (80 \text{ psf})(7 \text{ ft}) = 0.560 \text{ k/ft}$$
$$w_{D,wall} = (15 \text{ ft})(25 \text{ psf}) = 0.375 \text{ k/ft}$$
$$w_L = (49.1 \text{ psf})(7 \text{ ft}) = 0.344 \text{ k/ft}$$
$$w_U = 1.2(w_{D,floor} + w_{D,wall}) + 1.6 w_L$$
$$= 1.2(0.560 \text{ k/ft} + 0.375 \text{ k/ft}) + 1.6(0.342 \text{ k/ft}) = 1.67 \text{ k/ft}$$

Notice how easy it was to just combine the floor and wall loads, since they are both uniformly distributed dead loads.

Case 1 of Table 3-23 applies for getting the load effects:

$$V_{max,U} = \frac{w_U l}{2} = \frac{(1.67 \text{ k/ft})(30 \text{ ft})}{2} = \mathbf{25.1} \text{ kips}$$

$$M_{max,U} = \frac{w_U l^2}{8} = \frac{(1.67 \text{ k/ft})(30 \text{ ft})^2}{8} = \mathbf{188} \text{ k-ft}$$

Example 8.11 Computing Ultimate Demands in Spandrel Girders

Compute the ultimate demands on the indicated spandrel girder if the floor dead load is 80 psf, the floor live load is 50 psf, and the exterior wall weight is 25 psf.

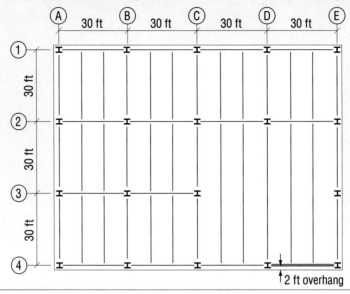

Step 1 - Identify the tributary area for the point loads

From the figure, the tributary area for one point load is:

$$A_{t,1} = (10 \text{ ft})(\frac{60 \text{ ft}}{2} + 2) = 320 \text{ ft}^2$$

You'll notice that I'm treating the slab overhang the same way as I'm treating floor on the other side. It would be more accurate to treat the overhang seperately and calculate it as a uniform distributed load (rather than part of the point loads), but this represents more work and the resulting load effects will be essentially the same once we round our final answer.

$$A_t = 2(320 \text{ ft}^2) = (640 \text{ ft}^2)$$

Step 2 - Reduce the live load

$$L = (50 \text{ psf}) \left(0.25 + \frac{15}{\sqrt{2(640)}} \right) = (50 \text{ psf})(0.669)$$

This is above the lower limit so go ahead with:

$$L = (50 \text{ psf})(0.669) = 33.5 \text{ psf}$$

Step 3 - Calculate the wall load

$$W_{t,wall} = 15 \text{ ft}$$

The wall load on the spandrel beam is a uniformly distributed dead load and is equal to the tributary wall width multiplied by the wall weight in psf.

$$w_{D,wall} = (15 \text{ ft})(25 \text{ psf}) = 0.375 \text{ k/ft}$$

Example Continued

Step 4 - Compute and factor the load effects

The point floor loads are:

$$P_{D,floor} = (80 \text{ psf})(320 \text{ ft}^2) = 25.6 \text{ kips}$$
$$P_L = (33.5 \text{ psf})(320 \text{ ft}^2) = 10.7 \text{ kips}$$

The distributed load from the wall is:

$$w_{D,wall} = 0.375 \text{ k/ft}$$

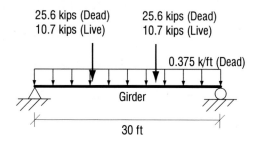

25.6 kips (Dead)   25.6 kips (Dead)
10.7 kips (Live)   10.7 kips (Live)

0.375 k/ft (Dead)

Girder

30 ft

The principle of superposition can be used to calculate the ultimate load effects. We will compute the ultimate effects for just the point loads, and just the distributed load, and then combine them.

Point Loads Only

$$P_U = 1.2P_{D,floor} + 1.6P_L = 1.2(25.6 \text{ kips}) + 1.6(10.7 \text{ kips}) = 47.8 \text{ kips}$$

Case 9 of Table 3-23 applies:

$$V_{max,U} = P_U = 47.8 \text{ kips}$$

$$M_{max,U} = P_U a = (47.8 \text{ kips})(10 \text{ ft}) = 478 \text{ k-ft}$$

Distributed Loads Only

$$w_U = 1.2w_{D,wall} = 1.2(0.375 \text{ k/ft}) = 0.45 \text{ k/ft}$$

Case 1 of Table 3-23 applies for getting the load effects:

$$V_{max,U} = \frac{w_U l}{2} = \frac{(0.45 \text{ k/ft})(30 \text{ ft})}{2} = 6.75 \text{ kips}$$

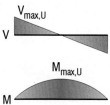

$$M_{max,U} = \frac{w_U l^2}{8} = \frac{(0.45 \text{ k/ft})(30 \text{ ft})^2}{8} = 50.6 \text{ k-ft}$$

All Loads Together

When the shear and moment diagrams are combined, the maximum shear will be at the supports, and the maximum moment at midspan. The values for these maximum load effects are:

$$V_{max,U} = 47.8 \text{ kips} + 6.75 \text{ kips} = \textbf{54.6 kips}$$
$$M_{max,U} = 478 \text{ k-ft} + 50.6 \text{ k-ft} = \textbf{529 k-ft}$$

- Why do spandrel girders have both point loads and distributed loads?

weight of floor that goes past the girder (pour stop), & wall

8.8 Deflections

When a beam is loaded, even under just its own weight, it will experience some amount of deflection. The magnitude of the deflection depends on the load, the moment of inertia of the beam, the length of the beam, and the modulus of elasticity of the material. The procedures for calculating beam deflections are developed in Mechanics textbooks. The deflections for common situations have already been derived and are given in Table 3-23.

Excessive deflection is called a serviceability limit state, since deflections need to be controlled under day-to-day loads. Since the limits on deflection are service-load deflection limits, unfactored loads should be used for deflection calculations.

Example 8.12 Calculating Beam Deflection

Calculate the live load deflection at the midspan of the beam.

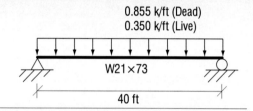

0.855 k/ft (Dead)
0.350 k/ft (Live)

W21×73

40 ft

Case 1 of Table 3-23 gives the equation for the maximum deflection of the beam, which occurs at the midspan. The equation is:

$$\Delta_{max} = \frac{5wl^4}{384EI}$$

When using the equation, it is common to make mistakes when putting in the load and converting units. For this problem the load should be the unfactored live load, since the problem is asking for the live load deflection. With regards to units, it is best to convert all the lengths to inches.

$$\Delta_{max} = \frac{5\left(0.35\frac{k}{ft}\right)\left(\frac{ft}{12\ in.}\right)(40 \times 12\ in.)^4}{384(29,000\ ksi)(1600\ in.^4)} = \mathbf{0.43}\ in.$$

- What are two common mistakes when computing beam deflections?

−have to use unfactored loads

−putting in load & converting units in $\Delta max = \frac{5wl^4}{384EI}$

8.9 Limit States

The previous sections have discussed the demands on beams. Now that you know how to compute demands (deflections, shear forces and bending moments), we are ready to start discussing beam capacity.

The capacity of a beam is governed by one of five limit states. These limit states are:
1. Yielding limit state (plastic hinge formation)
2. Lateral torsional buckling
3. Local buckling
4. Shear yielding in the web
5. Excessive elastic deflection

The figures below illustrate what these limit states look like when reached.

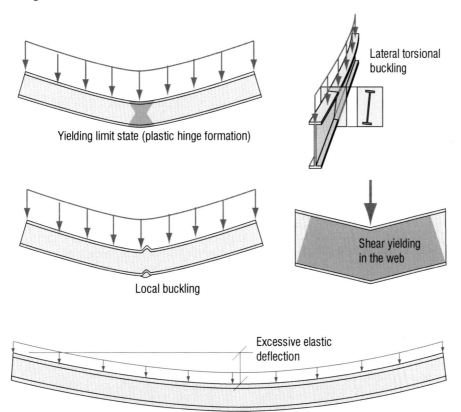

Yielding limit state (plastic hinge formation)

Lateral torsional buckling

Local buckling

Shear yielding in the web

Excessive elastic deflection

In following sections, these limit states will be discussed in turn. The nominal resistance (capacity) of a beam for each state will be developed.

You Should Know

- What are the limit states for beams?

8.10 Normal Stresses

Before we consider the five limit states for beams, it will be helpful to review the stress state in typical beams. This material is covered in Mechanics, and you may need to refer back to a text from that course if the following information feels unfamiliar.

The bending moments in a beam are resisted by normal stresses. Consider the beam below that is subject to a uniform load. The bending moment diagram is shown for the beam. Below the bending moment diagram is a figure that shows the normal stresses at a few cross sections along the beam. At each location, part of the cross section is in tension and part in compression. The resultant forces at each cross section, from the tension and compression stresses, form a force couple that is equal in magnitude to the bending moment at that location in the beam.

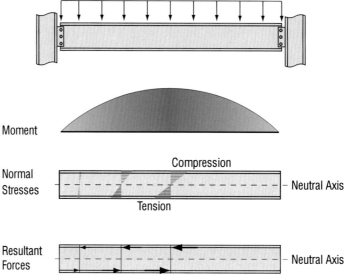

Typical elastic beam theory gives us the relationship between the normal stresses at a cross section of a beam, f_b, and the bending moment, M, at the location of the cross section.

$$f_b = \frac{-My}{I}$$

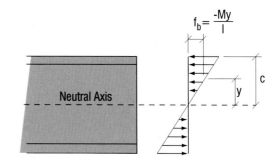

where y is the distance from the neutral axis to the point of interest, and I is the moment of inertia of the cross section. The dimension c shown in the figure to the right is the maximum possible value for y.

Example 8.13 Computing the Normal Stresses in Beams

A simply-supported W14×22 beam is 30 ft long has a uniform load of 0.75 k/ft. Compute the maximum normal stress in the steel.

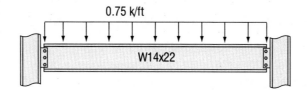

0.75 k/ft

W14x22

Step 1 - Calculate the maximum moment

The maximum normal stress will occur at the cross section where the moment is greatest. The maximum moment occurs at midspan and is equal to:

$$M_{max} = \frac{w_U l^2}{8} = \frac{(0.75 \text{ k/ft})(30 \text{ ft})^2}{8} = 84.4 \text{ k-ft}$$

Step 2 - Calculate/plot the normal stress at the midspan cross section

The equation for the normal stress is:

$$f = \frac{-My}{I}$$

where

$M = M_{max} = 84.4$ k-ft
$I = I_x = 199$ in.^{4} (from Table 1-1)
and y varies.

Step 3 - Calculate the maximum normal stress

The maximum normal stress occurs when y is greatest - at the extreme fiber from the neutral axis.

$$y_{max} = \frac{d}{2} = \frac{13.7 \text{ in.}}{2} = 6.85 \text{ in.}$$

$$f_{max} = \frac{[(84.4 \text{ k-ft})(12 \text{ in./ft})](6.85 \text{ in.})}{199 \text{ in.}^4} = \mathbf{34.86} \text{ ksi}$$

As in the example above, we are often interested in the maximum normal stress at a beam cross section. This maximum normal stress will be equal to:

$$f_{max} = \frac{Mc}{I} = \frac{M}{\left(\frac{I}{c}\right)} = \frac{M}{S}$$

where c is the distance to the point furthest from the neutral axis. The term I/c is called the elastic section modulus and is designated S.

A beam will begin to yield if f_{max} reaches F_y. The moment corresponding to this first yielding is designated M_y and is calculated as:

$$M_y = F_y S$$

Example 8.14 Computing the Yield Moment

What moment will cause a W14×22 beam to begin to yield?

Step 1 - Look up the value for the elastic section modulus

It is generally safe to assume that beams are oriented such that they are bending about the strong axis. This makes the pertinent section modulus S_x. The value can be looked up in Table 1-1.

$$S_x = 29.0 \text{ in.}^3$$

Step 2 - Compute the moment that causes yielding

The beam will begin to yield if the moment reaches M_y.

$$M_y = F_y S_x = (50 \text{ ksi})(29.0 \text{ in.}^3) = 1450 \text{ k-in.} = \textbf{121 k-ft}$$

where moment is highest

You Should Know

- Where are the normal stresses the highest in a uniformly-loaded beam?
- If the beam in Example 8.12 had been a W18×35, would the maximum normal stress have been higher or lower than it was for the W14×22?
- What moment would cause a W18×35 to begin to yield?

8.11 Plastic Moment Capacity

Steel beams can actually carry moments that are greater than M_y. The figure below shows what happens to the stress profile of a wide flange cross section as the moment increases.

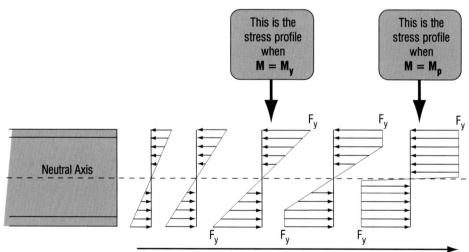

Changes in the stress profile as the moment in the beam increases

The profile in the center corresponds with first yielding (M_y). As the applied moment increases the stress can't get any higher on the edges, yielding spreads towards the center of the beam. The stress profile at the far right, represents the state of a beam when its entire cross section has yielded, half in tension and half in compression. The moment corresponding to this profile is called the plastic moment and is designated M_p.

You need to know how to compute M_p for beams of any cross section. The basic steps are:
1. Identify the location of the neutral axis when the beam is entirely yielded.
2. Compute the magnitudes of the tension and compression resultants.
3. Identify the location of the tension and compression resultants.
4. Compute M_p as the moment from the tension-compression couple.

The example on the next pages illustrates how the steps for computing M_p are applied for the case of a tee. The steps are easier to apply for more common beam shapes where the cross section is doubly symmetric.

Example 8.15 What a Plastic Hinge Looks Like

What does a beam look like when a plastic hinge forms?

The figure below shows a W36×256 beam that is cantilevered from a heavy column. The flanges of this beam were cut on purpose to make a region with reduced cross section. The end of the cantilevered beam (not shown) has a point load that is causing bending moments in the beam. The point load has increased to the level that a plastic hinge has formed in the region with the reduced cross-section.

Flanges were cut near the connection to make a reduced cross-section.

Flaking of the painted mill scale (outer layer of the beam), is a manifestation of yielding.

The entire cross section of the beam is yielded. The beam will experience significant deflection if the loading is increased at all.

Example 8.16 Computing the Plastic Moment for a Beam

Compute M_p for a WT18×128 used as a beam?

Step 1 - Identify the location of the neutral axis when the tee is fully yielded

When the WT18×128 is fully yielded in bending, half in tension and half in compression, the neutral axis will divide the cross section into two equal **areas**. This is the only way that the tension and compression resultant forces can be equal

The area of a WT18×128 is:

$$A = 37.7 \text{ in.}^2$$

so half is:

$$0.5 \times A = 18.85 \text{ in.}^2$$

For tees in general, the plastic neutral axis might be in the flange or web. In this case:

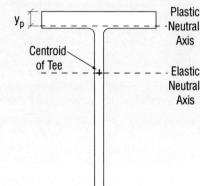

$$y_p = \frac{18.85 \text{ in.}^2}{12.2 \text{ in.}} = 1.545 \text{ in.}$$

The flange thickness for a WT18×128 is 1.73 in.

Note: The plastic neutral axis is different from the elastic neutral axis for tees. The elastic neutral axis is located at the *centroid* of the tee cross section. After the tee begins to yield, the neutral axis migrates until it reaches the plastic neutral axis location calculated above.

Step 2 - Compute the magnitudes of the tension and compression resultants

When M_p is reached, the entire cross section is yielded, half in tension half in compression. The tension and compression resultant forces, T and C, are simply:

$$T = C = (F_y)(A/2)$$
$$T = C = (50 \text{ ksi})(18.85 \text{ in.}^2) = 942.5 \text{ kips}$$

Step 3 - Compute the location of the tension and compression resultants

Since the stress is uniform over the cross-section (equal to F_y everywhere), the resultants will be located at the centroids of the top half and the bottom half.
The distance to the centroid for the top half is easily computed

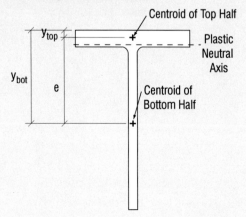

$$y_{top} = \frac{1.545 \text{ in.}}{2} = 0.773 \text{ in.}$$

Example Continued

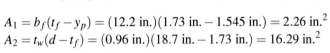

The distance to the centroid of the bottom half can be computed as:

$$y_{bot} = \frac{A_1 y_1 + A_2 y_2}{A_1 + A_2} \text{ where:}$$

$$A_1 = b_f(t_f - y_p) = (12.2 \text{ in.})(1.73 \text{ in.} - 1.545 \text{ in.}) = 2.26 \text{ in.}^2$$
$$A_2 = t_w(d - t_f) = (0.96 \text{ in.})(18.7 \text{ in.} - 1.73 \text{ in.}) = 16.29 \text{ in.}^2$$

$$y_1 = y_p + \frac{(t_f - y_p)}{2} = (1.545 \text{ in.}) + \frac{(1.73 \text{ in.} - 1.545 \text{ in.})}{2} = 1.64 \text{ in.}$$
$$y_2 = t_f + \frac{(d - t_f)}{2} = (1.73 \text{ in.}) + \frac{(18.7 \text{ in.} - 1.73 \text{ in.})}{2} = 10.22 \text{ in.}$$

Note that $A_1 + A_2$ is a little less than $0.5 \times A$. This is because we have not accounted for the fillets between the flange and the web. For calculations like this, it is impractical to try to consider them. We will accept that our calculation will have a small error (probably less than 1%).

$$y_{bot} = \frac{A_1 y_1 + A_2 y_2}{A_1 + A_2} = \frac{(2.26 \text{ in.}^2)(1.64 \text{ in.}) + (16.29 \text{ in.}^2)(10.22 \text{ in.})}{2.26 \text{ in.}^2 + 16.29 \text{ in.}^2}$$

$$y_{bot} = 9.17 \text{ in.}$$

Step 4 - Compute the moment from the tension-compression resultant couple

Stress Profile   Resultant Forces

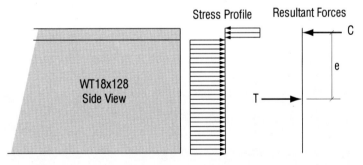

The moment from a force couple is equal to the magnitude of the forces multiplied by the distance between them. The distance between the force resultants is:

$$e = y_{bot} - y_{top} = 9.17 \text{ in.} - 0.773 \text{ in.} = 8.40 \text{ in.}$$

Since the magnitude of the forces is T (or C):

$$M_p = Te = (942.5 \text{ kips})(8.40 \text{ in.}) = 660 \text{ k-ft}$$

- What does the stress profile look like when a plastic hinge forms?
- Why does the plastic neutral axis have to divide the shape into two equal areas?
- What are the four general steps for getting M_p?

8.12 Plastic Section Modulus

In the previous section we defined the plastic moment, M_p, and outlined the general steps for computing M_p for any cross section. M_p can be written as:

$$M_p = F_y(A/2)e$$

where e is the distance between the centroids of the top and bottom halves of the cross section. For convenience, we define:

$$Z = (A/2)e$$

and we call Z the plastic section modulus. Now, the plastic moment can be simply written as the yield stress multiplied by the plastic section modulus:

$$M_p = F_y Z$$

Example 8.17 Computing the Plastic Section Modulus

Compute the plastic section modulus, Z, for a WT18×128.

Step 1 - Calculate half the area

To compute Z, you only need two things. The first is half of the cross-sectional area. For a WT18×128:

$$\frac{A}{2} = \frac{37.7 \text{ in.}^2}{2} = 18.85 \text{ in.}^2$$

Step 2 - Compute the distance between centroids

The second thing you need to compute Z is the distance between the centroids of the top and bottom halves. This was done for the WT18×128 in Steps 3 and 4 of Example 8.16:

$$e = 8.40 \text{ in.}$$

Step 3 - Compute the plastic section modulus
$$Z = (A/2)e = (18.85 \text{ in.}^2)(8.40 \text{ in.}) = 158 \text{ in.}^3$$

Note that the units for Z are in.^{3}. Also remember that this value of Z has some error because the fillets were not accounted for when computing e.

Study the Manual

The Manual lists values for Z for the standard shapes. Turn to Table 1-8 and look for the WT18×128.

Notice in the top-left corner of the page there is a diagram showing the tee; the plastic neutral axis (PNA) is indicated and the dimension to the PNA is y_p.

- From Table 1-8, what is y_p for the WT18×128?

- How does this value compare with the value calculated in Step 1 of Example 8.16?

When bending is about the X-X axis, the Z with respect to the X-X axis is used to compute M_p. The value of Z for the X-X axis is called Z_x.

- What is the tabulated value for Z_x for the WT18×128?

- How does the tabulated value for Z_x for the WT18×128 differ from what was calculated in Step 3 of Example 8.17?

It is important to understand the difference between the plastic section modulus, Z, and the elastic section modulus, S. The plastic section modulus is multiplied by F_y to get the plastic moment, M_p, which corresponds to yielding of the entire cross-section. The elastic section modulus is multiplied by F_y to get the moment at first-yield, M_y, which corresponds to yielding at the extreme fiber of the cross-section.

The ratio Z/S is called the *shape factor*. The shape factor will also be the ratio of M_p/M_y. This ratio is a measure of how much additional moment capacity is available after a beam begins to yield at the extreme fiber.

Example 8.18 Computing the Shape Factor

What is the shape factor for a W12×96 bending about the strong axis?

Step 1 - Look up Z and S

Look up the plastic section modulus and elastic section modulus from Table 1-1. For the X-X axis of a W12×96:

$$Z = 147 \text{ in.}^3$$
$$S = 131 \text{ in.}^3$$

Step 2 - Compute the shape factor

$$\frac{Z}{S} = \frac{147 \text{ in.}^3}{131 \text{ in.}^3} = \textbf{1.12}$$

You Should Know

- How is the plastic section modulus calculated?
- Where can you look up the plastic section modulus for standard shapes?
- How do you compute the shape factor?

8.13 Yielding Limit State

The previous three sections have provided the background to understand the yielding limit state for beams. The yielding limit state for beams occurs when M_p is reached at any point in the beam and a plastic hinge forms. For a simply supported beam, the formation of one plastic hinge will lead to excessive deformation and possibly collapse.

Yielding limit state
(plastic hinge formation)

Study the Manual

Turn to Chapter F of the Specification (page 16.1-44).

- What is the title of the chapter?

There are many sub-sections in Chapter F, each dealing with particular types of shapes. The most common beam shapes are wide-flange shapes that have thick enough flanges and webs that we don't need to worry about local buckling when the flanges and webs are thick enough they are called "compact."

- Which section in Chapter F deals with the most common beam shapes?

Study the Manual

Turn to §F 2. of the Specification.

This section covers the most common beams. The first limit state is covered in §F 2.1. and is called the yielding limit state. Eqn. F2-1 gives the nominal moment capacity, M_n, for the yielding limit state.

- Write the equation for M_n for the yielding limit state?

- How does this equation relate to the material covered in the previous pages of *Build with Steel*?

- What is the ϕ factor for the yielding limit state [see §F 1.(1)]?

The yielding limit state is easy to calculate and tables have been developed so that ϕM_n for the yielding limit state can be simply looked-up.

Example 8.19 Computing the Capacity for the Yielding Limit State

Compute ϕM_n for the yielding limit state for a W12×58 beam.

$$\phi M_n = 0.9 M_p = 0.9(F_y Z_x) \qquad \text{(Eqn. F2-1)}$$
$$\phi M_n = 0.9(50 \text{ ksi})(86.4 \text{ in.}^3) = 3888 \text{ k-in.} = \textbf{324} \text{ k-ft}$$

Study the Manual

Turn to Table 3-2 in the Manual. This table is referred to as the "Z_x Table."

Table 3-2 lists all of the wide-flange shapes, from greatest to lowest Z_x.

- Which wide-flange has the greatest Z_x?

- Which wide-flange has the lowest Z_x?

There is a column in the table that gives ϕM_p ($\phi_b M_{px}$) for all of the shapes. For the yielding limit state, ϕM_n is equal to ϕM_p so the capacity for the yielding limit state can be read directly from the table.

Find the W12×58 in Table 3-2.

- What is the listed value for $\phi_b M_{px}$?

- How does it compare with ϕM_n calculated in Example 8.19?

Notice how the shapes are grouped in Table 3-2. For example, the W12×58 is in a group bounded by W21×44 at the top and W16×45 at the bottom. The shapes at the top of each group are printed in bold-faced type.

- How does the weight for the bold-faced shapes compare with the weights of the other shapes in the same group?

- How can lighter shapes have higher Z_x and $\phi_b M_{px}$ than heavier shapes?

Example 8.20 Computing the Capacity for the Yielding Limit State

What is the lightest wide-flange shape that has ϕM_n for the yielding limit state greater than 1800 k-ft?

We recognize that ϕM_n for the yielding limit state is equal to ϕM_p ($\phi_b M_{px}$).

Turning to Table 3-2 and scanning down the $\phi_b M_{px}$ column, we can find a group of shapes that has yielding limit state capacities around 1800 k-ft. The group begins with W36×135 (bold-faced) and ends with W24×162.

The shape with $\phi_b M_{px}$ nearest to 1800 k-ft is the W12×279, but that is not what the question was asking. We've been asked to find the lightest wide-flange shape with ϕM_n greater than 1800 k-ft. The lightest shape will be the bold-faced one: the W36×135. Note that the W36×135 weighs 144 lbs/ft less than the W12×279.

You Should Know

- How do you compute the capacity for the yielding limit state for a beam?
- How are the shapes organized in Table 3-2?
- What do the bold-faced entries in Table 3-2 mean?

8.14 Lateral-Torsional Buckling

The next limit state we will consider for beams is called lateral torsional buckling (LTB). This limit state is illustrated below. On the left, a beam is shown prior to loading. The × at each end designates that the top flange is constrained from translating to the left or right at the ends. The distance between the flange constraints is designated the unbraced length. When a distributed load is applied, the top flange of the beam is in compression and the bottom flange in tension (center figure). Think of the compression flange like a column. If the applied load increases, the compression stress in the top flange will increase. At some load, the compression stress in the top flange will be high enough to cause buckling. Since the compression flange is restrained by the web, it will buckle perpendicular to the web. At the same time, the tension flange is stable and will want to remain in place. The result is that the cross-section will translate and twist - hence lateral torsional buckling (LTB).

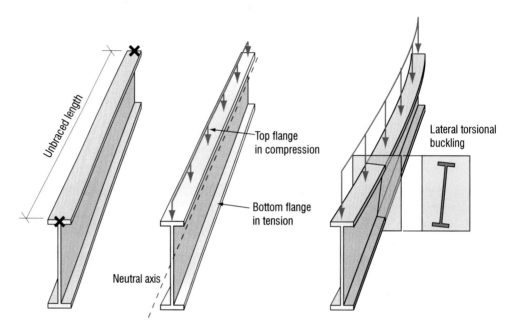

The bending moment that a beam can resist before it experiences LTB depends on:
1. The beam cross-section
2. The unbraced length
3. The moment gradient

These three things will be considered one at a time.

The cross-section of a beam heavily influences the lateral torsional buckling capacity. The cross-sections shown to the right are naturally resistant to LTB. Pipes, HSSs, and other shapes with closed cross-sections do not experience lateral torsional buckling, partly because the closed cross-section makes them very stiff torsionally. Other shapes that do not experience LTB are channels and I-shapes *that are bent about their weak axis.*

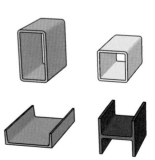

Not Susceptible to LTB

The shapes most susceptible to LTB are the ones most often used as beams. These are *I*-shaped shapes that are much deeper than they are wide.

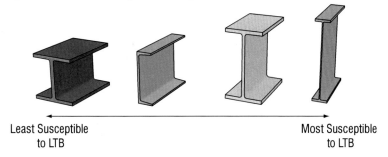

Least Susceptible to LTB   Most Susceptible to LTB

You may wonder why we use deep I-shapes for beams when they are the most susceptible to LTB. Deep I-shaped cross-sections will have a high moment of inertia (I_x) relative to their cross-sectional area (A). This characteristics gives them vertical stiffness, which is important for controlling beam deflections. High I_x also makes flange stresses low. The problems with LTB for I-shapes can be mitigated by controlling the unbraced length.

Study the Manual

Turn to the User Note Table at the beginning of Chapter F of the Specification.

In the table, there are pictures to indicate which Section in Chapter F pertains to which kinds of shapes used as beams.

- What is the last column in the Table?

Notice which types of shapes have LTB listed as a pertinent limit state?

- Are angles and tees susceptible to lateral torsional buckling?

You Should Know

- Why do wide-flange beams twist when they buckle in bending? → *compression flange is stable & will buckle ⊥ to web*
- What three characteristics influence lateral torsional buckling capacity of a beam?
- Why are closed cross-sections resistant to lateral torsional buckling? → *closed makes them stiff*
- Which is probably more susceptible to LTB if all things are equal other than cross-section, a W12×53 or a W14×53? *or bent about their weak axis*

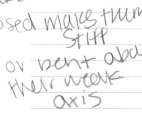

8.15 Unbraced Length

In addition to the cross-section, the unbraced length of a beam heavily influences the lateral torsional buckling capacity of the beam. The unbraced length is defined as the distance between bracing points for the *compression flange* of a beam and is designated L_b.

Example 8.21 Determining the Unbraced Length of a Beam

In the picture below, the columns are 30 ft. apart, and the floor beams are equally spaced. Assuming that the floor beams provide restraint to the girder top flange, what is the unbraced length, L_b, for the girder between the columns?

The length of the girder is 30 ft. because it spans between the columns. The unbraced length of the girder is 10 ft. because the floor beams restrain the top flange at the third points. The connections at each end of the girder will also provide restraint for the top flange.

In figures, we indicate the restraint to the compression flange with an ×. The girder above might be depicted as:

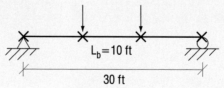

If there are no intermediate restraints for the compression flange of a beam, perhaps as in the case of the floor beams in the example above, then the unbraced length will be equal to the total length.

The plot below shows the nominal moment capacity for a group of beams that all have the same cross-section but have different unbraced lengths. The plot shows that, in general, the longer the unbraced length, L_b, the lower will be the lateral torsional buckling capacity.

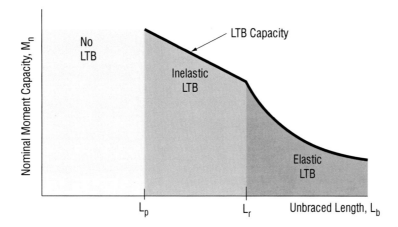

From the plot we observe that for small values of L_b (less than some value designated L_p), LTB does not occur and the moment capacity of the beams will be limited by something else (the yielding limit state). For beams with very high L_b (greater than some value designated L_r) the moment capacity is limited by elastic LTB and diminishes with increased unbraced length. For intermediate values of L_b, inelastic LTB occurs, which means that the compression flange begins to yield and then buckles.

The derivation of the lateral torsional buckling equations are beyond the scope of a first undergraduate course. Chapter F of the Specification provides the equations that define the relationship between M_n and L_b for any beam cross-section.

Study the Manual

Turn to §F2.2. in the Specification. This section explains how to compute the nominal moment capacity for lateral-torsional buckling.

Read §F2.2.(a)

- What happens for values of L_b that are less than L_p?

Read §F2.2.(b)

- Which line on the figure above represents Eqn. F2-2?

- Which terms in Eqn. F2-2 have already been defined?

- Which terms in Eqn. F2-2 are unfamiliar?

Look at §F2.2.(c)

- Which line on the figure above represents Eqn. F2-3?

Keep reading through §F2.2. until you reach the equations for computing L_p and L_r. These two lengths are required in Eqn. F2-2 and are calculated using Eqns. F2-5 and F2-6. You will rarely need to use Eqns. F2-5 and F2-6 because values for L_p and L_r for all the wide-flange shapes are listed in Table 3-2.

Example 8.22 Calculating the Lateral Torsional Buckling Capacity

A W14×74 girder is 30 ft. long and has lateral restraint at the third points. Compute ϕM_n for the lateral torsional buckling limit state (assuming C_b=1.0).

Step 1 - Determine Lb

The first step is to determine L_b. Since the compression flange is braced at the third points:

$$L_b = \frac{30\ \text{ft}}{3} = 10\ \text{ft}$$

Step 2 - Determine Lp and Lr

In order to know what equation applies, we need to know how L_b compares with L_p and L_r. These lengths can be determined using Eqns. F2-5 and F2-6, but it is faster to look them up in the Z_x table. For the W14×74:

$$L_p = 8.76\ \text{ft}$$
$$L_r = 31.0\ \text{ft}$$

L_b is between L_p and L_r.

Step 3 - Compute the nominal moment capacity

Since L_b is between L_p and L_r, Eqn. F2-2 applies for calculating the nominal moment capacity. It has a number of terms which can be computed individually and then combined in the equation.

$C_b = 1.0$ (given in the problem statement)
$M_p = F_y Z_x = (50\ \text{ksi})(126\ \text{in.}^3) = 6300\text{k-in} = 525\ \text{k-ft}$
$F_y S_x = (50\ \text{ksi})(112\ \text{in.}^3) = 5600\text{k-in} = 466.7\ \text{k-ft}$

The other terms were determined in Steps 1 and 2. All the terms can now be combined to compute the nominal moment capacity.

$$M_n = C_b\left[M_p - (M_p - 0.7F_y S_x)\left(\frac{L_b - L_p}{L_r - L_p}\right)\right] \leq M_p$$

$$M_n = 1.0\left[(525\ \text{k-ft}) - \left((525\ \text{k-ft}) - 0.7(466.7\ \text{k-ft})\right)\left(\frac{10\ \text{ft} - 8.76\ \text{ft}}{31.0\ \text{ft} - 8.76\ \text{ft}}\right)\right]$$

$$M_n = 514\ \text{k-ft} \leq 525\ \text{k-ft}$$

The expression above means that the nominal capacity for LTB can never exceed M_p. Since the left side is lesser:

$$M_n = 514\ \text{k-ft}$$

Step 4 - Factor the nominal moment capacity

$$\phi M_n = (0.9)(514\ \text{k-ft}) = \textbf{463}\ \text{k-ft}$$

Table 3-10 in the Manual can be used to determine factored moment capacities for LTB without doing calculations.

Study the Manual

Turn to Table 3-10 in the Manual.

This table is more than 30 pages long! In the table are the ϕM_n-L_b curves for the wide-flange shapes typically used as beams. A simplified version of the table is shown in the schematic below.

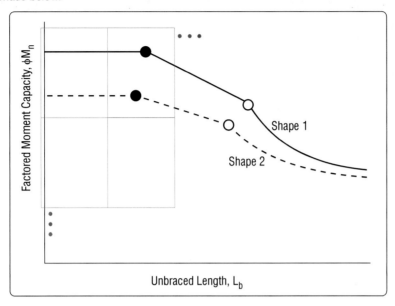

The lines in the table are the ϕM_n-L_b curves . Each page of the table only shows part of the ϕM_n-L_b space. The red rectangles in the schematic above represent individual pages of the table. The lines on each page of the table have the shape names written next to them so you know which shape the line pertains to. Some lines are dashed and some are solid this will be discussed later when we talk about beam design.

On the ϕM_n-L_b curve for each shape, there is a solid black circle and an open circle at different points along the curve. The solid circle appears at L_p for the shape, and the open circle appears at L_r.

Look at the top left corner of any page in Table 3-10.

- What F_y is assumed in the table?

- What C_b is assumed in the table?

Turn to page 3-122 of the Manual. Find the line on the page corresponding to a W14×74 in the lower left corner of the page.

- For $L_b = 10$ ft, what is the value for ϕM_n for a W14×74?

- How does the value read from the table compare with the value calculated in Example 8.22?

This section will conclude with an example showing how Table 3-10 can be used to determine ϕM_n for the lateral torsion buckling limit state.

Example 8.23 Determining Factored Capacity for LTB Using Table 3-10

The two beams are both W18×86. Determine ϕM_n for each beam for the lateral torsional buckling limit state (assuming $C_b = 1.0$).

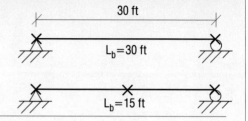

Step 1 - Look up capacity when Lb=30 ft

It takes some practice to find particular shapes in Table 3-10 because there are so many. It may feel like looking for a needle in a haystack. As you glance through pages, observe the beam weights and unbraced lengths. Turn to the right for lower beam weights.

Look at page 3-125 in the Manual to find the W18×86 with $L_b = 30$ ft. The factored capacity is read to be:

$\phi M_n = \mathbf{406}$ k-ft

Note that we are to the right of the open circle on the curve, meaning that for $L_b = 30$ ft the beam would experience elastic LTB.

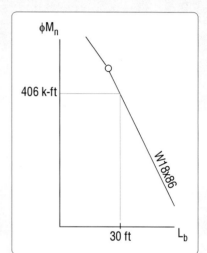

Step 2 - Look up capacity when Lb=15 ft

We will need to turn a few pages to the left to find the W18×86 with $L_b = 15$ ft.

Look at page 3-120 in the Manual. The factored capacity is read to be:

$\phi M_n = \mathbf{620}$ k-ft

Note that we are to the right of the closed circle and to the left of the open circle, meaning that for $L_b = 15$ ft the beam would experience inelastic LTB.

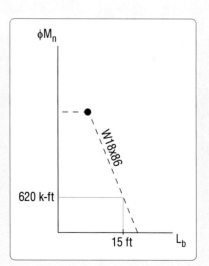

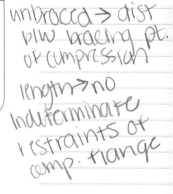

You Should Know

- What is the difference between the length of a beam and the unbraced length of a beam?
- For what values of L_b will a beam experience elastic lateral torsional buckling?
- Where can you look up the value of L_p for a beam?
- How could you determine L_r for a beam from Table 3-10?
- What are two ways to determine ϕM_n for the lateral torsional buckling limit state?

8.16 Moment Gradient

The previous two sections have shown how cross-section and unbraced length influence the lateral-torsional buckling capacity of beams. This section will discuss moment gradient, which is the third beam characteristic that influences LTB capacity.

Consider the three beams below. All three beams have the same cross-section, unbraced length, and maximum moment; but all three beams are not equally susceptible to lateral torsional buckling. The difference between the beams is the moment gradient.

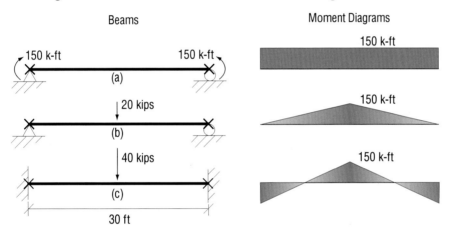

Moment gradient increases a beam's lateral torsional buckling capacity as easily illustrated by comparing beams (a) and (c). In the figures below, the beams have shading to indicate compression regions.

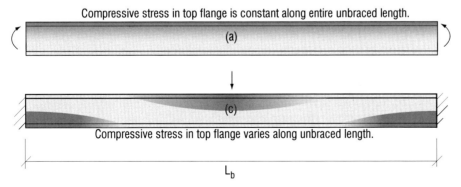

Even though both beams have the same unbraced length, only part of the top flange for beam (c) is even in compression. In other words, in beam (c) the length of the top flange that wants to buckle is less than L_b because of the moment gradient.

179

The beneficial effects of moment gradient are accounted for by the C_b factor. In previous examples, C_b was conservatively assumed to be equal to 1.0. §F1.(2) of the Manual explains how to compute C_b.

Study the Manual

Turn to §F1.(3) of the Specification. Read through the equation for C_b and the definitions of the terms in the C_b equation.

- What is M_A?

- When would M_C and M_{max} be equal?

The procedures for computing C_b are illustrated in the following examples.

Example 8.24 Computing the Cb Factor for a Beam

Compute the C_b factor for the left un-braced segment of the beam.

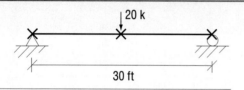

30 ft

Step 1 - Draw the moment diagram for the beam

C_b is based on the shape of the moment diagram. The first step is to draw the moment diagram for the beam.

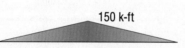

150 k-ft

Step 2 - Calculate moments for the unbraced length of interest

The C_b factor is calculated for a specific unbraced length of the beam. The beam in this problem has lateral restraint at the midspan, dividing the beam into two equal unbraced lengths.

We are interested in the left segment. For the C_b equation we need the maximum moment and the moments at the quarterpoints.

$M_{max} = 150$ k-ft
$M_a = 37.5$ k-ft
$M_b = 75$ k-ft
$M_c = 112.5$ k-ft

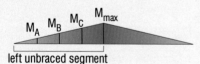

left unbraced segment

Step 3 - Compute Cb

We can now compute C_b using equation F1-1. We will assume the beam is made from a doubly symmetric shape so $R_m = 1.0$

$$C_b = \frac{12.5 M_{max}}{2.5 M_{max} + 3 M_A + 4 M_B + 3 M_C} R_m \leq 3.0$$

$$C_b = \frac{12.5(150 \text{ k-ft})}{2.5(150 \text{ k-ft}) + 3(37.5 \text{ k-ft}) + 4(75 \text{ k-ft}) + 3(112.5 \text{ k-ft})} 1.0 \leq 3.0$$

$C_b = 1.67 \leq 3.0$
$C_b = \mathbf{1.67}$

When computing C_b remember that the moments M_{max}, M_A, M_B, and M_C are defined to be the absolute value of the moments at the quarter points (see §F1.).

The C_b factors for common situations are given in Table 3-1 of the Manual.

Study the Manual

Turn to Table 3-1 in the Manual (page 3-18).

The third column in the table provides C_b values for various segments of common beams. The second beam (going down) is like the one in Example 8.24 that has a single point load in the middle and is laterally restrained in the middle and the ends.

- How does the C_b factor for the left segment of this beam compare with that calculated in Example 8.24?

- Why is the C_b factor the same for the left and right segment of this beam?

Look at the uniformly loaded beam towards the bottom of the table. Notice that for the center unbraced segments, the C_b factor is close to 1.0. That is because the moment is nearly constant over these segments, so there is no moment gradient.

- What is C_b for a uniformly loaded beam with no lateral restraint between the supports?

When there is a moment gradient, C_b will be greater than 1.0, amplifying the lateral torsional buckling capacity of the beam.

Example 8.25 Computing LTB Capacity When Cb Is Greater Than 1.0

Compute ϕM_n for LTB for a W14×74 girder with L_b=15 ft, and C_b=1.67 using Eqn. F2-2.

$$M_n = C_b \left[M_p - (M_p - 0.7 F_y S_x) \left(\frac{L_b - L_p}{L_r - L_p} \right) \right] \leq M_p$$

$$M_n = 1.67 \left[(525 \text{ k-ft}) - \left((525 \text{ k-ft}) - 0.7(466.7 \text{ k-ft}) \right) \left(\frac{15 \text{ ft} - 8.76 \text{ ft}}{31.76 \text{ ft} - 8.76 \text{ ft}} \right) \right] \leq M_p$$

$$M_n = 787 \text{ k-ft} \leq 525 \text{ k-ft}$$

Notice that the left side of the expression exceeds the right (M_p). This will often happen when C_b is more than 1.0 . It means that the moment to cause lateral torsional buckling is greater than the plastic moment capacity. In other words, it means that lateral torsional buckling will not occur for the beam because the yielding limit state will be reached first. So:

$$M_n = 525 \text{ k-ft (governed by yielding not LTB)}$$

$$\phi M_n = 0.9(525 \text{ k-ft}) = \mathbf{473} \text{ k-ft}$$

It is usually faster to get ϕM_n using Table 3-10, rather than using the equations in §F2.2. of the Specification. However, when C_b is not 1.0, an adjustment needs to be made for values read from Table 3-10, since the table assumes C_b=1.0. Values read from the Table are multiplied by C_b, and then checked to see that they have not exceeded ϕM_p. This procedure is illustrated in the following example.

Example 8.26 Determining LTB Capacity When Cb Is Greater Than 1.0

Determine ϕM_n for LTB for a W14×74 girder with L_b=15 ft, and C_b=1.67 using Table 3-10.

Step 1 - Get LTB capacity if Cb=1.0

The first step is to look up the value for ϕM_n from Table 3-10, assuming for the moment that $C_b = 1.0$. For a W14×74 with $L_b = 15$ ft:

$$\phi M_{n,Cb=1} = 422 \text{ k-ft}$$

Note that we are careful to designate that this is ϕM_n for $C_b = 1.0$ as assumed in the table.

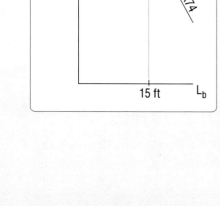

Step 2 - Adjust to account for Cb

The nominal capacity accounting for C_b is simply:

$$\phi M_n = C_b(\phi M_{n,Cb=1}) \leq \phi M_p$$

From the Z_x Table:

$$\phi M_p = 473 \text{ k-ft}$$

So we have:

$$\phi M_n = 1.67(422 \text{ k-ft}) \leq 473 \text{ k-ft}$$
$$\phi M_n = 705 \text{ k-ft} \leq 473 \text{ k-ft}$$

Notice that the left side of the expression exceeds the right. This will often happen when C_b is more than 1.0. It means that the moment to cause lateral torsional buckling is greater than the plastic moment capacity. In other words, it means that lateral torsional buckling will not occur for the beam because the yielding limit state will be reached first. So:

$$\phi M_n = \phi M_p = \mathbf{473} \text{ k-ft}$$

You Should Know

- Why is moment gradient beneficial to lateral torsional buckling capacity?
- What values of M_{max}, M_A, M_B, and M_C will give a C_b factor of 1.0?
- Where can you look up values of C_b for common cases?
- Why is beam capacity not limited by the lateral torsional buckling limit state when C_b is large?

8.17 Local Buckling

The previous sections have addressed lateral torsion buckling (LTB) which is a global buckling failure. In LTB, cross-sections along the beam do not distort; they simply translate and rotate relative to each other (below left).

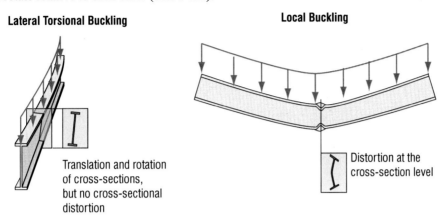

Lateral Torsional Buckling

Translation and rotation of cross-sections, but no cross-sectional distortion

Local Buckling

Distortion at the cross-section level

Local buckling (above right) is different, and is the third limit state that will be discussed for beams. Local buckling involves distortion at the cross-sectional level that leads to overall failure of the beam.

For an I-shaped cross-section, local buckling may initiate in any element of the cross-section. If local buckling initiates in the web it is called web local buckling (WLB); if it initiates in a flange it is called flange local buckling (FLB).

Like columns, local buckling is only an issue for beams that have elements with λ greater than a prescribed limit. In beams, local buckling will not occur prior to yielding if the elements of the cross-section have λ less than λ_p, making the elements compact (see below). However, if λ exceeds λ_p for any elements of the cross-section then local buckling may govern and ϕM_n needs to be calculated for the pertinent local buckling limit state.

The procedure for checking local buckling in beams can be summarized in three steps that need to be performed for each element of the cross-section:

1. Determine λ.
2. Determine λ_p.
3. If $\lambda < \lambda_p$, there is no local buckling of that element (DONE). If $\lambda > \lambda_p$, compute ϕM_n corresponding to local buckling of the element.

The equations for λ_p for various cross-sectional elements are given in Table B4.1b. The format of Table B4.1b is the same as for Table B4.1a which we used to check for local buckling in columns, back in Chapter 6. The following examples show how to check for local buckling issues in beams.

Example 8.27 Checking a Beam for Local Buckling

Determine if local buckling might occur for a W12×50 beam.

Step 1 - Check for flange local buckling

To check if flange local buckling will occur, we follow the steps outlined on the previous page. First we determine λ for the flange. This is most easily done by reading the value from Table 1-1.

$$\lambda = \frac{b}{t} = \frac{b_f}{2t_f} = 6.31$$

Next we need to calculate the appropriate value for λ_p. In Table B4.1b, Case 10 will apply since we are dealing with a beam flange for a W12x50 (rolled I-shaped section):

$$\lambda_p = 0.38\sqrt{E/F_y} = 0.38\sqrt{(29000 \text{ ksi})/(50 \text{ ksi})} = 9.15$$

Since $\lambda < \lambda_p$, the flanges are *compact* so flange local buckling will not occur.

Step 2 - Check for web local buckling

Following the same steps as for above, but for the web:

$$\lambda = \frac{h}{t_w} = 26.8 \quad \text{(Case 15 in Table B4.1b, and looking up value in Table 1-1)}$$
$$\lambda_p = 3.76\sqrt{E/F_y} = 3.76\sqrt{(29000 \text{ ksi})/(50 \text{ ksi})} = 90.6$$

Since $\lambda < \lambda_p$, the web is *compact* so web local buckling will not occur.

The check done in Example 8.27 has already been performed for all the standard beam shapes (assuming the standard material). Those shapes which have λ greater than λ_p, are indicated with footnotes in Tables 1-1 through 1-6.

Example 8.28 Checking a Beam for Local Buckling Using Footnotes

Determine if local buckling might occur for a W12×65 beam.

In Table 1-1, footnote *f* is referenced for the W12×65. The footnote says "Shape exceeds compact limit for flexure with F_y=50 ksi." This means that λ is greater than λ_p for the flange and that ϕM_n needs to be calculated for flange local buckling (FLB).

In the previous example, it was determined that ϕM_n needed to be computed for flange local buckling. The procedure for computing ϕM_n for flange local buckling is given in §F3.2 of the Manual.

You Should Know

- What is the difference between lateral-torsional buckling and local buckling?
- How do you know if local buckling will occur?
- What part of the Specification explains how to compute the local buckling capacity for wide-flange shapes with flanges that have λ greater than λ_p?

[handwritten margin notes:] LTB → global buckling ix-sec translate or rotate relative to eachother local → distortion & failure of beam λ > than limit

8.18 Shear Capacity

Much earlier in the chapter we observed that two load effects in beams were bending moments and shear forces (M_u and V_u). The capacities that have been discussed thus far (ϕM_n for yielding limit state, ϕM_n for LTB, and ϕM_n for local buckling) are all moment-resisting capacities. In this section we will discuss the shear capacity of beams and how to compute ϕV_n that can be compared with V_u.

The first step to developing the shear capacity of a beam, ϕV_n, is to recognize how shear stresses are distributed in a beam. Consider the I-shaped beam below that is subjected to a uniform load. The shear diagram is shown for the beam. The shear force in the beam at each location along the length is resisted by shear stresses in the cross-section. Below the shear diagram is a figure that illustrates the shear stresses at a few cross sections along the beam. The maximum shear stresses occur at the section near the support where the shear force is highest. At that critical cross section, the maximum shear stress is in the center of the web, although the shear is nearly constant over the depth of the web.

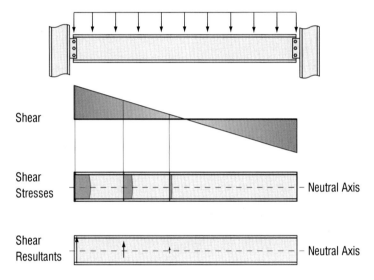

The distribution of shear stress shown above is specific for an I-shaped beam. For other cross sections, the distribution of shear stress is different, as explained in most Mechanics textbooks.

For I-shaped cross-sections, the flanges carry negligible shear, and the shear stress in the web is nearly constant. Thus the shear capacity corresponding to yielding of the web is simply the web area multiplied by the shear yield stress of the material.

Study the Manual

Turn to Chapter G of the Specification (page 16.1-67).

- What is the title of the Chapter?

Read §G2.1.

- What is the general equation for the nominal shear strength of a web? How does it correspond to the discussion above?

The term C_v accounts for buckling that may occur prior to yielding. For hot-rolled shapes, such buckling never occurs and C_v is taken as 1.0. The resistant factor, ϕ, is also taken as 1.0 for hot-rolled I-shapes.

Example 8.29 Computing the Shear Capacity for a Beam

What is the factored shear capacity, ϕV_n, for a W12×50 beam?

Step 1 - Compute the web area

The shear capacity is related to the web area defined as:
$$A_w = dt_w = (12.2 \text{ in.})(0.370 \text{ in.}) = 4.51 \text{ in.}^2$$

Step 2 - Compute the nominal shear capacity

The nominal capacity is given by Eqn. G2-1:
$$V_n = 0.6F_y A_w C_v$$

The term C_v accounts for web buckling, but will be equal to 1.0 for all the standard hot-rolled shapes.
$$V_n = 0.6(50 \text{ ksi})(4.51 \text{ in.}^2)(1.0) = 135 \text{ kips}$$

Step 3 - Factor the nominal shear capacity

For standard hot-rolled shapes, $\phi = 1.0$ for shear yielding. The commentary of the Specification says this is justified by experimental data and the minor consequences of shear yielding.
$$\phi V_n = (1.0)(135 \text{ kips}) = \mathbf{135} \text{ kips}$$

The calculation above is not normally performed because tabulated values are available in the Manual. The shear capacities for wide-flange shapes are given in the last column of the Z_x Table (Table 3-2).

Example 8.30 Checking a Beam for Local Buckling Using Footnotes

What is the factored shear capacity, ϕV_n, for a W12×50 beam?

From the Z_x Table, $\phi V_n = 135$ kips for a W12×50 beam; this is the same as the value computed in Example 8.27.

We have confined our discussion to the shear capacity of standard hot-rolled shapes. For other situations refer to §G2. through §G8. of the Specification.

You Should Know

- What part of an *I*-shaped beam has the highest shear stresses?
- What does the C_v factor account for?
- What is the fastest way to determine the shear capacity for a wide-flanged shape?

[handwritten: near the support]

[handwritten: accounts for buckling that more occurs prior to yielding]

8.19 Deflection Limits

The final limit state for beams that will be discussed in this chapter is excessive deflection. All beams experience some deflection when loaded - excessive deflections are those that damage finishes, annoy occupants, or result in unacceptable vibrations.

The International Building Code (IBC) prescribes deflection limits for structural members. For floor and roof beams, deflections under the service live load generally should not exceed $L/360$, where L is the span of the beam. There is another limit on service dead-plus-live-load deflection ($L/240$) but dead load deflections are typically cambered out, so the live load criteria ($L/360$) generally governs in design. For cantilever spans, L is taken as twice the length of the cantilever.

Example 8.31 Calculating Live Load Deflection Limits

A simply-supported floor beam is 40 ft long. What is the maximum permitted deflection under the service live load?

The maximum permitted deflection is:
$$L/360 = (40 \text{ ft})/360 = 0.11 \text{ ft} = \textbf{1.33 in.}$$
During design, the live load deflection of the beam will need to be compared with this limiting value.

In the following sections on design, there are examples that demonstrate how deflection limits are checked against demands and how they may govern the design of a beam.

You Should Know

- What is the limit for live load deflection of beams? → excessive deflection
- Why don't we worry as much about dead load deflections? → cambered out
- What value should be used for L when checking deflection limits for cantilever spans?
  2×L of cantilever

8.20 Design

With an understanding of how to compute beam demands and beam capacities, we are ready to discuss beam design. The general steps in beam design are the same as for other steel members:

1. Compute demands (M_u, V_u).
2. Pick a shape to try.
3. Compute the capacity of the shape and compare with demands.
4. Finalize the design or iterate to find a better design.

Step 2 can be challenging because there are several limit states that may govern the size of the beam. A good approach is to begin by guessing which limit state will govern. Most beams are governed by the yielding limit state or LTB. If L_b is greater than 3 ft then LTB may govern, and it is best to pick a shape from Table 3-10. Otherwise it is generally best to pick a shape from the Z_x Table.

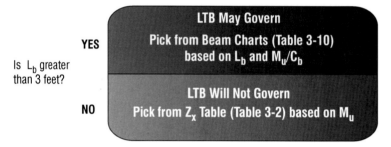

Is L_b greater than 3 feet?

YES — **LTB May Govern** — Pick from Beam Charts (Table 3-10) based on L_b and M_u/C_b

NO — **LTB Will Not Govern** — Pick from Z_x Table (Table 3-2) based on M_u

The following examples will illustrate how this approach, and the general steps outlined above, can be used to design beams.

Example 8.32 Beam Design

Pick a beam size that will work for all of the 38 ft long floor beams. The floor overhangs the exterior beams by 1.5 ft. The story height for the building is 15 ft. Assume that the floor beams have lateral restraint provided at the midpoints. The loads are:

Floor Dead: 80 psf
Floor Live: 50 psf
Ext. Wall: 20 psf

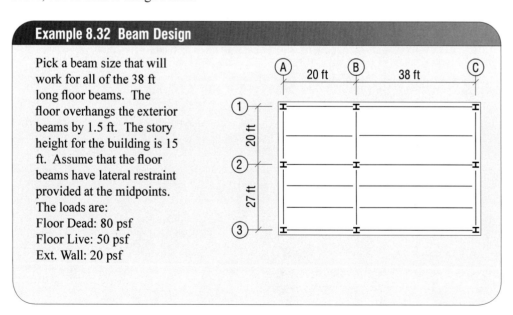

Example Continued

Step 1 - Compute demands

1a - Identify the critical floor beam

There are (6) floor beams shown that are 38 ft long. First, we need to determine which floor beam will have the greatest demands. Of the interior floor beams, the one running along gridline 1.5 would have the greatest tributary width (10 ft). The critical spandrel beam runs along gridline 1. It only has a tributary width of 6.5 ft, but it carries exterior wall weight. It is not obvious which will govern, but a quick calculation can be done to check.

$$w_{D,wall} = (15 \text{ ft})(20 \text{ psf}) = 0.30 \text{ k/ft}$$
$$w_{D,3.5-ft-of-floor} = (3.5 \text{ ft})(80 \text{ psf}) = 0.28 \text{ k/ft}$$

The dead loads on the two beams (critical interior and critical spandrel) will be similar as suggested by the calculations above, but the interior beam will have 3.5 tributary feet more for live load. From these rough calculations it is clear that the critical interior floor beam will have the greatest demands.

1b - Reduce the live load

$$A_t = (10 \text{ ft})(38 \text{ ft}) = 380 \text{ ft}^2$$
$$L = (50 \text{ psf})\left(0.25 + \frac{15}{\sqrt{2(380)}}\right) = (50 \text{ psf})(0.794) = 39.7 \text{ psf}$$

1c - Get factored load effects

$$w_D = (10 \text{ ft})(80 \text{ psf}) = 0.8 \text{ k/ft}$$
$$w_L = (10 \text{ ft})(39.7 \text{ psf}) = 0.397 \text{ k/ft}$$
$$w_U = 1.2w_D + 1.6w_L = 1.2(0.8 \text{ k/ft}) + 1.6(0.397 \text{ k/ft}) = 1.60 \text{ k/ft}$$
$$M_U = \frac{w_U L^2}{8} = \frac{(1.6 \text{ k/ft})(38 \text{ ft})^2}{8} = 289 \text{ k-ft}$$
$$V_U = \frac{w_U L}{2} = \frac{(1.6 \text{ k/ft})(38 \text{ ft})}{2} = 30.4 \text{ kips}$$

Step 2 - Pick a shape to try

2a - Guess which limit state will govern

Now that the demands are known, we need to pick a shape to try. Our method for picking a shape will depend on which limit state we think will govern. Since L_b is 19 ft, LTB will likely govern. We should go to Table 3-10 to find a shape to try.

2b - Determine Cb

Before entering Table 3-10, we should determine C_b for the beam. The beam will have two unbraced segments since it is supported at the midspan, each 19 ft long. From Table 3-1, C_b =1.30 for each segment.

continued on next page

2c - Pick a shape from Table 3.10

For design, we will enter Table 3.10 with our unbraced length (19 ft) and moment demand divided by C_b.

$$\frac{M_U}{C_b} = \frac{289 \text{ k-ft}}{1.3} = 222 \text{ k-ft}$$

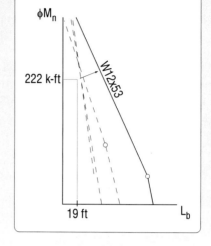

We divide M_U by C_b because we know that the values in the Table will get amplified by C_b in the next step. After finding the point (19 ft, 222 k-ft) we move up and to the right in the table until we hit a solid line. The solid lines represent the lightest shapes for a given L_b and demand. For this case, the first solid line is for W12×53.

So, our trial shape will be W12×53.

Step 3 - Compute capacity and compare with demands

With a trial shape selected, we can now compute capacities and compare them with demands.

3a - Check yielding limit state

$$\phi M_n = \phi M_p = 292 \text{ k-ft (from Table 3-2)}$$
$$292 \text{ k-ft} > 289 \text{ k-ft (OK)}$$

3b - Check LTB

For a W12×53 with $L_b = 19$.

$$\phi M_{n,Cb=1} = 236 \text{ k-ft}$$
$$\phi M_n = C_b(\phi M_{n,Cb=1}) \leq \phi M_p$$
$$\phi M_n = 1.3(236 \text{ k-ft}) \leq 292 \text{ k-ft}$$
$$\phi M_n = 307 \text{ k-ft} \leq 292 \text{ k-ft}$$

When the left side is bigger, it means that the LTB capacity exceeds that of the yielding limit state. Yielding limit state governs, but is still OK.

3c - Check local buckling

In Table 1-1 there are no footnotes next to the W12×53. Flanges and web are compact so there is no local buckling.

3d - Check shear

The shear capacity can be compared with the shear demand from Step 1.

$$\phi V_n = 125 \text{ kips (from Table 3-2)}$$
$$125 \text{ kips} > 30.4 \text{ kips (OK)}$$

Example Continued

3e - Check deflection

The service live load is:
$$w_L = (10 \text{ ft})(39.7 \text{ psf}) = 0.397 \text{ k/ft}$$

The live load deflection at mid-span is:
$$\delta_L = \frac{5w_L L^4}{384EI} = \frac{5(0.397/12 \text{ k/in.})(38 \times 12 \text{ in})^4}{384(29000 \text{ ksi})(425 \text{ in.}^4)} = 1.51 \text{ in.}$$

The permitted live load deflection is:
$$\frac{L}{360} = \frac{38 \times 12 \text{ in}}{360} = 1.27 \text{ in}$$

1.51 in. > 1.27 in. (NO GOOD)

The live load deflection is too big so the W12×53 will not work for the beam.

Step 4 - Finalize the design or iterate to find a better design

We are going to have to pick a different shape to try since the W12×53 did not work. Since deflection governed, it is helpful to calculate what I_{req} we need to satisfy the deflection limit. An easy way to get I_{req} is to scale our previous I by our deflection demand/capacity ratio:

$$I_{req} = (425 \text{ in.}^4)\frac{1.51 \text{ in.}}{1.27 \text{ in.}} = 505 \text{ in.}^4$$

Now, going back to Table 3-10, we notice that one of the dashed lines we skipped over is the W14×53. This shape is dashed in the table because the W12×53 was the same weight but had greater LTB capacity. In retrospect, the W14×53 obviously would have been the better choice. Before doing any calculations for the W14×53 it is a good idea to look up I. From Table 1-1, $I = 541 \text{ in.}^4$, which is bigger than I_{req}, so the W14×53 will work for deflection. Summarizing the capacities for the limit states for the W14×53:

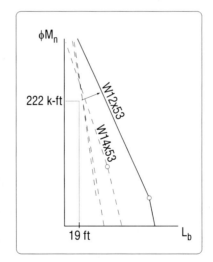

Yielding: $\phi M_n = \phi M_p = $ **327** k-ft

LTB: $\phi M_n = C_b(\phi M_{n,Cb=1}) \leq \phi M_p$

$\phi M_n = 299$ k-ft ≤ 327 k-ft

$\phi M_n = $ **299** k-ft (OK since greater than M_U)

Local Buckling: OK no footnote in Table 1-1

Shear: $\phi V_n = $ **155** kips (OK since greater than V_U)

Deflection: $\delta_L = $ **1.19** in (OK since less than 1.27 in.)

Use W14×53.

The next example illustrates the design of a beam with a short unbraced length.

Example 8.33 Beam Design - Top Flange Continuously Restrained

Pick a beam size that will work for all of the 38 ft long floor beams. The floor overhangs the exterior beams by 1.5 ft. The story height for the building is 15 ft. Assume that the floor beams have continuous lateral restraint (L_b=0). The loads are:

Floor Dead: 80 psf
Floor Live: 50 psf
Ext. Wall: 20 psf

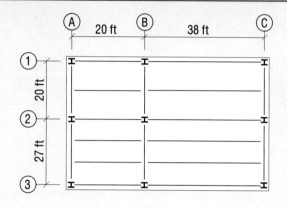

Step 1 - Compute demands

The demands on the critical beam were computed in the previous example.

$$M_U = \frac{w_U L^2}{8} = \frac{(1.6 \text{ k/ft})(38 \text{ ft})^2}{8} = 289 \text{ k-ft}$$

$$V_U = \frac{w_U L}{2} = \frac{(1.6 \text{ k/ft})(38 \text{ ft})}{2} = 30.4 \text{ kips}$$

Step 2 - Pick a shape to try

2a - Guess which limit state will govern

Since L_b is small we will guess that the yielding limit state will govern and use the Z_x Table (Table 3-2) to get a trial shape.

2b - Pick a shape from Table 3-2

Entering Table 3-2 we scan down the $\phi_b M_p$ column looking for shapes with capacity a little bigger than 289 k-ft. There is a group of shapes, bounded by W18×40 and W10×60 that have about the right capacity. The W18×40 is bold-faced meaning that it is the lightest shape in the group.

Try W18×40.

Step 3 - Compute capacity and compare with demands

With a trial shape selected, we can now compute capacities and compare them with demands.

3a - Check yielding limit state

$$\phi M_n = \phi M_p = 294 \text{ k-ft (from Table 3-2)}$$
$$294 \text{ k-ft} > 289 \text{ k-ft (OK)}$$

3b - Check LTB

LTB is not applicable since the beam is continuously restrained.

3c - Check local buckling

In Table 1-1 there is a footnote next to the W18×40, but it relates to slenderness in compression (if the shape were used as a column). The flanges and web are compact for flexure so there is no local buckling.

3d - Check shear

$$\phi V_n = 169 \text{ kips (from Table 3-2)}$$
$$169 \text{ kips} > 30.4 \text{ kips (OK)}$$

3e - Check deflection

The service live load is:

$$w_L = (10 \text{ ft})(39.7 \text{ psf}) = 0.397 \text{ k/ft}$$

The live load deflection at mid-span is:

$$\delta_L = \frac{5 w_L L^4}{384 EI} = \frac{5(0.397/12 \text{ k/in.})(38 \times 12 \text{ in})^4}{384(29000 \text{ ksi})(612 \text{ in.}^4)} = 1.05 \text{ in.}$$

The permitted live load deflection is:

$$\frac{L}{360} = \frac{38 \times 12 \text{ in}}{360} = 1.27 \text{ in}$$

1.05 in. < 1.27 in. (OK)

Step 4 - Finalize the design or iterate to find a better design

Use $W18 \times 40$.

Note: In comparing this solution with the previous example we see that we can save 13 lbs/ft on our beam weight if we can provide continous restraint to compression flanges of the floor beams.

The final example (next page) is the design of a girder. The configuration is the same as the previous examples, but the loads have been changed.

Example 8.34 Girder Design - Top Flange Continuously Restrained

Pick a girder size that will work for all of the girders. The floor overhangs the exterior beams by 1.5 ft. The story height for the building is 15 ft. Assume that the girders have continuous lateral restraint (L_b=0). At the top flange:
Floor Dead: 80 psf
Floor Live: 100 psf (not reducible)
Ext. Wall: 20 psf

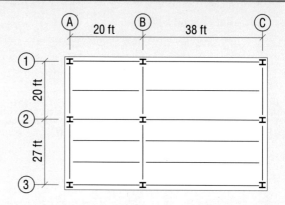

Step 1 - Compute demands

1a - Identify the critical girder

There are (6) girders for the floor. The floor live loads are large so by inspection the interior girders will have greater demands than the ones on the perimeter. The girder that spans 27 ft, along gridline B is the critical girder.

1b - Reduce the live load

The problem statement said live loads could not be reduced. This is often the case for public assembly areas.

1c - Get factored load effects

The tributary area for one point load at the third point of the girder is:

$$A_{t,1} = [(27 \text{ ft})/3][(38 \text{ ft})/2 + (20 \text{ ft})/2] = 261 \text{ ft}^2$$

The magnitudes of the point loads at the third-points of the girder are:

$$P_D = (80 \text{ psf})(261 \text{ ft}^2) = 20.88 \text{ kips}$$
$$P_L = (100 \text{ psf})(261 \text{ ft}^2) = 26.1 \text{ kips}$$
$$P_U = 1.2P_D + 1.6P_L = 66.8 \text{ kips}$$

The load effects are:

$$M_U = 601 \text{ k-ft}$$
$$V_U = 66.8 \text{ kips}$$

Step 2 - Pick a shape to try

2a - Guess which limit state will govern

Since L_b is less than 3 ft (the top flange is continously restrained) we know that LTB will not govern. We will begin by trying a shape from the Z_x table.

2b - Pick a shape from Table 3-2

Entering Table 3-2 we scan down the $\phi_b M_p$ column looking for shapes with capacity a little bigger than 601 k-ft. The lightest shape with $\phi_b M_p$ greater than 601 k-ft is W24x68.

Try W24x68.

Example Continued

Step 3 - Compute capacity and compare with demands

With a trial shape selected, we can now compute capacities and compare them with demands.

3a - Check yielding limit state

$$\phi M_n = \phi M_p = 664 \text{ k-ft (from Table 3-2)}$$
$$664 \text{ k-ft} > 601 \text{ k-ft (OK)}$$

3b - Check LTB

LTB is not applicable because the girder top flange is continously laterally restrained.

3c - Check local buckling

In Table 1-1 there is a footnote c next to the W24×68. This indicates that the shape is slender for compression and would pertain if we were using the shape for a column. Since we are using it as a beam, the footnote that would suggest a local buckling issue is f which says the shape exceeds the compact limit for flexure. There is no footnote f indicated, so local buckling will not govern beam capacity.

3d - Check shear

The shear capacity can be compared with the shear demand from Step 1.

$$\phi V_n = 295 \text{ kips (from Table 3-2)}$$
$$295 \text{ kips} > 66.8 \text{ kips (OK)}$$

3e - Check deflection

The maximum live load deflection from the two P_L point loads is easily determined using Case 9 from Table 3-23:

$$\delta_L = \frac{P_L L^3}{28EI} = \frac{(26.1 \text{ kips})(27 \times 12 \text{ in})^3}{28(29000 \text{ ksi})(1830 \text{ in.}^3)} = 0.60 \text{ in.}$$

The permitted live load deflection is:

$$\frac{L}{360} = \frac{27 \times 12 \text{ in}}{360} = 0.90 \text{ in}$$

$$0.60 \text{ in.} < 0.90 \text{ in. (OK)}$$

Step 4 - Finalize the design or iterate to find a better design

It may be desirable to use a heavier, shallower beam in order to minimize the thickness of the floor system, but in the absence of such constraints the W24x68 seems to work fine.

Use $W24 \times 68$.

Remember This

- Loads are transmitted to floor beams by the slab on metal deck.
- Floor beams transmit loads to girders or columns.
- Exterior girders will have loads from the exterior wall.
- Important load effects for beams are bending moments and shear forces. The maximum factored bending moment for a beam will generally govern the design.
- Five limit states for beams are: yielding, lateral torsional buckling, local buckling, shear yielding, and excessive elastic deflection.
- The plastic moment corresponds to yielding of the entire cross-section and is the maximum moment a beam can carry.
- Lateral torsional buckling (LTB) capacity depends on the cross-section, the unbraced length, and the moment gradient.
- Most of the standard hot-rolled shapes are not limited by local buckling.
- Excessive deflection is a serviceability limit state and should be checked using unfactored loads (usually the unfactored live loads).
- In beam design, it is generally best to begin by assuming that yielding or LTB will govern.

This page blank.

A steel girder bridge is shored up during construction. The inset shows the top of a girder before the concrete deck was poured. Hundreds of steel studs, welded to the top of each girder, serve to tie the concrete deck and steel girders together. When the steel and concrete are integrated, the girders are considered composite beams.

Studs are welded through the deck to the beams below, eventually tying together the slab and beams.

9. Composite Beams

Consider This

- What is a composite beam?
- How are demands on composite beams different from demands on bare steel beams?
- How do composite beams fail? What are the limit states?
- How many studs do you need for a composite beam?
- What is the difference between fully and partially composite beams? Why are partially composite beams more common?
- How do you compute the flexural capacity of a composite beam?
- What is cambering? How does it result in lighter beams?
- What tables in the Manual can help you to design composite beams?

9.1 Overview

Chapter 8 explained how to design steel beams, but in many situations it is more economical to use composite beams. A composite beam has elements made from more than one material. In civil structures, the most common type of composite beam consists of a concrete flange integrated with a steel shape.

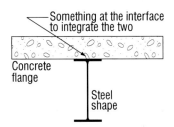

In a typical building, slab-on-metal-deck floors are used to span between floor beams. If these concrete floors, that are needed anyway, are integrated with the steel beams below, then the beams become composite beams. The most common way to integrate the concrete floor and steel beams is using studs as shown in the picture at the top of the page. The studs are welded to the steel beam through the deck; after the concrete floor is poured and cured, the studs transfer shear forces between the concrete floor and the steel beam, facilitating composite action.

Composite beams are also used in steel bridges. When steel girders are integrated with a concrete deck, then less steel is required for the girders. There is always cost associated with providing the connection (the studs), but the savings in steel often justifies the cost of the studs.

The following two sections will explain how to compute the demands on composite beams. Then several sections will explain what the limit states are for composite beams and how to compute the ultimate capacity. Finally, composite beam design will be explained, and we will explore the resources in the Manual that facilitate design.

You Should Know

- What are composite beams?
- How are steel beams and concrete floors/decks integrated?
- What is the benefit of using composite beams?

9.2 Factored Demands

Composite beams are designed to resist the factored load effects. As with regular beams, the load effects of primary interest are the maximum bending moment and shear forces. The procedures for computing M_u and V_u are the same for composite beams as they were for regular beams. Tributary width, or areas, are usually used to get distributed loads or point loads, which are then used to calculate the load effects.

Example 9.1 Calculating Demands on Composite Beams

The beams in the floor below will be composite beams. Compute the ultimate demands on the indicated composite beam if the floor dead load is 90 psf and the floor live load is 50 psf.

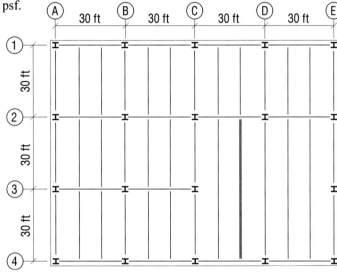

Step 1 - Get the tributary width and area

$$W_t = 10 \text{ ft}$$
$$A_t = (10 \text{ ft})(60 \text{ ft}) = 600 \text{ ft}^2$$

Step 2 - Reduce the live load

The live load reduction for the beam is:

$$L = (50 \text{ psf})\left(0.25 + \frac{15}{\sqrt{2(600)}} \right) = (50 \text{ psf})(0.683)$$

$$L = (50 \text{ psf})(0.638) = 34.2 \text{ psf}$$

Step 3 - Compute and factor the load effects

$$w_D = (90 \text{ psf})(10 \text{ ft}) = 0.90 \text{ k/ft}$$
$$w_L = (34.2 \text{ psf})(10 \text{ ft}) = 0.342 \text{ k/ft}$$
$$w_U = 1.2(0.90 \text{ k/ft}) + 1.6(0.342 \text{ k/ft}) = 1.63 \text{ k/ft}$$

$$V_U = \frac{w_U l}{2} = \frac{(1.63 \text{ k/ft})(60 \text{ ft})}{2} = \textbf{48.9 kips}$$

$$M_U = \frac{w_U l^2}{8} = \frac{(1.63 \text{ k/ft})(60 \text{ ft})^2}{8} = \textbf{734 k-ft}$$

9.3 Pre-Composite Demands

A composite beam is not a composite beam until after the concrete cures. Prior to that time it is a bare steel beam. The bare steel beam must support the wet concrete demands, M_{wc} and V_{wc}, until the concrete cures and the composite beam reaches its full strength.

Neither *ASCE 7* nor the *Specification* prescribes how the wet concrete demands must be calculated or factored. In the following examples, the effects from the wet concrete weight are simply factored by 1.2 and no live load is considered. This is not to imply that such an approach is better than another; actual practice varies.

Example 9.2 Tributary Area and Tributary Width for Floor Beams

If the wet concrete floor weight is 65 psf, compute the wet concrete demands, M_{wc} and V_{wc}, for the beam in Example 9.1.

Step 1 - Get the tributary width
$$W_t = 10 \text{ ft}$$

Step 2 - Compute wet concrete load effects

There are no rules about how to compute wet concrete demands. We will just do something reasonable by factoring the wet weight up a little to account for uncertainty and incidental live load.

$$w_{wc} = 1.2(65 \text{ psf})(10 \text{ ft}) = 0.78 \text{ k/ft}$$

$$V_{wc} = \frac{w_{wc}l}{2} = \frac{(0.78 \text{ k/ft})(60 \text{ ft})}{2} = 23.4 \text{ kips}$$

$$M_{wc} = \frac{w_{wc}l^2}{8} = \frac{(0.78 \text{ k/ft})(60 \text{ ft})^2}{8} = 351 \text{ k-ft}$$

In the previous chapter, the wet concrete demands were not important because they were always less than the ultimate demands (M_u and V_u) that the bare steel beam needed to support. For composite beams we will have two checks to make: the bare steel beam under M_{wc} and V_{wc}, and the composite beam under M_u and V_u.

9.4 Limit States

Now that you know how to compute the flexural demands on composite beams (M_u and M_{wc}) let's turn our attention to the flexural capacity of composite beams (ϕM_n). The flexural capacity of a composite beam will be the lowest value of ϕM_n computed considering three limit states:

          1. Concrete crushing
          2. Tensile yielding of the steel section
          3. Shear strength of studs (or other anchors)

These three limit states are illustrated below. For a particular composite beam, the governing limit state (the one that would actually occur if we loaded the beam to failure) depends on the relative strengths of the slab, steel shape, and studs.

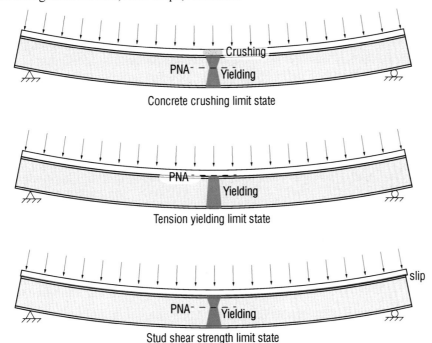

Concrete crushing limit state

Tension yielding limit state

Stud shear strength limit state

From the illustrations above, notice that all of the limit states involve the formation of a plastic hinge in the steel beam. What differs is the location of the plastic neutral axis (PNA) and how much of the beam is yielding in tension and compression.

There are several details you need to learn in order to compute the value of ϕM_n for each of the limit states. The following sections delve into those details. As we get into the details, try to keep in mind the big picture which is computing ϕM_n.

You Should Know

- What are the three limit states for composite beams?
- If the steel yields for all the limit states, what is the difference between the "tension yielding" limit state and the others?
- Besides the slab not crushing, what is the difference between the concrete crushing and stud shear strength limit states from the illustrations above?

9.5 Slab Effect without Connectors

In order to better understand the three limit states for composite beams, it is important to first understand the basic idea of how composite beams work. Let's begin by considering an idealized beam that is **non-composite**. This beam consists of a steel beam supporting a concrete beam [see (a) below] with **nothing tying the two together**.

If a small load were applied to the center of this idealized system, the beams would deflect and have the mid-span stress distribution shown in (b). Notice that there will be some slip at the interface. From the stress distribution we see that the two beams are sharing the load, but acting independently. Each beam has a neutral axis, with compression stresses above and tensile stresses below.

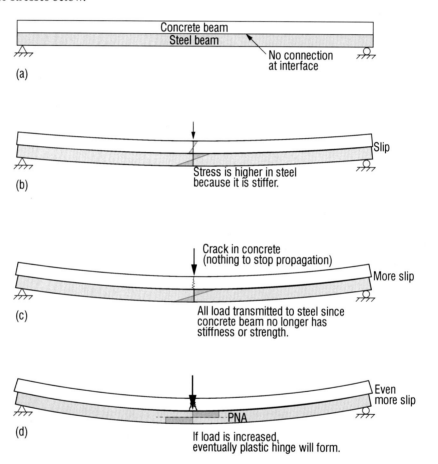

If the load is increased, at some point the concrete beam will crack, beginning at the bottom where the tension is highest. There will be nothing to arrest the development of the crack, and it will propagate through the concrete beam (c). All the load will then be transferred to the steel beam.

Under further loading, the bare steel beam will eventually form a plastic hinge, with the plastic neutral axis (PNA) in the middle. Thus the ultimate capacity of the non-composite systems is simply the capacity of the bare steel beam.

You Should Know

- Why doesn't the concrete contribute to ϕM_n for non-composite beams?

9.6 Slab Effect with Connectors

Now that we have considered the non-composite case, where there was no connection between the concrete and steel, let's consider a case with some connectors. Consider the system below where the concrete and steel beams are tied to each other by only two studs (a). Under a small load, the studs prevent slip between the concrete and steel. This results in a different stress distribution than was observed under the small load for the non-composite case [compare (b) below with (b) on the previous page]. Rather than having two neutral axes, one in the concrete beam and one in the steel, there is only one neutral axis that is located in the steel beam; all of the concrete beam is in compression. There is a discontinuity in the stress plot (b) at the interface of the steel and concrete, because the steel is much stiffer (the concrete and steel have the same strain at the interface, but the stress in the steel is higher because E is greater).

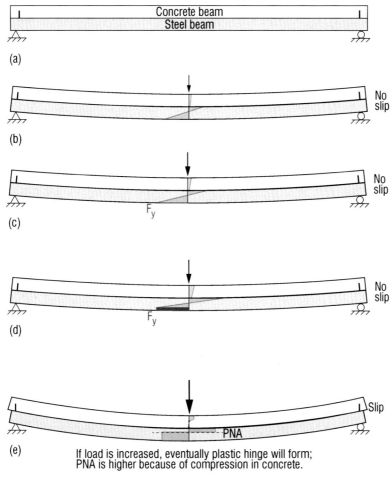

(a)

(b) No slip

(c) F_y — No slip

(d) F_y — No slip

(e) Slip — PNA

If load is increased, eventually plastic hinge will form; PNA is higher because of compression in concrete.

As the load is increased, at some point the studs will begin to yield or crush the surrounding concrete. This permits some slip to occur which causes the concrete beam to crack at the bottom. Still, the studs arrest the crack to some extent, such that the top of the concrete beam is still resisting compression (c).

If the load is increased, the steel beam will eventually form a plastic hinge (d). The plastic neutral axis will be somewhat higher, however, than it was for the non-composite case, because of the compression that is in the concrete.

This type of system is called a *partially composite* beam, because the concrete is contributing but enough studs were not provided to completely prevent slip. The moment capacity, ϕM_n, for partially composite beams is governed by the Stud Shear Strength Limit State.

As a final case, consider the system shown below where enough studs are provided so that slip never occurs (a). Under a small load, the stress distribution is similar to the partial composite beam (b).

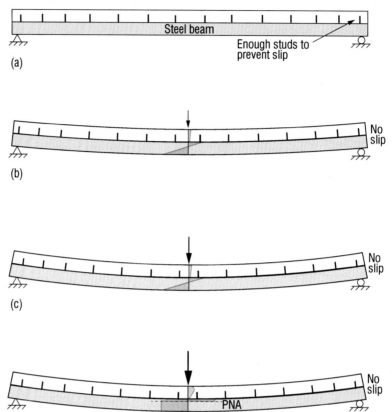

(a)

(b)

(c)

(d)

Under increasing load, the PNA will rise until either the concrete crushes in compression, or the entire steel beam is yielded.

As the load increases, no slipping occurs, so the stresses simply get larger with the same distribution (c).

If the load continues to increase, the steel will begin to yield. A plastic hinge will form in the steel beam. If the load continues to increase, the PNA will migrate up as the compression in the concrete continues to grow (d). In other words, less of the steel needs to be in compression because there is greater compression in the concrete. Eventually, one of two things will happen if the load continues to increase. Either the concrete will crush in compression, or the PNA will migrate all the way to the top of the steel beam, such that the steel shape is fully yielded in tension. These are two ultimate cases, and additional load cannot be resisted by the beam.

When enough studs are provided to completely prevent slip, the system is said to be *fully composite*. The moment capacity for fully composite beams is governed by either the Concrete Crushing Limit State or the Tension Yielding Limit State.

You Should Know

- How do studs facilitate concrete participation?
- What is the difference between a fully composite and a partially composite beam?
- How is the ultimate stress distribution different for fully and partially composite beams?

9.7 Governing Limit State

We have discussed three limit states for composite beams. By considering the maximum force that can develop in the studs for each limit state, we can determine which governs.

Consider the composite beam to the right with the moment diagram shown. When the load is increased such that the beam reaches its ultimate capacity, the normal stress distribution at the location of maximum moment will look something like (b). This figure is showing the general idea of the stress distribution; the location of the PNA will vary, depending on which limit state is governing.

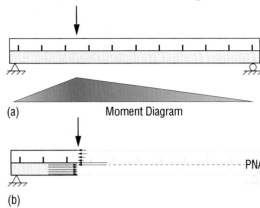

(a)   Moment Diagram

(b)   PNA

If the magnitudes of the stresses and the location of the PNA were known, we could compute the resultants of the stresses shown in (c) [enlarged as compared to (a) and (b)]. In the figure, C_c is the total compression force in all of the concrete at the cross-section; C_s is the total compression force in the steel; and T_s is the total tension force in the steel at the cross-section. From horizontal equilibrium we observe that T_s must be equal to C_c plus C_s.

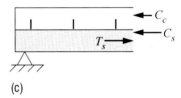

(c)

Finally, consider the free-body diagram shown in (d) where we cut through the studs. Here we introduce another resultant force, V', which is the combined shear in the studs between the point of maximum and zero moment. From this free-body diagram we observe that V' is equal to C_c.

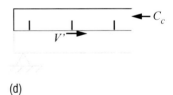

(d)

Example 9.3 Calculating Resultants in Composite Beams

A particular composite beam has a concrete slab that would crush if C_c ever reached 100 kips; however, the studs would fail if V' ever reached 90 kips. What are the maximum possible values for C_c, and V' based on the given information?

From equilibrium, C_c and V' must always be equal. If the maximum force that can develop for V' is 90 kips, then 90 kips is also the maximum possible value for C_c. In other words, the concrete can never reach its compressive strength because the studs would fail first. **Max possible C_c = Max possible V' = 90 kips.**

Capacity

For each of the three limit states, there is a corresponding maximum possible value for V'. The table below summarizs these critical values and explains why they are the maximums.

Limit State	Max Value for V'	Reasoning
Concrete Crushing	$0.85f'_c A_c$	Since V' is always equal to C_c, V' can never be greater than the concrete crushing capacity. The concrete will crush if C_c ever reaches $0.85f'_c A_c$ (as will be explained in a following section). Thus, if the governing limit state is concrete crushing, the maximum value for V' will be $0.85f'_c A_c$.
Tension Yielding	$F_y A_g$	The tension yielding limit state occurs if the PNA reaches the top of the steel and the entire steel shape is yielded in tension, meaning that $T_s = F_y A_g$. If this were to occur, then C_s would equal 0, and C_c would be equal to T_s [see free-body diagram (c) on the previous page]. If C_c is equal to T_s then V' is also (since V' is always the same as C_c). Thus, if the governing limit state is tension yielding, the maximum value for V' will be $F_y A_g$.
Stud Shear Strength	ΣQ_n	Q_n is the shear capacity for one stud (as will be explained in a following section). ΣQ_n is the sum of the capacities of the studs between the points of maximum and zero moment. The shear resultant in the studs, V', cannot be greater than the capacity of the studs. Thus, if the governing limit state is stud shear strength, the maximum value of V' will be ΣQ_n.

You can determine which limit state will govern for a particular composite beam by computing $0.85f'_c A_c$, $F_y A_g$, and ΣQ_n; whichever of the three is lowest, is the greatest value that V' can ever reach and indicates the governing limit state.

Example 9.4 Determining the Governing Limit State in Composite Beams

The following have been calculated for a particular composite beam:
$$0.85f'_c A_c = 1500 \text{ kips}$$
$$F_y A_g = 840 \text{ kips}$$
$$\Sigma Q_n = 932 \text{ kips}$$
What is the value for V' when the beam reaches its ultimate capacity? What is the governing limit state? Is the beam fully or partially composite?

The value for V' when the composite beam reaches its ultimate capacity will be the lesser of the three max values; $V' = \mathbf{840}$ **kips**. The governing limit state is **Tension Yielding** and the beam is considered **fully composite**; beams are partially composite if the Stud Shear Strength Limit State governs.

From your experience with tension members, you know how to compute F_yA_g for a steel shape. The next sections will explain how to compute $0.85f'_cA_c$ and ΣQ_n so you can do the check that was demonstrated in the previous example.

9.8 Effective Width and Thickness of Concrete Slab

The concrete flange in a composite beam is considered crushed if the resultant force in the concrete, C_c, ever reaches $0.85f'_cA_c$. The $0.85f'_c$ term is the effective concrete crushing stress and A_c is the effective area of the concrete flange.

Example 9.5 Calculating Resultants in Composite Beams

If f'_c is the compression strength of concrete, why do we use $0.85f'_c$ as the effective concrete crushing stress?

The mechanical properties of concrete are determined by loading concrete cylinders in compression. The picture to the right shows a typical concrete cylinder test. The stress-strain results from a typical cylinder test are shown below. Notice how the stress drops for strains beyond 0.002. We generally consider the concrete crushed at a strain of 0.003.

The strain in a composite beam flange will vary with the maximum strain at the top. The stress of $0.85f'_c$ is a reasonable estimate of the *average* stress over a concrete flange when it finally crushes (strain reaches 0.003 at the extreme fiber).

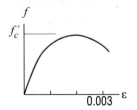

Capacity

There are two things that you need to know in order to compute A_c (the effective area of the concrete flange). They are the *effective width* and the *effective thickness*. We will start by discussing effective width.

Composite beams are usually made by integrating steel beams into a concrete floor or deck. Depending on the spacing of the beams and the layout of the system, only part of the concrete floor can be considered to act compositely with a particular steel beam. The figure below illustrates how only part of the concrete is considered effective for each beam. The effective width is computed separately for each beam and is a function of the beam span, beam spacing, and edge distances.

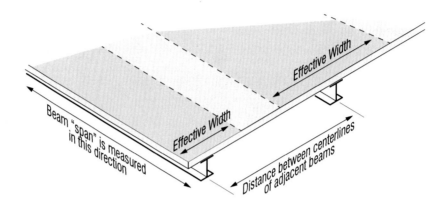

Study the Manual

Turn to §I3.1a. in the Specification (bottom of page 16.1-88) and read the definition of effective width.

* The effective width is the sum of what two things?

The figure below illustrates the three things that are considered when computing the effective width on each side of a composite beam.

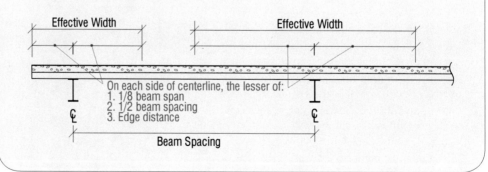

The example on the next page demonstrates how effective widths are calculated.

Example 9.6 Calculating the Effective Width of Composite Beams

Determine the effective width of concrete for the indicated beam and girder.

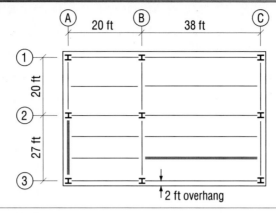

Step 1 - Get the effective width for the floor beam.

To get the effective width for the floor beam, we need to sum the effective width on each side of the floor beam centerline. The effective width for *one* side of the floor beam will be the lesser of:

$$\text{one-eighth of the beam span} = \frac{38 \text{ ft}}{8} = 4.75 \text{ ft}$$

$$\text{one-half the distance to centerline of adjacent beam} = \frac{9 \text{ ft}}{2} = 4.5 \text{ ft}$$

the distance to the edge of the slab = 11 ft for one side, and 40 ft for the other

In this case, the one-half the distance to the centerline of adjacent beam governs for both sides. The total effective width of the floor beam is:

$$2(4.5 \text{ ft}) = \mathbf{9} \text{ ft}$$

Step 2 - Get the effective width for the spandrel girder

Again we need to sum the effective width on each side of the girder centerline. The effective width for *one* side of the spandrel girder will be the lesser of:

$$\text{one-eighth of the beam span} = \frac{27 \text{ ft}}{8} = 3.375 \text{ ft}$$

$$\text{one-half the distance to centerline of adjacent beam} = \frac{20 \text{ ft}}{2} = 10 \text{ ft}$$

the distance to the edge of the slab = 2 ft for left side (slab overhang)
$$= 60 \text{ ft for right side}$$

In this case, different criteria govern the effective width on each side of the beam. Edge distance governs on the left side, and one-eighth span governs to the right. The total effective width of the spandrel girder is:

$$2 \text{ ft} + 3.375 \text{ ft} = \mathbf{5.375} \text{ ft}$$

The concrete area, A_c, is computed by multiplying the effective width by the effective thickness of the concrete. When the concrete slab has been poured over corrugated metal deck, then the thickness of the concrete will vary throughout the slab and along the composite beams. For floor beams, where the deck flutes run perpendicular to the beam, only the concrete above the flutes should be considered when computing A_c. For girders, where the deck flutes run parallel to the beam, an average concrete thickness may be used.

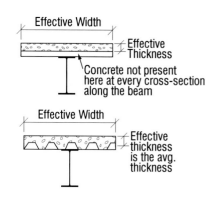

Example 9.7 Computing the Concrete Area and Crushing Force

The slab-on-metal-deck for the building in Example 9.6 has the profile shown to the right. The strength of the concrete ,f'_c , is 3000 psi.

3.5 in.
3 in.

Compute $0.85f'_c A_c$ for the beams in Example 9.6.

Step 1 - Compute for the 38 ft long floor beam

In order to get A_c we need to know the effective width of the beam and the appropriate thickness to use. The effective width of the floor beam was determined in Example 9.6:

effective width = 9 ft

Since the flutes of the metal deck will run perpendicular to the floor beam, we only consider the concrete above the flutes when computing A_c. For half of the cross-sections along the beam, there is not concrete below the top of the flutes.

effective thickness = 3.5 in.

Finally, making the calculations and being careful with units:

$$A_c = (9 \times 12 \text{ in.})(3.5 \text{ in.}) = 378 \text{ in.}^2$$

$$0.85 f'_c A_c = 0.85(3000 \text{ psi})(319.2 \text{ in.}^2) = \textbf{964 kips}$$

Step 2 - Compute for the spandrel girder

effective width = 5.375 ft (see Example 9.6)

Since the flutes of the metal deck will run parallel to the girder the concrete area is the same at every cross-section.

$$\text{effective thickness} = \text{avg. thickness} = \frac{3.5 + 6.5}{2} = 5.0 \text{ in.}$$

$$A_c = (5.375 \times 12 \text{ in.})(5.0 \text{ in.}) = 322.5 \text{ in.}^2$$

$$0.85 f'_c A_c = 0.85(3000 \text{ psi})(354.8 \text{ in.}^2) = \textbf{822 kips}$$

9.9 Stud Strength

In order to determine which limit state will govern for a composite beam, you need to compute $0.85f'_cA_c$, F_yA_g, and ΣQ_n. This section and the following will explain how ΣQ_n is computed.

The example on the next page illustrates how the capacity of an individual stud is calculated.

Example 9.8 Computing the Capacity of an Individual Stud (Deck Parallel)

What is the nominal shear capacity, Q_n, for a 3/4 in. diameter stud welded to the indicated girder?

The deck profile is shown to the right. The concrete is lightweight (110 pcf) with $f'_c = 3000$ psi.

The stud is made from steel with $F_u = 65$ ksi.

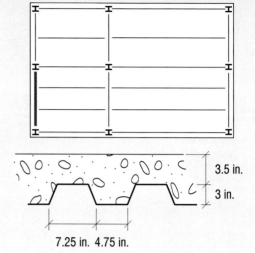

3.5 in.

3 in.

7.25 in. 4.75 in.

Step 1 - Compute the left side of Eqn. I8-1

The capacity of an individual stud, Q_n, is given by Eqn. I8-1. The left side of Eqn. I8-1 depends on three values, A_{sa}, f'_c, and E_c.

$$A_{sa} = \frac{\pi(3/4 \text{ in.})^2}{4} = 0.442 \text{ in.}^2$$

$$f'_c = 3000 \text{ psi} = 3 \text{ ksi} \qquad \text{(given)}$$

$$E_c = w_c^{1.5}\sqrt{f'_c} = (110)^{1.5}\sqrt{3} = 1998 \text{ ksi}$$

Note that dimensions aren't dealt with truly in the equation for E_c. You have to put w_c in pcf, and f'_c in ksi and then you get E_c in ksi.

So left side of Eqn I8-1 yields:

$$0.5A_{sa}\sqrt{f'_c E_c} = 0.5(0.442)\sqrt{(3)(1998)} = 17.1 \text{ kips}$$

Again, the dimensions aren't dealt with truly in the above equation. You have to put A_{sa} in inches^2, and f'_c and E_c in ksi, and then you get Q_n in kips.

Step 2 - Compute the right side of Eqn. I8-1

The right side of Eqn. I8-1 has two factors, R_g and R_p that adjust stud strength depending on the type and orientation of the deck that is present. The user note on page 16.1-98 of the Manual provides values for R_g and R_p.

From the user note, R_g and R_p depend on whether the deck is oriented parallel or perpendicular to the steel shape. In this example the stud is welded to a girder. The deck will generally be parallel to girders because it spans between adjacent floor beams. When the deck is parallel to the steel shape, as in our case, the value for R_g depends on the ratio w_r/h_r (see user note). These terms are defined at the bottom of the user note and illustrated in the figure at the top of the next page.

Example Continued

For the given deck:

$$h_r = 3 \text{ in.}$$

$$w_r = \frac{4.75 \text{ in.} + 7.25 \text{ in.}}{2} = 6 \text{ in.}$$

$$\frac{w_r}{h_r} = \frac{6 \text{ in.}}{3 \text{ in.}} = 2$$

h_r, nominal rib height

w_r, Average width of concrete rib

Since w_r/h_r is greater than 1.5, from the user note:

$$R_g = 1.0$$
$$R_p = 0.75$$

Now the right side of Eqn. I8-1 can be computed as:

$$R_g R_p A_{sa} F_u = (1.0)(0.75)(0.442 \text{ in.}^2)(65 \text{ ksi}) = 21.5 \text{ kips}$$

Step 3 - Compute Q_n

Combining the work from the previous two steps.

$$Q_n = 17.1 \text{ kips} \le 21.5 \text{ kips}$$
$$Q_n = \mathbf{17.1} \text{ kips}$$

Table 3-21 in the Manual has tabulated values for Q_n for common situations like the previous example.

Study the Manual

Turn to Table 3-21 in the Manual (page 3-209).

The table has some similarity to the user note on page 16.1-98, but has values listed for Q_n.

- What is Q_n for a 3/4 in. diameter stud, in 110 pcf concrete with $f'_c = 3$ ksi, and located on a girder that runs parallel to the deck (with $w_r/h_r > 1.5$)?

- How does this value compare with the Q_n computed in the previous example?

The example on the next page illustrates how the Table 3-21 can be used to quickly determine individual stud capacity.

Example 9.9 Capacity of an Individual Stud (Deck Perpendicular)

What is the capacity, Q_n, for a 3/4 in. diameter stud welded to the indicated floor beam? There will be no more than one stud per rib for this beam.

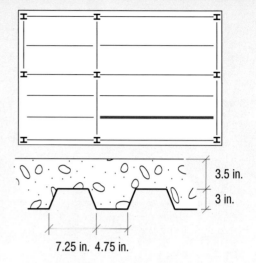

The deck profile is shown to the right. The concrete is lightweight (110 pcf) with $f'_c = 3000$ psi.

The stud is made from steel with $F_u = 65$ ksi.

3.5 in.

3 in.

7.25 in. 4.75 in.

Step 1 - Determine R_g and R_p

In this case the stud is welded to a floor beam so the deck will be perpendicular to the steel shape. From the User Note on page 16.1-98, R_g and R_p depend on the number of anchors occupying the same decking rib. In the given information we are told that no more than one stud will be welded per rib. So:

$$R_g = 1.0$$
$$R_p = 0.6^+$$

From the footnote in the User Note: the 0.6^+ means that the value can be increased to 0.75 when e_{mid-ht} is greater than or equal to 2 in. The dimension e_{mid-ht} is described in the text above the User Note, and illustrated in the figure to the right.

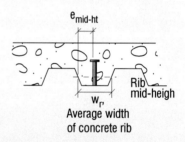

e_{mid-ht}

Rib
mid-heigh

w_r
Average width
of concrete rib

For the given deck, if the stud is located in the middle of the rib:

$$e_{mid-ht} = \frac{w_r}{2} - \frac{stud\,diameter}{2} = \frac{6\ in.}{2} - \frac{3/4\ in.}{2} = 2.625\ in.$$

Since e_{mid-ht} is greater than 2 we say the stud is "strong" and:

$$R_p = 0.75$$

Step 2 - Look up Q_n in Table 3-21

Turning to Table 3-21 we can look up the value for Q_n based on the given information and what was determined in Step 1. For lightweight concrete, $f'_c = 3$ ksi, Deck Perpendicular, 1 Strong stud per rib, and 3/4 in. diameter:

$$Q_n = \textbf{17.1 kips}$$

Note: In this example the values for R_g and R_p did not impact the final result because the left side of Eqn. I8-1 governs for this particular stud.

9.10 Summing Stud Strength

ΣQ_n is calculated by summing the capacities of some, not all, of the studs along a beam.

To understand why ΣQ_n is defined the way it is, consider the two composite beams shown below. The beam on the left has a distributed load. If this beam were cut through the studs, the resulting free-body diagram is shown below. In order to have horizontal equilibrium, the sum of the shear forces in the studs must be zero. This is the first hint at why we don't sum *all* of the stud shear forces when computing ΣQ_n. Notice from the free-body diagram that the point at which the stud shear forces switch direction is the point of maximum moment. ΣQ_n for this beam would be the sum of Q_n for half of the studs on the beam, since half of the studs are located between the point of maximum positive moment and the point of zero moment.

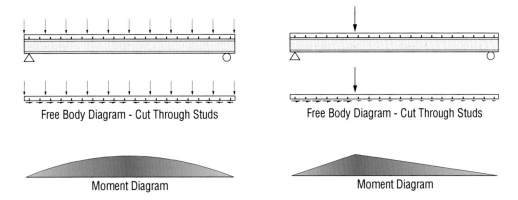

Free Body Diagram - Cut Through Studs   Free Body Diagram - Cut Through Studs

Moment Diagram   Moment Diagram

Now consider the beam on the right with the single point load. In order for the stud shear forces to sum to zero and change direction at the point of maximum moment, the shear must be greater in the studs located left of the point load. ΣQ_n for this beam would be the sum of Q_n for the studs to the left of the point load (as suggested in the figure). The studs to the left of the load would fail before the studs to the right.

Example 9.10 Computing Summation of Stud Strength

The indicated girder has (21) 3/4 in. dia. studs spaced evenly along the span. What is ΣQ_n for the girder?

The deck profile is shown to the right. The concrete is lightweight (110 pcf) with $f'_c = 3000$ psi.

The studs are made from steel with $F_u = 65$ ksi.

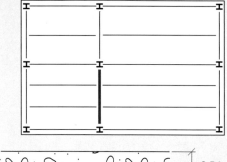

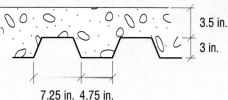

3.5 in.

3 in.

7.25 in. 4.75 in.

Step 1 - Determine Q_n for one stud

Q_n for one stud on a girder with this deck was determined in a previous example:

$$Q_n = 17.1 \text{ kips}$$

Step 2 - Determine the number of studs between the points of maximum and zero moment

The shape of the moment diagram for the girder is shown to the right. There are two segments of the beam, one on the left and one on the right, where the moment ranges from zero to maximum.

Moment Diagram

Each of these segments will have one third of the total number of studs (7 studs). Either can be thought of as the critical segment for computing ΣQ_n.

Step 3 - Compute Summation of Q_n

The sum of the strength of the studs on a critical segment is:

$$\Sigma Q_n = (7 \text{ studs})(17.1 \text{ kips/stud}) = \textbf{120 kips}$$

You Should Know

- Why doesn't it make sense to sum up the shear capacity of all the studs in a composite beam?
- In floor beams with a uniformly distributed load and uniformly spaced studs, what percentage of the studs should be summed to get ΣQ_n?

9.11 Governing V' Value

Now that you know how to compute $0.85f'_cA_c$, F_yA_g, and ΣQ_n you can determine what the ultimate value of V' will be for a composite beam and what limit state will govern. The entire procedure is demonstrated in the example below.

Example 9.11 Computing V' and the Governing Limit State

The indicated beam is a W18×60 with (76) 3/4 in. dia. studs spaced evenly along the span (two studs per rib).

The deck profile is shown to the right. The concrete is normal weight (145 pcf) with $f'_c = 4$ ksi.

The studs are made from steel with $F_u = 65$ ksi.

What is the ultimate value for V' for the beam and what limit state governs the capacity?

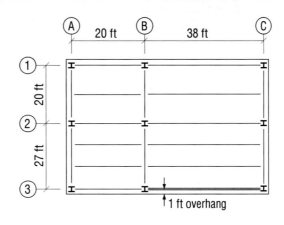

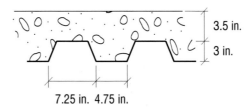

Step 1 - Recognize the overall procedure

The overall procedure is to compute the three values of V' corresponding to the three different limit states:

$$V' = 0.85f'_cA_c \text{ (Concrete Crushing)}$$
$$V' = F_yA_S \text{ (Tension Yielding)}$$
$$V' = \Sigma Q_n \text{ (Stud Shear Strength)}$$

The lowest value of V' indicates the governing limit state.

Step 2 - Compute $0.85f'_cA_c$

2a - Determine the effective width, b_e

The effective width *on each side* of the beam centerline is governed by one of three things: one-eigth the span, one-half the spacing, and the edge distance.

$$\text{one-eighth of the beam span} = \frac{38 \text{ ft}}{8} = 4.75 \text{ ft} = 57 \text{ in.}$$

$$\text{one-half the dist. to centerline of adjacent beam} = \frac{9 \text{ ft}}{2} = 4.5 \text{ ft} = 54 \text{ in.}$$

$$\text{the distance to the edge of the slab} = 1 \text{ ft} = 12 \text{ in.}$$

continued on next page

Example Continued

The effective width for the "inside" of the beam is governed by the second criteria, and the effective width for the "outside" of the beam is governed by the last. The total effective width is:

$$b_e = 54 \text{ in.} + 12 \text{ in.} = 66 \text{ in.}$$

2b - Determine the effective thickness

In this case, since the flutes of the deck will run perpendicular to the floor beam, we only consider the concrete above the flutes when computing the effective thickness:

effective thickness = 3.5 in.

2c - Calculate the effective area and $0.85 f_c' A_c$

$$A_c = (66 \text{ in.})(3.5 \text{ in.}) = 231 \text{ in.}^2$$
$$0.85 f_c' A_c - 0.85(4 \text{ ksi})(231 \text{ in.}^2) = \textbf{785} \text{ kips}$$

Step 3 - Compute $F_y A_s$

This is the easiest of the three limiting values for V' to compute:

$$F_y A_s = (50 \text{ ksi})(17.6 \text{ in.}^2) = \textbf{880} \text{ kips}$$

Step 4 - Compute ΣQ_n

4a - Determine Q_n

The capacity of a single stud can be determined using Table 3-21. To determine if the studs are "strong" or "weak" we need to see if e_{mid-ht} is greater than 2 inches. This procedure was demonstrated in Example 9.9 for this same deck, and the studs were found to be "strong". From Table 3-21 for deck perpendicular, strong studs, 2 per rib, 3/4 in diameter, normal weight concrete, and $f_c' = 4$ ksi:

$$Q_n = 18.3 \text{ kips/stud}$$

4b - Determine ΣQ_n

ΣQ_n is the sum of the capacity of the studs located between the points of zero and maximum. The floor beam is reasonably assumed to carry a uniform load such that the maximum moment occurs mid-span. Since there are (76) studs total on the beam, (38) studs will be located between the points of zero and maximum moment.

$$\Sigma Q_n = (38 \text{ studs})(18.3 \text{ kips/stud}) = \textbf{695} \text{ kips}$$

Step 5 - Determine what governs

Summarizing our work from the previous steps:

$$0.85 f_c' A_c = 785 \text{ kips}$$
$$F_y A_s = 880 \text{ kips}$$
$$\Sigma Q_n = 695 \text{ kips}$$

Comparing the three, the stud shear strength governs and $V' = \textbf{695}$ kips.

9.12 Normal Force Resultants

We have accomplished a lot thus far, but there is still more work to do to reach the objective of determining ϕM_n. The next step, after determining the governing limit state is to get the values for the ultimate stress resultants C_c, C_s, and T_s.

Ultimate Stress Resultants at Critical Section

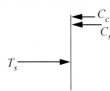

For each limit state, one of the stress resultants will be known and the others can be easily derived. The values for the resultants are given in the table and figure below.

Limit State	Known Resultant
Concrete Crushing	$C_c = 0.85f'_c A_c$
Tension Yielding	$T_s = F_y A_g$
Stud Shear Strength	$C_c = \Sigma Q_n$

Concrete Crushing Governs

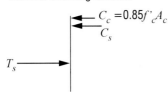

$$0.85f'_c A_c = T_s - C_s \quad \text{(Eq. 1)}$$
$$T_s + C_s = F_y A_g \quad \text{(Eq. 2)}$$
$$T_s = \frac{0.85f'_c A_c + F_y A_g}{2} \quad \text{(solving Eqs. 1 and 2)}$$
$$C_s = \frac{F_y A_g - 0.85f'_c A_c}{2} \quad \text{(solving Eqs. 1 and 2)}$$

Tension Yielding Governs

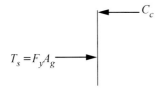

$$C_c = T_s - C_s \quad \text{(Eq. 1)}$$
$$C_s = 0 \quad \text{(Eq. 2)}$$
$$C_c = T_s = F_y A_g \quad \text{(solving Eqs. 1 and 2)}$$

Stud Shear Strength Governs

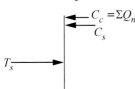

$$\Sigma Q_n = T_s - C_s \quad \text{(Eq. 1)}$$
$$T_s + C_s = F_y A_g \quad \text{(Eq. 2)}$$
$$T_s = \frac{\Sigma Q_n + F_y A_g}{2} \quad \text{(solving Eqs. 1 and 2)}$$
$$C_s = \frac{F_y A_g - \Sigma Q_n}{2} \quad \text{(solving Eqs. 1 and 2)}$$

Example 9.12 Computing Force Resultants

The indicated beam is a W18×60 with (76) 3/4 in. dia. studs spaced evenly along the span (two studs per rib).

The deck profile is shown to the right. The concrete is normal weight (145 pcf) with $f'_c = 4$ ksi.

The studs are made from steel with $F_u = 65$ ksi.

If the beam were loaded to failure, what would be the ultimate values for the force resultants at the critical section?

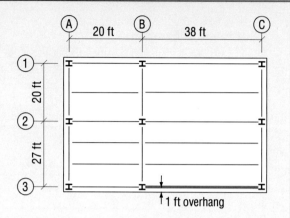

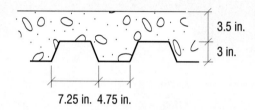

7.25 in. 4.75 in.

Step 1 - Identify the governing limit state and known force resultant

In the previous example it was determined that the capacity of this beam is governed by the Stud Shear Strength Limit State. The ultimate value for V' will be ΣQ_n. Since C_c is always equal to V':

$$C_c = V' = \Sigma Q_n = 695 \text{ kips (from previous example)}$$

Step 2 - Compute the other force resultants

The other force resultants are related to C_c by horizontal equilibrium. T_s and C_s are also related to each other because they sum to $F_y A_g$ (since the whole cross section is yielded). From these relationships, equations for T_s and C_s were derived on the previous page.

$$T_s = \frac{\Sigma Q_n + F_y A_g}{2} = \frac{695 \text{ kips} + (50 \text{ ksi})(17.6 \text{ in.}^2)}{2} = 787.5 \text{ kips}$$

$$C_s = \frac{F_y A_g - \Sigma Q_n}{2} = \frac{(50 \text{ ksi})(17.6 \text{ in.}^2) - 695 \text{ kips}}{2} = 92.5 \text{ kips}$$

You Should Know

- In the previous example, if C_s is 92.5 kips, where is the PNA?
- Which resultant is known when the governing limit state is tension yielding?

9.13 Nominal Moment Capacity

Our general strategy for computing the moment capacity for a composite beam is to compute the values of T_s, C_c, and C_s corresponding to the ultimate stress state. The moment on the cross-section caused by these three resultants *is* the nominal moment capacity, M_n, of the beam:

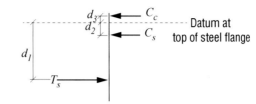

Ultimate Stress Resultants

$$M_n = T_s d_1 - C_s d_2 + C_c d_3$$

The previous sections have outlined the procedures for calculating T_s, C_c, and C_s. However, in order to compute the nominal moment, M_n, we also need to know the locations of the resultants (d_1, d_2, and d_3).

The distances d_1 and d_2 are determined based on the centroids of the areas of steel in tension and compression. This is demonstrated in the example that follows.

The distance d_3 is calculated as:

$$d_3 = t_{total} - \frac{a}{2}$$

where t_{total} is the total slab thickness and a is the depth of the equivalent stress block in the concrete. You need to have a class in reinforced concrete to fully understand the concept behind a, but it is computed as:

$$a = \frac{C_c}{0.85 f'_c b_e}$$

where b_e is the effective width of the concrete flange.

Example 9.13 Computing the Moment Capacity of a Composite Beam

Compute ϕM_n for the composite beam of the previous two examples.

Step 1 - Determine the governing limit state and force resultants
In the previous two examples the governing limit state was found to be the stud shear strength limit state and the ultimate force resultants were found to be:

$C_c = 695$ kips
$C_s = 92.5$ kips
$T_s = 787.5$ kips

Step 2 - Calculate the location of the concrete stress resultant, d_3
For this example, the location of C_c is the easiest of the three to compute. The location of the concrete stress resultant, d_3, is:

$$d_3 = t_{total} - \frac{a}{2}$$

where:

$$a = \frac{C_c}{0.85 f'_c b_e} = \frac{695 \text{ kips}}{0.85(4 \text{ ksi})(66 \text{ in.})} = 3.10 \text{ in.}$$

so:

$$d_3 = 6.5 \text{ in.} - \frac{3.10 \text{ in.}}{2} = 4.95 \text{ in.}$$

continued on next page

223

Example Continued

Step 3 - Compute the location of the compression steel resultant, d_2

3a - Determine the PNA

The first step in determining d_2 is to locate the plastic neutral axis (PNA). Suppose for a moment that the PNA were located immediately below the top flange. If that were the case:

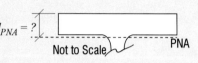

$$C_s = F_y(b_f t_f) = (50 \text{ ksi})[(7.56 \text{ in.})(0.695 \text{ in.})] = 263 \text{ kips.}$$

Now we know from our previous work that C_s is much less than that (it is 92.5 kips), meaning that the PNA is higher. Since the PNA is *in* the top flange C_s will be:

$$C_s = F_y(b_f d_{PNA})$$

so:

$$d_{PNA} = \frac{C_s}{F_y b_f} = \frac{92.5 \text{ kips}}{(50 \text{ ksi})(7.56 \text{ in.})} = 0.245 \text{ in.}$$

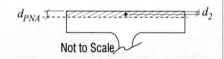

3b - Calculate d_2

The resultant C_s will act at the centroid of the area that is in compression. From the figure to the right we can see that:

$$d_2 = \frac{d_{PNA}}{2} = \frac{0.245 \text{ in.}}{2} = 0.122 \text{ in.}$$

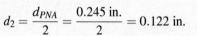

In this case it was relatively easy to determine d_2 because the PNA was in the top flange. If the PNA were in the web, the process would be more complicated, similar to what will be done for d_1 in the next step.

Step 4 - Compute the location of the tension steel resultant, d_1

The tension steel resultant will act through the centroid of the tension steel area (since the stress over the area is uniform). The centroid can be calculated by idealizing the section with three rectangles.

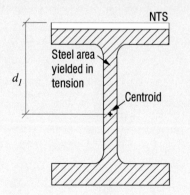

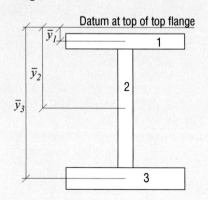

Example Continued

The area and $\bar{y}$ for each of the rectangles are:

$A_1 = b_f(t_f - d_{PNA}) = (7.56 \text{ in.})(0.695 \text{ in.} - 0.245 \text{ in.}) = 3.402 \text{ in.}^2$
$A_2 = t_w(d - 2t_f) = (0.415 \text{ in.})[18.2 \text{ in.} - 2(0.695 \text{ in.})] = 6.976 \text{ in.}^2$
$A_3 = b_f(t_f) = (7.56 \text{ in.})(0.695 \text{ in.}) = 5.254 \text{ in.}^2$

$\bar{y}_1 = d_{PNA} + \dfrac{t_f - d_{PNA}}{2} = 0.245 \text{ in.} + \dfrac{0.695 \text{ in.} - 0.245 \text{ in.}}{2} = 0.47 \text{ in.}$

$\bar{y}_2 = \dfrac{d}{2} = \dfrac{18.2 \text{ in.}}{2} = 9.1 \text{ in.}$

$\bar{y}_3 = d - \dfrac{t_f}{2} = 18.2 \text{ in.} - \dfrac{0.695 \text{ in.}}{2} = 17.853 \text{ in.}$

So the distance to the centroid for the combined area is:

$d_1 = \dfrac{A_1\bar{y}_1 + A_2\bar{y}_2 + A_3\bar{y}_3}{A_1 + A_2 + A_3} = 10.16 \text{ in.}$

Step 5 - Calculate the moment capacity

The nominal moment capacity is:

$M_n = T_s d_1 - C_s d_2 + C_c d_3$
$M_n = (787.5 \text{ kips})(10.16 \text{ in.}) - (92.5 \text{ kips})(0.122 \text{ in.}) + (695 \text{ kips})(4.95 \text{ in.})$
$M_n = 11430 \text{ kip-in.} = 952 \text{ kip-ft}$

And finally, from Section I3 of the Specification:

$\phi_b = 0.90$

so

$\phi_b M_n = (0.90)(952 \text{ kip-ft}) = \mathbf{857} \text{ kip-ft}$

You Should Know

- In what ways is it easier to compute $\phi_b M_n$, if the tension yielding state governs? There are two primary ones you should identify.
- In the previous example, how did we know that the PNA was located in the top flange?

9.14 Tables

The previous six sections have outlined the procedures for determining what limit state will govern for a composite beam and what the flexural capacity will be. Table 3-19 in the Manual provides values of $\phi_b M_n$ for thousands of composite beams. These values were determined using the procedures that have been described.

Study the Manual

Turn to Table 3-19 in the Manual (page 3-158). This is an incredibly powerful table, but requires some explanation.

Notice on the left of the table is a column indicating specific steel beams. Not all wide flange shapes are included in the Table, just those that are most likely to be used as beams.

- Is W36×800 included in Table 3-19? Why or why not?

The other column in Table 3-19 that you should already be familiar with is the third one from the left for $\phi_b M_p$. This is simply the plastic moment capacity of the bare steel shape. The values are the same as those listed in the Z_x table, and are repeated in Table 3-19 for convenience.

Some explanation is provided in the footnotes for some of the other columns.

- From footnote a, what is $Y1$?

- We defined this dimension earlier; what notation did we use?

- From footnote b, what is $Y2$?

- We defined this dimension earlier; what notation did we use?

Compare Equations 3-6 and 3-7 on page 3-13 of the Manual, with the equations for d_3 and a given a few pages ago in Build With Steel.

- How are they the same? How are they different?

Notice that values in Table 3-19 don't seem to depend on the strength of the concrete or the effective width of the concrete flange. The influence of these parameters is accounted for with $Y2$.

Perhaps the easiest way to explain how Table 3-19 works, is to apply it to an example that you are already familiar with. The following example demonstrates how Table 3-19 can be used to obtain the capacity of a composite beam.

Example 9.14 Using Table 3-19 to Determine Moment Capacity

The indicated beam is a W18×60 with (76) 3/4 in. dia. studs spaced evenly along the span (two studs per rib).

The deck profile is shown to the right. The concrete is normal weight (145 pcf) with $f'_c = 4$ ksi.

The studs are made from steel with $F_u = 65$ ksi.

What is $\phi_b M_n$ for the beam as determined using Table 3-19?

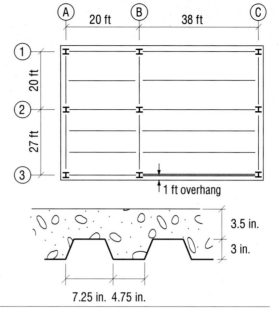

Step 1 - Calculate the effective width of the concrete

This calculation was done for this very beam in a previous example:

$b = 66$ in.

Step 2 - Calculate ΣQ_n

This calculation was done for this very beam in a previous example:

$\Sigma Q_n = 695$ kips

Step 3 - Calculate the distance to the compression concrete resultant, $Y2$

3a - Calculate the depth of the equivalent concrete stress block

Using Eqn. 3-7:

$$a = \frac{\Sigma Q_n}{0.85 f'_c b} = \frac{695 \text{ kips}}{0.85(4 \text{ ksi})(66 \text{ in.})} = 3.10 \text{ in.}$$

Note that this is the same value for a as obtained in the previous example.

3b - Get $Y2$

Using Eqn. 3-6:

$$Y2 = Y_{con} - \frac{a}{2} = 6.5 \text{ in.} - \frac{3.10 \text{ in.}}{2} = 4.95 \text{ in.}$$

Note that this is the same value for the distance to the concrete compression resultant (d_3) as in the previous example.

Step 4 - Enter Table 3-19 with the steel shape and ΣQ_n

We are now ready to enter Table 3-19. First we will identify which page has information for W18×60 beams. It is page 3-180 and the pertinent portion of the table is at the top.

continued on next page

Example Continued

The pertinent rows of the table depend on our value for ΣQ_n. For our beam, $\Sigma Q_n = 695$ kips. When we compare that with the values listed, it falls between 749 and 617 (the second and third rows of the table). This means that we will interpolate between these two rows to obtain the capacity for our beam.

The $Y1$ column of the table isn't required for this problem, but it is good to know what it indicates. $Y1$ is the d_{PNA} which corresponds with a particular value of ΣQ_n. In a previous example we computed d_{PNA} ($Y1$) to be 0.245 in. for this beam. As we look at the table, we see that this $Y1$ value falls between the second and third rows of the table (0.174 and 0.348 in.) just as our ΣQ_n did. If we hadn't known $Y1$ previously, we could have gotten it from the table once we knew ΣQ_n, by interpolating between 0.174 and 0.348 inches.

Step 5 - Look up the moment capacity based on ΣQ_n and $Y2$

Now that the pertinent rows have been identified, all that remains is to identify which column(s) has the value(s) of $\phi_b M_n$ that applies.

Values of $\phi_b M_n$ are given for particular values of $Y2$ in the columns of the table. We are fortunate, for this particular problem, that our value of $Y2$ (4.95 in.) is close enough to correspond directly with one of the columns ($Y2 = 5$). $\phi_b M_n$ for our beam will be obtained by interpolating between the values of the second and third row of the $Y2 = 5$ column.

$$\phi_b M_n = 829 \text{ k-ft} + (880 \text{ k-ft} - 829 \text{ k-ft}) \left(\frac{695 \text{ kips} - 617 \text{ kips}}{749 \text{ kips} - 617 \text{ kips}} \right) = \mathbf{859} \text{ k-ft}$$

Note: this is essentially the answer we obtained for $\phi_b M_n$ in the previous example, but using the table was much easier because we did not have to determine locations for the centroids for the steel compression and tension resultants.

You Should Know

- What information do you need to know before you can look up the capacity for a composite beam in Table 3-19?
- Which rows of Table 3-19 would correspond to the case when enough studs are provided that the Tension Yielding Limit State governs? Hint: what is the value of Y1 if the tension limit state governs?

9.15 Partially Composite Beams

The values in Table 3-19, show that there are diminishing returns for adding more and more studs to a beam.

Example 9.15 Using Table 3-19 to Compare Composite Beams

What is $\phi_b M_n$ for the beam in the previous example if there were only half as many studs?

Redoing Calculations if only half the studs are provided

The steps in the previous example are repeated, but with new numbers reflecting half as many studs.

$$b = 66 \text{ in.}$$
$$\Sigma Q_n = 347 \text{ kips}$$
$$a = \frac{\Sigma Q_n}{0.85 f'_c b} = \frac{347 \text{ kips}}{0.85(4 \text{ ksi})(66 \text{ in.})} = 1.55 \text{ in.}$$
$$Y2 = Y_{con} - \frac{a}{2} = 6.5 \text{ in.} - \frac{1.55 \text{ in.}}{2} = 5.73 \text{ in.}$$

Reading Table 3-19 we need to interpolate twice: between the 5th and 6th rows of the table, and between the $Y2 = 5.5$ and 6 columns.

$$\phi_b M_n = \textbf{735} \text{ k-ft}$$

Note: this is 85% of the capacity of the beam from the previous example, even though only half as many studs are provided.

Another way to look at it is that the first (38) studs on the beam increase the capacity from 461 k-ft ($\phi_b M_p$) to 735 k-ft, but the next (38) would only increase the capacity up to 859 k-ft, and about (20) more studs would be required to get full composite action. Since there are diminishing returns with additional studs, it is less common to use fully composite beams.

This concludes our discussion of the flexural capacity of composite beams.

The shear capacity of composite beams is generally computed considering the web of the steel shape alone and is usually much greater than demands.

You Should Know

- Why are partially composite beams used more often than fully composite beams?
- In what table would you look up the shear capacity for a composite beam?

9.16 Cambering

Cambering may influence the design of composite beams so we will begin our discussion of design by explaining what cambering is. Steel beams that support concrete decks may be cambered (bent) upward, so that when the concrete is placed, the deflected beam will be essentially level. Thus, the camber for a beam is generally determined based on anticipated dead load deflections.

Cambered beam → Level after dead load applied

Since cambering requires additional labor during fabrication, it is not always the most economical approach to controlling deflections. In some situations it will be more economical to specify a heavier beam (spend more on the steel), so that cambering is not required. The relative economy of cambering depends on a variety of factors including the price of steel, the particular fabricator, the design loads, and the beam spans.

There are minimums and maximums on specified camber. Engineers should not specify camber if less than 3/4 in. is required, knowing that when cambering is not specified, beams will be fabricated with the natural camber up. On the other extreme, engineers should not specify excessive camber recognizing that fabricators have limits on how much camber they can induce (usually up to 3 or 4 inches). Engineers often specify camber such that a small amount remains (1/2 in.) after the dead load is applied.

In the composite beam design examples that follow, we will assume that cambering is economical and that we are trying to keep required camber to less than three inches. The validity of these assumptions will vary in practice, depending on the design context.

Example 9.16 Beam Design

A 40 ft long floor composite beam has the following distributed loads. If the shape is a W18×60, specify a reasonable camber for the beam.

w_D: 0.80 k/ft
w_L: 0.40 k/ft

Step 1 - Compute dead load deflection

Since the point of cambering is to offset dead load deflections, it is helpful to begin by computing the deflection caused by the dead load.

$$\delta_D = \frac{5w_D l^4}{384EI} = \frac{5(0.80 \text{ k/ft})(\text{ft}/12 \text{ in.})(40 \times 12 \text{ in.})^4}{384(29000 \text{ ksi})(800 \text{ in.}^4)} = 1.99 \text{ in.}$$

Step 2 - Decide on the camber

Since the dead load deflection is greater than 3/4 in. it is reasonable to specify camber. Camber is generally specified in 1/4 in. increments. Reasonable values for this particular beam would include anything in the neighborhood of the dead load deflection, including 1.75 in., 2 in., 2.25 in., or 2.5 in. The "right" camber depends on the engineer's preference and cambering objectives. We'll say: camber = **2.25 in.**

You Should Know

- How do you compute a reasonable amount of beam camber?
- Does it always save money to camber the beams?

9.17 Design

With an understanding of how to compute composite beam demands and capacities, we are ready to discuss composite beam design. The general steps in beam design are the same as for other steel members:

1. Compute demands (M_u, M_{wc}).
2. Pick a shape and number of studs to try.
3. Determine the capacity of the shape and compare with demands.
4. Finalize the design or iterate to find a better design.

Steps 2 and 3 can be performed by using Table 3-19 in the Manual. When picking shapes use beam depths around L/24 so that excessive cambering will not be required. Also, assume a is 1 in. when picking shapes to try; you can calculate the precise value later after you've settled on a shape.

The procedures for designing composite beams are illustrated in the following example.

Example 9.17 Beam Design

Design the 38 ft long floor beams as composite beams. Specify the steel shape and total number of studs.

The loads are:
Floor Dead: 80 psf
Floor Live: 50 psf
Ext. Wall: 20 psf

The deck has the profile shown. The concrete is lightweight with f'_c= 3 ksi. Use 3/4 in. dia. studs with F_y=65 ksi.

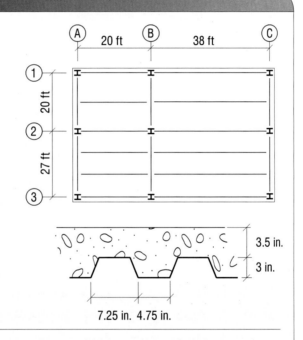

Step 1 - Compute demands

1a - Identify the critical floor beam

There are (6) floor beams shown that are 38 ft long. First, we need to determine which floor beam will have the greatest demands. Of the interior floor beams, the one running along gridline 1.5 would have the greatest tributary width (10 ft). The critical spandrel beam runs along gridline 1. It only has a tributary width of 6.5 ft, but it carries exterior wall weight. It is not obvious which will govern, but a quick calculation can be done to check.

$$w_{D,wall} = (15 \text{ ft})(20 \text{ psf}) = 0.30 \text{ k/ft}$$
$$w_{D,3.5-ft-of-floor} = (3.5 \text{ ft})(80 \text{ psf}) = 0.28 \text{ k/ft}$$

The dead loads on the two beams (critical interior and critical spandrel) will be similar as suggested by the calculation above, but the interior beam will have 3.5 tributary feet more for live load. From these rough calculations it is clear that the critical interior floor beam will have the greatest demands.

continued on next page

231

Example Continued

Of course, the interior beam will also have a greater effective width of concrete to help meet the demands, so it may not be obvious that it will govern. From experience, the effective width of the exterior beam is sufficient to prevent it from being the critical case. We will design the interior beam, and then could come back and check to verify if the design is adequate for the exterior.

1b - Reduce the live load

$$A_t = (10 \text{ ft})(38 \text{ ft}) = 380 \text{ ft}^2$$

$$L = (50 \text{ psf})\left(0.25 + \frac{15}{\sqrt{2(380)}}\right) = (50 \text{ psf})(0.794) = 39.7 \text{ psf}$$

1c - Get factored load effects

$$w_D = (10 \text{ ft})(80 \text{ psf}) = 0.8 \text{ k/ft}$$
$$w_L = (10 \text{ ft})(39.7 \text{ psf}) = 0.397 \text{ k/ft}$$
$$w_U = 1.2w_D + 1.6w_L = 1.2(0.8 \text{ k/ft}) + 1.6(0.397 \text{ k/ft}) = 1.60 \text{ k/ft}$$
$$M_U = \frac{w_U L^2}{8} = \frac{(1.6 \text{ k/ft})(38 \text{ ft})^2}{8} = 289 \text{ k-ft}$$
$$V_U = \frac{w_U L}{2} = \frac{(1.6 \text{ k/ft})(38 \text{ ft})}{2} = 30.4 \text{ kips}$$

1d - Compute wet concrete load effects

$$w_{wc} = 1.2(80 \text{ psf})(10 \text{ ft}) = 0.96 \text{ k/ft}$$
$$M_{wc} = \frac{w_{wc} L^2}{8} = \frac{(0.96 \text{ k/ft})(38 \text{ ft})^2}{8} = 173 \text{ k-ft}$$
$$V_{wc} = \frac{w_{wc} L}{2} = \frac{(0.96 \text{ k/ft})(38 \text{ ft})}{2} = 18.2 \text{ kips}$$

Step 2 - Pick a shape to try

2a - Estimate beam depth and Y2

Now that the demands are known, we need to pick a shape to try. Before going to Table 3-19 we will estimate the depth of the steel shape and the distance $Y2$ using the recommendations that were given just prior to this example.

$$d \approx \frac{L}{24} = \frac{38 \times 12 \text{ in.}}{24} = 19 \text{ in. (look at W18x and W21x shapes)}$$

$$Y2 = Y_{conc} - \frac{a}{2} \approx 6.5 \text{ in.} - \frac{1 \text{ in.}}{2} = 6.0 \text{ in.}$$

2b - Identify some options from Table 3-19

With rough beam sizes and an estimate of $Y2$ we can explore options using Table 3-19.

The lightest W18× is the W18×35 on page 3-182 of Table 3-19. From the $\phi_b M_n$ values listed in the $Y2 = 6$ column, there is more than adequate capacity even if the minimum ΣQ_n is provided (372 k-ft > M_u).

The lightest W21× is the W21×44 on page 3-178 of Table 3-19. From the $\phi_b M_n$ values listed in the $Y2 = 6$ column, there is much greater capacity than necessary, even if the minimum ΣQ_n is provided (530 k-ft >> M_u).

Example Continued

At this point we are tempted to try W16× since the smallest W18× and
W21× have excess capacity. We will eventually see that the required camber
is almost excessive even for the the W18×, so we will not explore any W16×
shapes.

In summary, our options are:

W21×44 with $\Sigma Q_n = 163$ kips $\phi_b M_n \approx 530$ k-ft
W18×35 with $\Sigma Q_n = 129$ kips $\phi_b M_n \approx 372$ k-ft

You may wonder if we could use lower values of ΣQ_n (which will mean
fewer studs) with the shapes above in order to get capacities nearer to our
demands. The use of partially composite beams with $\Sigma Q_n < 0.25 F_y A_s$ is
discouraged, which is why lower values are not provided in Table 3-19. The
options remain as stated above.

2c - Pick a shape

We will try W18×35 with $\Sigma Q_n \geq 129$ kips.

Step 3 - Compute capacity and compare with demands

With a trial shape selected, we can now compute capacities and compare them
with demands. We will need to do some initial work to get the real value of a.
We assumed it was equal to 1 in. in order to get a preliminary value for $Y2$.

3a - Determine the effective width of the slab

The effective width *on each side* of the beam centerline is governed by one of
two things: one-eight the span, or one-half the spacing. The edge distance is
not pertinent for interior beams.

$$\text{one-eight of the beam span} = \frac{38 \text{ ft}}{8} = 4.75 \text{ ft} = 57 \text{ in.}$$

$$\text{one-half the dist. to centerline of adjacent beam} = \frac{10 \text{ ft}}{2} = 5 \text{ ft} = 60 \text{ in.}$$

The effective width on both sides is governed by the first criteria, so the total
effective width is:

$$b = 57 \text{ in.} + 57 \text{ in.} = 114 \text{ in.}$$

3b - Determine the number of studs and ΣQ_n

The beam we are designing is a floor beam so the deck flutes will run
perpendicular to the beam. Since the flutes of the deck are spaced one foot
apart it is only possible to place studs at one foot increments.

To determine an appropriate number of studs, it is helpful to compute Q_n.
From Table 3-21 for lightweight concrete, $f'_c = 3$ ksi, Deck Perpendicular, 1
strong stud per rib, and 3/4 in. diameter:

$$Q_n = 17.1 \text{ kips/stud}$$

If studs were placed every other flute (two feet on center) then we would have
(19) total for the beam. Since the beam is uniformly loaded, the point of
maximum moment would be in the middle and the number of studs between
there and the point of zero moment (either end) would be (9) studs.

continued on next page

Example Continued

$\Sigma Q_n = (17.1 \text{ kips/stud})(9 \text{ studs}) = 153.9 \text{ kips}$

This is greater than 129 kips (which was all we needed for ΣQ_n) and will result in greater capacity than our preliminary estimate. At this point we are confident that the design will work; we will go ahead and compute $\phi_b M_n$ but we can tell by inspection that we will have more than enough capacity.

3c - Compute a

$$a = \frac{\Sigma Q_n}{0.85 f_c' b} = \frac{153.9 \text{ kips}}{0.85(3 \text{ ksi})(114 \text{ in.})} = 0.529 \text{ in.}$$

3d - Compute Y2

$$Y2 = Y_{conc} - \frac{a}{2} = 6.5 \text{ in.} - \frac{0.529 \text{ in.}}{2} = 6.24 \text{ in.}$$

3e - Read $\phi_b M_n$ from Table 3-19

To get a precise value of $\phi_b M_n$ we would need to interpolate between rows 6 and 7 (for the W18×35) AND interpolate again between the columns for $Y2 = 6$ and $Y2 = 6.5$. Since we know the capacity is much more than needed, we will simply read off the lowest value (associated with row 7, $Y2 = 6$) knowing that this is conservative.

$\phi_b M_n = 372 + \text{ k-ft}$
$372 \text{ k-ft} \geq 289 \text{ k-ft (OK)}$

3f - Check shear capacity

The shear capacity of the composite beam will be at least as great as the shear capacity of the bare steel beam. From Table 3-2:

$\phi_v V_{nx} = 159 \text{ kips} \geq 30.4 \text{ kips (OK)}$

3g - Check the beam under the wet concrete load

Now we need to check the strength of the bare steel beam to carry the wet concrete load. From the left-most column in Table 3-19 we read $\phi_b M_p$ for the bare beam. Since the top flange of the beam is tied-into and restrained-by the deck, lateral torsional buckling is prevented so:

$\phi_b M_n = \phi_b M_p = 249 \text{ k-ft (for bare steel beam)}$

Comparing this with M_{wc} computed in Step 1, we see the beam is more than adequate for the wet concrete load.

$249 \text{ k-ft} \geq 173 \text{ k-ft (OK)}$

By inspection the shear strength is also more than adequate.

3h - Compute required camber

The deflection from the wet concrete is typically cambered out so the beam will be essentially flat after the concrete is placed.

$$\delta_{wc} = \frac{5 w_{wc} l^4}{384 EI} = \frac{5(0.96 \text{ k/ft})(\text{ft}/12 \text{ in.})(38 \times 12 \text{ in.})^4}{384(29000 \text{ ksi})(510 \text{ in.}^4)} = 3.0 \text{ in.}$$

Step 4 - Finalize the design or iterate to find a better design

At this point our design is to use a W18×35 beam with (19) total studs (2 ft. on center). The capacity of this beam is greater than what is required and the required camber (3 in. for a 38 ft. beam) is reasonable. Shallower shapes would result in excessive cambering, and heavier shapes would be even more conservative.

9.18 Stud Spacing Requirements

In the previous example, stud spacing was highly constrained because the deck flutes were perpendicular to the beam. For girders, where the deck flutes typically run parallel to the steel shape, there is more flexibility for stud layout. When choosing the studs, it is important to keep spacing rules in mind.

Example 9.18 Composite Girder Design

Design the 27 ft long floor interior girder as a composite beam. Specify the steel shape, studs, and camber.

The loads are:
Floor Dead: 80 psf
Floor Live: 50 psf
Ext. Wall: 20 psf

The deck has the profile shown. The concrete is lightweight with f'_c=3 ksi. Use 3/4 in. dia. studs with F_y=65 ksi.

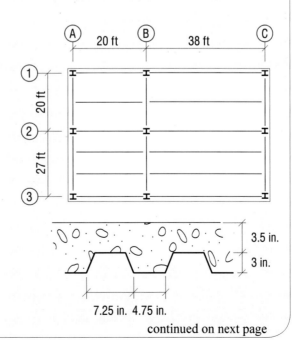

continued on next page

235

Example Continued

Step 1 - Compute demands

1a - Reduce the live load

$$A_t = (2/3)(27 \text{ ft})(20/2 \text{ ft} + 38/2 \text{ ft}) = 522 \text{ ft}^2$$

$$L = (50 \text{ psf})\left(0.25 + \frac{15}{\sqrt{2(522)}}\right) = (50 \text{ psf})(0.714) = 35.7 \text{ psf}$$

1b - Get factored load effects

The tributary areas for the point loads at the girder third-points will be:

$$A_{t,1} = A_t/2 = 261 \text{ ft}^2$$

The service point loads are:

$$P_D = (80 \text{ psf})(261 \text{ ft}^2) = 20.9 \text{ kips}$$
$$P_L = (35.7 \text{ psf})(261 \text{ ft}^2) = 9.32 \text{ kips}$$

Factoring the point loads gives:

$$P_U = 1.2P_D + 1.6P_L = 1.2(20.9 \text{ kips}) + 1.6(9.32 \text{ kips}) = 40.0 \text{ kips}$$

The corresponding maximum shear and bending moment are:

$$V_U = P_U = 40.0 \text{ kips}$$
$$M_U = P_U(27 \text{ ft}/3) = (40.0 \text{ kips})(27 \text{ ft}/3) = 360 \text{ k-ft}$$

1c - Compute wet concrete load effects

$$P_{wc} \approx 1.2P_D = 1.2(20.9 \text{ kips}) = 25.1 \text{ kips}$$
$$V_{wc} = P_{wc} = 25.1 \text{ kips}$$
$$M_{wc} = P_{wc}(27 \text{ ft}/3) = (25.1 \text{ kips})(27 \text{ ft}/3) = 226 \text{ k-ft}$$

Step 2 - Pick a shape to try

2a - Estimate beam depth and Y2

Now that the demands are known, we need to pick a shape to try. Before going to Table 3-19 we will estimate the depth of the steel shape and the distance $Y2$.

$$d \approx \frac{L}{24} = \frac{27 \times 12 \text{ in.}}{24} = 13.5 \text{ in. (look at W14} \times \text{ and W16} \times \text{ shapes)}$$

$$Y2 = Y_{conc} - \frac{a}{2} \approx 6.5 \text{ in.} - \frac{1 \text{ in.}}{2} = 6.0 \text{ in.}$$

2b - Identify some options from Table 3-19.

With rough beam sizes and an estimate of $Y2$ we can explore options using Table 3-19

There are several W14×s shown on page 3-185 of Table 3-19 that would work if enough studs are provided. The W14×34 has $\phi_b M_n = 381$ kips (see the $Y2 = 6$ column) if $\Sigma Q_n = 270$ kips.

Several W16×s could also work. The W16×36 has $\phi_b M_n = 389$ kips (see the $Y2 = 6$ column) if $\Sigma Q_n = 181$ kips.

It may also be worthwhile to consider the W18×35 since this shape was selected for the beams in the previous example. The W18×35 has $\phi_b M_n = 372$ kips (see the $Y2 = 6$ column) if $\Sigma Q_n = 129$ kips.

Example Continued

2c - Pick a shape

There are several shapes that would work here. We will try W18×35 with $\Sigma Q_n \geq 129$ kips. Some advantages of this choice are: it requires the fewest studs; and the shape is being used for the long beams (see previous example).

Step 3 - Compute capacity and compare with demands

With a trial shape selected, we can now compute capacities and compare them with demands. We will need to do some initial work to get the real value of a. We assumed it was equal to 1 in. in order to get a preliminary value for $Y2$.

3a - Determine the effective width of the slab

The effective width *on each side* of the beam centerline is governed by one of two things: one-eight the span, or one-half the spacing. The edge distance is not pertinent for interior beams.

$$\text{one-eight of the beam span} = \frac{27 \text{ ft}}{8} = 3.375 \text{ ft} = 40.5 \text{ in.}$$

$$\text{one-half the dist. to centerline of adjacent beam} = \frac{20 \text{ ft}}{2} = 10 \text{ ft} = 120 \text{ in.}$$

This is for the left side of the beam, the right side would be greater.

The effective width on both sides is governed by the first criteria, so the total effective width is:

$$b = 40.5 \text{ in.} + 40.5 \text{ in.} = 81 \text{ in.}$$

3b - Determine the number of studs and ΣQ_n

To determine an appropriate number of studs, it is helpful to compute Q_n. From Table 3-21 for lightweight concrete, $f_c' = 3$ ksi, Deck Parallel, and 3/4 in. diameter:

$$Q_n = 17.1 \text{ kips/stud}$$

The required number of studs such that $\Sigma Q_n \geq 129$ kips is:

$$N = \frac{\Sigma Q_n}{Q_n} = \frac{129 \text{ kips}}{17.1 \text{ kips/stud}} = 7.5 \text{ studs}$$

We will try (8) studs on each segment of the beam where the moment goes from zero to maximum. No studs are required in the center third of the girder where the moment is constant (although we may place some for good measure).

$$\Sigma Q_n = (17.1 \text{ kips/stud})(8.0 \text{ studs}) = 137 \text{ kips}$$

There will be (7) spaces between the (8) studs, making the spacing:

$$s = \frac{9 \text{ ft}}{7} = 1.28 \text{ ft} = 15 \text{ in.}$$

The spacing, s, is greater than the minimum spacing (six stud diameters), and less than the maximum (36 in.) so the design is compliant.

continued on next page

Example Continued

3c - Compute a

$$a = \frac{\Sigma Q_n}{0.85 f'_c b} = \frac{137 \text{ kips}}{0.85(3 \text{ ksi})(81 \text{ in.})} = 0.663 \text{ in.}$$

3d - Compute Y2

$$Y2 = Y_{conc} - \frac{a}{2} = 6.5 \text{ in.} - \frac{0.663 \text{ in.}}{2} = 6.16 \text{ in.}$$

3e - Read $\phi_b M_n$ from Table 3-19

To get a precise value of $\phi_b M_n$ we would need to interpolate between rows 6 and 7 (for the W18×35) AND interpolate again between the columns for $Y2 = 6$ and $Y2 = 6.5$.

Since we know the capacity is more than needed, we will simply read off the lowest value (associated with row 7, $Y2 = 6$) knowing that this is conservative.

$$\phi_b M_n = 372 + \text{ k-ft}$$
$$372 \text{ k-ft} \geq 360 \text{ k-ft (OK)}$$

3f - Check shear capacity

The shear capacity of the composite beam will be at least as great as the shear capacity of the bare steel beam. From Table 3-2:

$$\phi_v V_{nx} = 159 \text{ kips} \geq 40.0 \text{ kips (OK)}$$

3g - Check the beam under the wet concrete load

Now we need to check the strength of the bare steel beam to carry the wet concrete load. From the left-most column in Table 3-19 we read $\phi_b M_p$ for the bare beam. Since the top flange of the beam is tied-into and restrained-by the deck, lateral torsional buckling is prevented so:

$$\phi_b M_n = \phi_b M_p = 249 \text{ k-ft (for bare steel beam)}$$

Comparing this with M_{wc} computed in Step 1, we see the beam flexural strength is more than adequate for the wet concrete load.

$$249 \text{ k-ft} \geq 226 \text{ k-ft (OK)}$$

By inspection the shear strength is also more than adequate.

3h - Compute required camber

The deflection from the wet concrete is typically cambered out so the beam will be essentially flat after the concrete is placed.

$$\delta_{wc} = \frac{P_{wc} l^3}{28 EI} = \frac{(25.1 \text{ kips})(27 \times 12 \text{ in.})^3}{28(29000 \text{ ksi})(510 \text{ in.}^4)} = 2.0 \text{ in.}$$

Step 4 - Finalize the design or iterate to find a better design

At this point our design is to use a W18×35 beam with (16) total studs [(8) on each end third]. The capacity of this beam is greater than what is required and the required camber (2 in. for a 27 ft. beam) is reasonable. Shallower shapes could also work, but would require more studs and camber and would not have much weight savings.

You Should Know

- Why did a end up being smaller in this example as compared to the previous one?
- How many different steel shapes could have been used for this composite beam?

Remember This

- Composite beams are steel beams that are integrated with a concrete slab (or slab-on-metal deck) via shear connectors (usually headed studs).
- Shear connectors are an added expense but often result in net savings because of reduced steel beam weights.
- The steel beam must be strong enough to support the construction loads until the concrete cures and composite behavior is realized.
- Three limit states for composite beams are concrete crushing, tension yielding, and stud shear strength.
- When the capacity of a composite beam is limited by concrete crushing or tension yielding, it is said to be fully composite. When the capacity is limited by stud shear strength it is said to be partially composite.
- The flexural capacity of composite beams is determined by calculating ultimate resultant forces in the concrete and steel, and then summing the moments of the resultants.
- The shear strength of the studs, ΣQ_n, is the strength of the studs located between the points of zero and maximum moment.
- The flexural capacity of composite beams can be determined relatively quickly using Table 3-19 in the Manual.

This perimeter frame is designed to resist wind and earthquake loads. The beams are welded to the columns to create a special moment resisting frame (SMRF). The beams and columns in the frame will have axial forces, shear forces, and bending moments making them more complicated to design than typical beams and columns.

These girders will have bending moments from gravity loads and axial forces from earthquake and wind.

10. Beam-Columns

10.1 Overview

In Chapters 6 and 7 you learned how to design members that have compressive axial forces. In Chapter 8 you learned how to design members that have bending moments. In this chapter you will learn how to design steel members that have both axial forces and bending moments; these members are called *beam-columns*.

Beam-columns are often found in the lateral-force resisting systems of steel buildings. The picture above shows floor girders that also serve as collectors. Gravity loads cause bending moments and shear forces in the girders while wind and seismic loads cause axial forces. When wind or seismic loads are present, these floor girders will have both axial force and bending moment and will function as beam-columns.

Collectors are floor beams or girders that transmit seismic forces to the lateral force resisting frames. When you look at a steel building, beams that have connections with more than one vertical line of bolts are often collectors. The additional bolts help transmit axial loads that are in the beams.

In addition to collectors, the members of moment-resisting frames, like the one shown to the right, will be beam-columns. Both gravity and lateral loads will cause axial forces and moments in the frame members.

Calculating demands in beam-columns requires special care because of second-order moments. These are additional moments that are generated by the axial forces.

Calculating capacities of beam-columns requires the use of interaction equations. These equations allow us to combine the column capacity and beam capacity of a member in order to get the beam-column capacity.

As with the previous chapters, the following sections will address demands, then capacities, and finally design.

You Should Know

- What kind of load effects do beam-columns have?
- What causes second-order moments?
- What do interaction equations do?

10.2 Computing Demands

In Chapter 3, you were introduced to four general steps in computing demands for LRFD:
1. Calculate the loads.
2. Calculate the load effects (structural analysis).
3. Combine the load effects using load factors and combinations.
4. Identify the maximum load effects.

Computing demands for beam-columns requires more effort than computing the demands for tension members, compression members, or beams. Step 2 is often more complicated because beam-columns may be part of indeterminate frames that require more advanced structural analysis. Getting the bending moments (Steps 2 and 3) is complicated by second-order effects. Finally, in Steps 3 and 4 it is not always obvious which load combination will govern.

The general steps for computing beam-column demands are:
1. Calculate the loads.
2. Calculate the load effects (structural analysis, often on indeterminate systems).
3. Combine the load effects using load factors and combinations and accounting for second-order effects.
4. Identify the maximum load effects.

The next several sections will demonstrate how these steps are applied to compute the demands in beam-columns.

> **You Should Know**
>
> • How is Step 3 in computing demands different for beam-columns?
> • Why is the structural analysis in Step 2 more complicated for beam-columns?

10.3 First-Order Load Effects

The first step in calculating beam-column demands is to determine the loads. Previous chapters have explained and demonstrated how to compute gravity loads. Procedures for computing earthquake and wind loads are given in ASCE 7.

Once the loads have been determined, the next step is to use structural analysis to determine the load effects (axial forces, shear forces, and bending moments). In some cases, the analysis can be performed using statics, as illustrated in the following example.

Example 10.1 Computing Load Effects in Beam-Columns

A collector is subjected to the loads shown below. Compute the load effects in the collector.

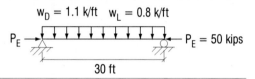

$w_D = 1.1$ k/ft $w_L = 0.8$ k/ft

P_E ← ... → $P_E = 50$ kips

30 ft

Step 1 - Identify the load effects that need to be calculated

In general, the load effects we are interested in are axial forces, shear forces, and bending moments. In this example, there are three different types of loads: dead, live, and earthquake. The nine load effects that need to be calculated then are:

$$P_D \quad V_D \quad M_D \quad P_L \quad V_L \quad M_L \quad P_E \quad V_E \quad M_E$$

Step 2 - Compute the dead load effects

The dead load is a distributed load. It will cause shear forces and bending moments, but no axial load effects.

$$P_D = 0 \text{ kips}$$

$$V_D = \frac{w_D L}{2} = \frac{(1.1 \text{ k/ft})(30 \text{ ft})}{2} = 16.5 \text{ kips}$$

$$M_D = \frac{w_D L^2}{8} = \frac{(1.1 \text{ k/ft})(30 \text{ ft})^2}{8} = 123.8 \text{ k-ft}$$

Step 3 - Compute the live load effects

The live load is also a distributed load, and the effects are computed in the same manner as the dead load effects.

$$P_L = 0 \text{ kips} \quad V_L = 12 \text{ kips} \quad M_L = 90 \text{ k-ft}$$

Step 4 - Compute earthquake load effects

If the earthquake loads were applied, and the dead and live were not, the only load effect would be axial force in the member.

$$P_E = 50 \text{ kips} \quad V_E = 0 \text{ kips} \quad M_E = 0 \text{ k-ft}$$

Example 10.2 Computing Load Effects in Indeterminate Systems

A frame is subjected to the loads shown. Compute the load effects in the beam.

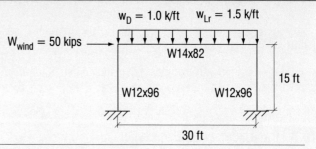

Step 1 - Identify the load effects that need to be calculated

The load effects we are interested in calculating are axial forces, shear forces, and bending moments. In this example, there are three different types of loads: dead, roof live, and wind. The nine load effects that need to be calculated for the beam are:

$$P_D \quad V_D \quad M_D \quad P_{Lr} \quad V_{Lr} \quad M_{Lr} \quad P_W \quad V_W \quad M_W$$

Step 2 - Compute the dead load effects

Using the stiffness method, a free-body diagram can be developed for the beam for the case when only the gravity loads are applied:

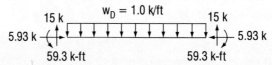

From the diagram:

$$P_D = 5.93 \text{ kips} \quad V_D = 15 \text{ kips} \quad M_D = 59.3 \text{ k-ft}$$

Note: In frames, the maximum beam and column moments generally occur at the ends. From the free-body diagram above it can be easily verified that this is the case.

Step 3 - Compute the roof live load effects

Using the stiffness method, a free-body diagram can be developed for the beam for the case when only the roof live loads are applied:

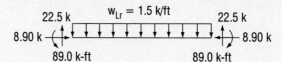

From the diagram:

$$P_{Lr} = 8.90 \text{ kips} \quad V_{Lr} = 22.5 \text{ kips} \quad M_{Lr} = 89.0 \text{ k-ft}$$

Example Continued

Step 4 - Compute the wind load effects

Using the stiffness method, a free-body diagram can be developed for the beam for the case when only the wind loads are applied:

104.9 k-ft   7.0 k

25 k ———————————— 25 k

7.0 k   104.9 k-ft

From the diagram:

$$P_W = 25 \text{ kips} \quad V_W = 7.0 \text{ kips} \quad M_W = 104.9 \text{ k-ft}$$

The previous two examples have illustrated how load effects are calculated for beam-columns. The next step is to factor and combine these effects using load combinations.

You Should Know

- How many load effects do you need to calculate? What does it depend on?
- How do you compute load effects for indeterminate systems?

10.4 Factored First-Order Load Effects

Load effects need to be combined using load combinations. Some students get confused and think that "combining" load effects means trying to add axial forces and bending moments. We can't do such a thing. When we "combine" load effects we only consider one effect at a time. We factor and add all the axial forces to get an ultimate axial force; we factor and add all the shear forces to get an ultimate shear force; and we factor and add all the moments to get an ultimate moment.

In applying the load combinations to beam-columns, our notation and procedure is different from what was done for other members. Previously, the ultimate axial force was designated P_u, and was equal to the axial force from the worst-case load combination. For example we might have written:

$$P_u = 1.2P_D + 1.6P_L + 0.5P_{Lr}$$

Previously, the ultimate moment was designated M_u and might have been calculated using a formula such as:

$$M_u = 1.2M_D + 1.6M_L$$

For beam-columns, the ultimate axial forces and bending moments are not designated with P_u and M_u; they are designated with P_r and M_r and there is a modified procedure for obtaining them. The reason that the notation and procedure are different for beam-columns is that beam columns have second-order effects (which will be discussed in detail in following sections).

Study the Manual

Turn to Chapter C in the Specification and read the first lines.

* How many sections are in the Chapter?

* What section deals with calculating demands (required strengths)?

Read the first three paragraphs of §C.1.

* What are the two types of second-order effects that must be considered?

Appendix 8 (page 16.1-237) describes an acceptable procedure for accounting for second-order effects. Read the first paragraph in Appendix 8.

* What is the general idea behind the method that is presented in Appendix 8?

Recall that M_r and P_r are the ultimate moment and axial force in a beam-column. Write the equations for M_r and P_r as given in §8.2.

$$M_r =$$
$$P_r =$$

In the equations for M_r and P_r you will note six unfamiliar terms (B_1, B_2, M_{nt}, M_{lt}, P_{nt}, and P_{lt}). You will also note that there are not any familiar load effects (like M_D or P_L) or load factors. We will discuss B_1 and B_2 in later sections but will address M_{nt}, M_{lt}, P_{nt}, and P_{lt} right now.

Scan ahead further in §8.2. until you arrive at the definitions for M_{nt}, M_{lt}, P_{nt}, and P_{lt}. Read the definitions for the terms.

* Write the definition for M_{nt}.

* How are the definitions for M_{lt}, P_{nt}, and P_{lt} similar?

Note that M_{nt}, M_{lt}, P_{nt}, and P_{lt} are calculated using load combinations.

It is important to know how to use load combinations to get M_{nt}, M_{lt}, P_{nt}, and P_{lt}, which are later combined to get M_r and P_r. The definitions for M_{nt}, M_{lt}, P_{nt}, and P_{lt} may be a bit puzzling, particularly for those who have not had an analysis course yet. For the symmetric systems that will be considered herein, three simple rules can be applied to get M_{nt}, M_{lt}, P_{nt}, and P_{lt} for a particular member. The rules are listed below, and illustrated in the following two examples:

Rule 1. All M and P load effects will contribute to either M_{nt}, M_{lt}, P_{nt}, and P_{lt}.
Rule 2. All M load effects will contribute to M_{nt} *except* those *in columns* caused by wind or earthquake loads.
Rule 3. All P load effects will contribute to P_{nt} *except* those *in columns* that are caused by wind or earthquake loads.

Example 10.3 Calculating Mnt, Mlt, Pnt, and Plt

Compute M_{nt}, M_{lt}, P_{nt}, and P_{lt} for the beam in the frame.

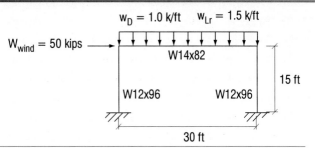

$W_{wind} = 50$ kips

$w_D = 1.0$ k/ft $w_{Lr} = 1.5$ k/ft

W14x82

15 ft

W12x96   W12x96

30 ft

Step 1 - Calculate the load effects for the beam in the frame

The first step is to get the load effects for the beam. This is the most time-consuming step, but was already done for this frame in Example 10.2. From that example, the load effects are:

$$P_D = 5.93 \text{ kips} \quad V_D = 15 \text{ kips} \quad M_D = 59.3 \text{ k-ft}$$
$$P_{Lr} = 8.90 \text{ kips} \quad V_{Lr} = 22.5 \text{ kips} \quad M_{Lr} = 89.0 \text{ k-ft}$$
$$P_W = 25 \text{ kips} \quad V_W = 7.0 \text{ kips} \quad M_W = 104.9 \text{ k-ft}$$

Note: In the remainder of this example we will not be using the shear forces. They can be combined using the methods shown in Chapter 8.

Step 2 - Indentify which load effects will contribute to M_{nt}, M_{lt}, P_{nt}, and P_{lt}

The rules outlined on the previous page can be used to see which load effects contribute to each term.

M_D and M_{Lr} and M_W will contribute to M_{nt} (see Rules 1 and 2).
P_D, P_{Lr}, and P_W will contribute to P_{nt} (see Rules 1 and 3).

In this example nothing will contribute to M_{lt} and P_{lt} since we are computing demands in a beam.

Step 3 - Calculate M_{nt}, M_{lt}, P_{nt}, and P_{lt} for pertinent load combinations

Now that we know which terms contribute to each, load combinations can be used to get M_{nt} and P_{nt}. Load combination 2 is not checked since it can be determined by inspection that load combination 3 would be more severe.

Load Combination 1
$$M_{nt} = 1.4M_D = 1.4(59.3 \text{ k-ft}) = 83.0 \text{ k-ft}$$
$$P_{nt} = 1.4P_D = 1.4(5.93 \text{ kips}) = 8.30 \text{ kips}$$

Load Combination 3
$$M_{nt} = 1.2M_D + 1.6M_{Lr} + 0.5M_W$$
$$= 1.2(59.3 \text{ k-ft}) + 1.6(89.0 \text{ k-ft}) + 0.5(104.9 \text{ k-ft}) = 266 \text{ k-ft}$$
$$P_{nt} = 1.2P_D + 1.6P_{Lr} + 0.5P_W$$
$$= 1.2(5.93 \text{ kips}) + 1.6(8.90 \text{ kips}) + 0.5(25 \text{ kips}) = 33.9 \text{ kips}$$

continued on next page

Load Combination 4
$$M_{nt} = 1.2M_D + 1.0M_W + 0.5M_{Lr}$$
$$= 1.2(59.3 \text{ k-ft}) + 1.0(104.9 \text{ k-ft}) + 0.5(89.0 \text{ k-ft}) = 220.6 \text{ k-ft}$$
$$P_{nt} = 1.2P_D + 1.0P_W + 0.5P_{Lr}$$
$$= 1.2(5.93 \text{ kips}) + 1.0(25 \text{ kips}) + 0.5(8.90 \text{ kips}) = 36.6 \text{ kips}$$

Step 4 - Identify which load combination governs
In the previous step, M_{nt} and P_{nt} were calculated for the three pertinent load combinations. It is clear that Load Combination 1 does not govern, because it yields lower values for M_{nt} and P_{nt} than Load Combination 3. However, it is not clear whether Load Combination 3 or 4 governs. Load Combination 3 has a higher value for M_{nt}, but Load Combination 4 has a higher value P_{nt}. Since it is unclear what governs, both will be retained for design. Later sections will show how we will use one combination for an initial design and then check the design with the other.

You Should Know

- What is M_{nt}, M_{lt}, P_{nt}, and P_{lt} for the beam in Example 10.1?

    $M_{nt} =$ $M_{lt} =$ $P_{nt} =$ $P_{lt} =$

- For beam-columns, why do we designate the ultimate moment and axial force M_r and P_r, rather than M_u and P_u?

10.5 Second-Order Load Effects

In the equations for M_r and P_r (§8.2) the factors B_1 and B_2 appear. This section will explain the theory behind B_1.

Consider a column that is initially bowed with a mid-height deflection of δ_o, as shown in the figure. Now suppose an axial load of P were applied to the member. When the axial load is applied, the mid-height deflection will increase by some amount, such that the deflection becomes δ_f. The increased deflection, from δ_o to δ_f, is a manifestation of bending moments caused by the axial load P. If the column were cut at mid-height (right figure) and moments were summed at the cut, we would find that $M = P\delta_f$.

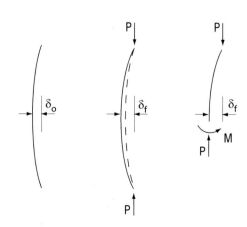

For the column on the bottom of the previous page we need to know δ_f in order to compute the moment caused by the axial load. It can be shown that the relationship between δ_o and δ_f is:

$$\delta_f = \delta_o \left[\frac{1}{1 - (P/P_e)} \right]$$

In the equation above, δ_f is expressed as the product of δ_o and an amplification factor (the term in the square bracket). The P_e that appears in the amplification factor is the Euler buckling load about the axis that is bowed.

Example 10.4 Computing Bending Moments Caused by Axial Loads

A W14×53 that is 30 ft long has a natural camber about the strong axis, such that it bows 0.25 in. at mid-span. If a 25 kip axial load is applied to the member, what are the mid-span deflection and bending moment?

Step 1 - Recognize that the load will not buckle the member

The 25 kips axial load is not big relative to the buckling strength of the member. If KL_x and KL_y equal 30 ft, the buckling capacity is 100 kips (from Table 4-1).

Step 2 - Compute the final mid-height deflection

The final mid-height deflection can be computed using the equation at the top of this page. We will compute P_e first since it is required in the equation.

$$P_e = \frac{\pi^2 EI}{(KL)^2} = \frac{\pi^2 (29000 \text{ ksi})(541 \text{ in.}^4)}{(30 \times 12 \text{ in.})^2} = 1194 \text{ kips}$$

$$\delta_f = \delta_o \left[\frac{1}{1 - (P/P_e)} \right] = (0.25 \text{ in.}) \left[\frac{1}{1 - (25 \text{ kips}/1194 \text{ kips})} \right] = \mathbf{0.255} \text{ in.}$$

Step 3 - Compute the moment at mid-height

$$M = P\delta_f = (25 \text{ kips})(0.255 \text{ in.}) = \mathbf{6.38} \text{ k-in.}$$

Note two things: 1) the moment of inertia for the strong axis was used in Step 2, because the initial deflection was bowing about the strong axis; 2) the amplification factor and calculated moment were small, because the applied axial load was small relative to the Euler buckling load.

Bending moments that are caused by an axial load, P, acting on a member with mid-span deflection, δ, are often referred to as P-δ moments, or P-δ effects.

You Should Know

- Why do axial loads amplify deflections?
- One member has an initial deflection of 0.5 in. and $P_e = 1000$ kips; another member has an initial deflection of 0.25 in. and $P_e = 100$ kips; which member would have the greatest moment if a 75 kips axial load were applied to both?
- What is a P-δ effect?

10.6 The B_1 Factor

Many beam-columns will have P-δ moments. Consider the beam shown on the right that has a certain amount of deflection under a transverse load, w. If an axial load, P, were combined with the transverse load, the deflection would increase following the principles discussed in the previous section.

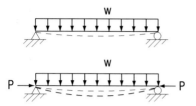

The bending moments caused by the transverse load are called first-order bending moments, because they are independent of the deformed geometry. The P-δ moments caused by the axial load are called *second-order* bending moments. The magnitudes of the second-order moments depend on the stiffness of the beam and how much it deflects under the transverse and axial loads.

Example 10.5 Computing Bending Moments Caused by Axial Loads

Compute the first-order and second-order moments for the W14×53 beam-column for Load Combination 5. What is the total bending moment at mid-span?

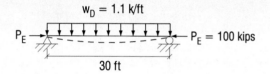

Step 1 - Calculate P and M from first-order analysis

The first-order P and M effects are simply:

$$M_D = \frac{w_D l^2}{8} = \frac{(1.1 \text{ k/ft})(30 \text{ ft})^2}{8} = 123.8 \text{ k-ft}$$

$$P_D = 0 \text{ kips}$$
$$M_E = 0 \text{ k-ft}$$
$$P_E = 100 \text{ kips}$$

Step 2 - Get first-order moment from Load Combination 5

M_{nt} and M_{lt} are the first-order moments that we obtain by using the load combinations. Using the rules from page 246 and the load factors from combination 5:

$$M_{nt} = 1.2M_D + 1.0M_E = 1.2(123.8 \text{ k-ft}) + 1.0(0) = 148.5 \text{ k-ft}$$

Note: All of the moment load effects contribute to M_{nt} because this is NOT a column in a moment frame (see rule 2).

We will need P_{nt} for the next step, so we'll compute it now while we're at it:

$$P_{nt} = 1.2P_D + 1.0P_E = 1.2(0) + 1.0(100 \text{ kips}) = 100 \text{ kips}$$

Step 3 - Compute the second-order moment

The beam will have $P - \delta$ moments because it deflects under the transverse load and there is an axial load applied. The maximum second-order moment occurs mid-span. In order to calculate it, we first need to compute the mid-span deflection after all the loads have been applied.

The deflection under only the factored transverse load is:

$$\delta_o = \frac{5w_u l^4}{384EI} = \frac{5[1.2 \times (1.1/12) \text{ k/in}](30 \times 12 \text{ in.})^4}{384(29000 \text{ ksi})(541 \text{in.}^4)} = 1.53 \text{ in.}$$

Example Continued

After the axial load is applied, the final deflection will be:

$$\delta_f = \delta_o \left[\frac{1}{1 - (P/P_e)} \right]$$

In the expression above, P is the factored axial force in the beam-column. The term P_e was computed for a 30 ft. long W14×53 beam in Example 10.4.

$$\delta_f = (1.53 \text{ in.}) \left[\frac{1}{1 - (100 \text{ kips}/1194 \text{ kips})} \right] = 1.67 \text{ in.}$$

Now the $P - \delta$ second-order moment at mid-span can be calculated:

$$M_{second-order} = P_{nt}\delta_f = (100 \text{ kips})(1.67 \text{ in.}) = 13.9 \text{ k-ft}$$

Step 4 - Get the total moment at mid-span

The total moment is obtained by adding the first-order and second-order moments:

$$M_r = M_{nt} + M_{second-order} = 148.5 \text{ k-ft} + 13.9 \text{ k-ft} = \mathbf{162.4} \text{ k-ft}$$

When computing beam-column demands, it is convenient to have an equation for the total moment, M_r, in terms of the first-order moment and an amplification factor. That is precisely what Eqn. A-8-1 in the Manual is. The amplification factor, B_1, accounts for P-δ second-order effects.

Study the Manual

Turn to Appendix 8 in the Specification and look at the equation for B_1 (page 16.1-238).

- How is this equation similar to the deflection amplification factor discussed in §10.5 of *Build With Steel*.

- What is the value for α when using LRFD?

The term C_m appears in the B_1 equation. C_m can be taken as 1.0 when there is transverse loading [see definition of C_m (b)]. It will be explained later.

- How is P_{e1} defined?

- How can P_r be estimated (see text at the end of the subsection, page 16.1-239)?

Finally, in looking at Eqn. A-8-3, note that B_1 must always be greater than 1. B_1 is intended to be an amplification factor; a value less than one would make it a de-amplification factor.

Demands

Example 10.6 Using an Amplification Factor to Get the Total Moment

Compute the total bending moment at mid-span for the W14×53 beam-column for Load Combination 5. Use an amplification factor to account for second-order effects.

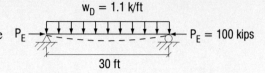

$w_D = 1.1$ k/ft
$P_E \rightarrow$ $\leftarrow P_E = 100$ kips
30 ft

Step 1 - Calculate P and M from first-order analysis

The first-order P and M effects are simply:

$$M_D = \frac{w_D l^2}{8} = \frac{(1.1 \text{ k/ft})(30 \text{ ft})^2}{8} = 123.8 \text{ k-ft}$$
$$P_D = 0 \text{ kips}$$
$$M_E = 0 \text{ k-ft}$$
$$P_E = 100 \text{ kips}$$

Step 2 - Get first-order effects from Load Combination 5

M_{nt}, M_{lt}, P_{nt}, and P_{lt} are the first-order effects that we obtain by using the load combinations. Using the rules from page 10.6 and the load factors from combination 5:

$$M_{nt} = 1.2 M_D + 1.0 M_E = 1.2(123.8 \text{ k-ft}) + 1.0(0) = 148.5 \text{ k-ft}$$

$$P_{nt} = 1.2 P_D + 1.0 P_E = 1.2(0) + 1.0(100 \text{ kips}) = 100 \text{ kips}$$

Step 3 - Compute the moment amplification factor

The equation for the total moment is:

$$M_r = B_1 M_{nt} + B_2 M_{lt}$$

We have not discussed B_2 yet, but it doesn't matter for this problem because $M_{lt} = 0$. The moment amplification factor, B_1, is calculated as:

$$B_1 = \frac{C_m}{1 - \alpha(P_r/P_{e1})} \qquad \text{(Eqn. C2-2)}$$
$$\alpha = 1.00 \qquad \text{(for LRFD)}$$
$$C_m = 1.00 \qquad \text{(for beam-column with transverse loading)}$$
$$P_r = P_{nt} + B_2 P_{lt} = 100 \text{ kips}$$
$$P_{e1} = \frac{\pi^2 EI}{(KL)^2} = \frac{\pi^2 (29000 \text{ ksi})(541 \text{ in.}^4)}{(30 \times 12 \text{ in.})^2} = 1194 \text{ kips}$$

So

$$B_1 = \frac{1.0}{1 - (1.0)[100 \text{ kips}/1194 \text{ kips}]} = 1.091$$

Step 4 - Get the total moment

The total moment is:

$$M_r = B_1 M_{nt} + B_2 M_{lt} = (1.091)(148.5 \text{ k-ft}) + 0 = \mathbf{162} \text{ k-ft}$$

Note that this is the same result as obtained in the previous example. Using a moment-amplification factor eliminates the need to compute the total deflection and the second-order moment.

10.7 The C_m Factor

Consider the three beam-columns shown below. Below each beam-column there are three moment diagrams. The first diagram (yellow) indicates the first-order moments in the beam-column. The second diagram (blue) indicates the second-order moments. Notice that the shape of the second-order moment diagram is always the same as the displaced shape of the member, since the second-order moment at any point is equal to the axial load multiplied by the displacement at that point. The last diagram for each beam-column (green) is the sum of the first and second-order moments. M_{nt} is used to designate the maximum first-order moment; M_r is used to designate the maximum total moment.

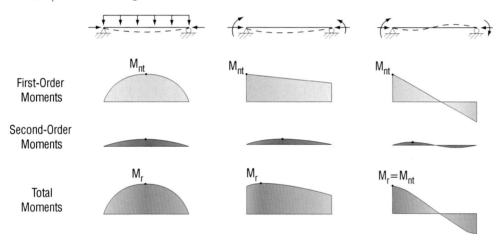

The beam-column on the left, is of the same kind as the ones considered in the previous two examples. Notice how the maximum first-order and maximum second-order moments occur at the same location (mid-span). It follows that when the first and second-order moments are combined, the maximum total moment will also occur at that location and will be equal in magnitude to the sum of the maximum first-order and maximum second-order moments.

For the other two beam-columns, the end moments cause something interesting to happen. In these cases, the maximum first-order and maximum second-order moments do not occur at the same location, and the maximum total moment will not be equal to the maximum first-order moment plus the maximum second-order moment. In fact, for the case on the right, when the first-order and second-order moments are combined, the maximum total moment is the same as the maximum first-order moment. The C_m factor that appears in Eqn. A-8-3 accounts for the effects of end moments on moment amplification.

Turn to the part of §8.2.1. of the Specification where C_m is defined (page 16.1-238).

- What is the equation given for C_m under definition (a)?

- By definition, which of the first-order end moments M_1 or M_2, is greatest in magnitude?

- By definition, how do you determine the sign of the ratio (M_1/M_2)?

Reverse curvature means that the deformed shaped of the member is like an S.

Read the definition (b) for C_m.

- For which of the three beam-columns on the previous page would this definition apply?

When C_m is taken as 1.0, either as calculated from definition (a) or as assumed in definition (b), it means that the first-order moments and second-order moments are maximum at the same location; therefore the moment amplification will be maximum.

Example 10.7 Computing Cm Factor

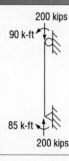

Compute C_m for the beam-column. The bending moments shown are first-order moments (M_{nt}) determined using a load combination.

Step 1 - Determine which definition to use

Since there is no transverse loading on the member, definition (i) applies.

Step 2 - Compute Cm

From definition (a):

$$C_m = 0.6 - 0.4(M_1/M_2)$$

For this member:

$$M_1/M_2 = -(85 \text{ k-ft}/90 \text{ k-ft}) = -0.944$$

The ratio is negative because the end moments put the member in single-curvature.

$$C_m = 0.6 - 0.4(M_1/M_2) = 0.6 - 0.4(-0.944) = \mathbf{0.978}$$

The next example illustrates how computing C_m fits into the bigger picture of computing amplified moments.

Example 10.8 Using Moment Amplification Factors with End Moments

A W14×53 column is 15 ft long and has the load effects shown. Compute the ultimate bending moment, taking into account second-order effects.

$M_D = 120$ k-ft
$M_L = 60$ k-ft
$P_D = 200$ kips
$P_L = 100$ kips

$M_D = 100$ k-ft
$M_L = 50$ k-ft
$P_D = 200$ kips
$P_L = 100$ kips

Step 1 - Get first-order effects from the critical load combination

By inspection, load combination 2 will govern. Factoring and combining the dead and live loads gives the effects shown to the right.

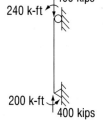

240 k-ft   400 kips

200 k-ft   400 kips

M_{nt} and P_{nt} are the maximum factored-and-combined effects from the dead and live loads:

$$M_{nt} = 1.2(120 \text{ k-ft}) + 1.6(60 \text{ k-ft}) = 240 \text{ k-ft}$$
$$P_{nt} = 1.2(200 \text{ kips}) + 1.6(100 \text{ kips}) = 400 \text{ kips}$$

Step 2 - Compute Cm

$$C_m = 0.6 - 0.4(M_1/M_2)$$
$$M_1/M_2 = (200 \text{ k-ft}/240 \text{ k-ft}) = 0.833$$

The ratio is positive because the end moments put the member into double curvature (displaced shape like an S).

$$C_m = 0.6 - 0.4(0.833) = 0.267$$

Step 3 - Compute the Euler buckling load about the axis that is bending

Assume that the column is oriented to resist moments about the strong axis.

$$P_{e1} = \frac{\pi^2 EI}{(KL)^2} = \frac{\pi^2 (29000 \text{ ksi})(541 \text{ in.}^4)}{(15 \times 12 \text{ in.})^2} = 4779 \text{ kips}$$

Step 4 - Compute the amplification factor

$$P_r = P_{nt} + B_2 P_{lt} = 400 \text{ kips} + 0 = 400 \text{ kips}$$
$$B_1 = \frac{C_m}{1 - (P_r/P_{e1})} \geq 1$$
$$B_1 = \frac{0.267}{1 - (400 \text{ kips}/4779 \text{ kips})} = 0.29 \geq 1$$
$$B_1 = 1$$

Notice that if the amplification factor is calculated to be less than 1.0, then it simply means there is no amplification and B_1 is taken as 1. It does not mean that the second-order effects reduce the maximum total moment.

Step 5 - Compute the ultimate moment

$$M_r = B_1 M_{nt} + B_2 M_{lt} = 1.0(240 \text{ k-ft}) + 0 = \mathbf{240} \text{ k-ft}$$

10.8 The B_2 Factor

The previous examples have considered members which have ends that do not translate relative to each other. The deflections that caused second-order effects were deflections of the member in between the joints. These deflections were designated with δ (right-top).

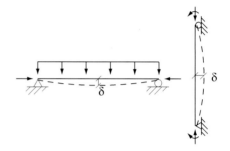

Columns in lateral force resisting frames have another type of deflection that needs to be considered. This is deflection of the joints relative to each other and is designated Δ.

Consider the columns shown in the figure to the right. The lateral load will cause first-order moments in the columns (indicated by the yellow moment diagrams). These moments result in a lateral translation (Δ_o) between the top and bottom of each column. First-order moments that cause lateral displacement of the ends of a member are designated M_{lt}.

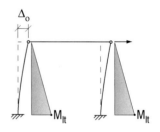

If axial loads are added to the system, at any location, they will cause second-order moments in the columns which will increase the deflection (Δ_f). Bending moments that are caused by an axial force, P, acting on a member with a relative joint displacement, Δ, are referred to as P-Δ moments, or P-Δ effects.

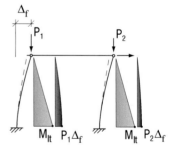

Just as the amplification factor B_1 accounts for P-δ effects, the amplification factor B_2 accounts for P-Δ effects.

The main differences between the equations for B_1 and B_2, are that the C_m factor is always 1.0 for B_2, and a sum of story vertical loads and buckling loads is used for B_2. The C_m factor is 1.0 because the maximum P-Δ moment always occurs at the same location as the maximum first-order moment, M_{lt}. The reason that entire story loads (P_{story}) and buckling loads ($P_{e\ story}$) are used is that axial loads anywhere in the system will influence the final deflection, Δ_f, which impacts the magnitude of the P-Δ moments for all members of the system. Similarly, the flexural stiffness of all the columns impacts Δ_f, which is why we also sum P_e.

Example 10.9 Using Moment Amplification Factors with End Moments

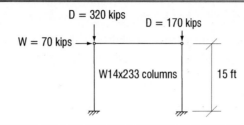

Compute the ultimate demands in the left column using load combination 4.

Step 1 - Calculate Ps and Ms from first-order analysis

The first-order effects in the left column are easily calculated in this case.

$$M_D = 0 \text{ k-ft}$$
$$P_D = 320 \text{ kips}$$

$$M_W = (35 \text{ kips})(15 \text{ ft}) = 525 \text{ k-ft}$$
$$P_W = 0 \text{ kips}$$

Step 2 - Sum first-order effects using load combination 4

M_{nt}, M_{lt}, P_{nt}, and P_{lt} are the first-order effects that we want to obtain using the load combination 4. Using the rules from page 10.6 and the load factors from combination 4:

$$M_{nt} = 1.2M_D = 0 \text{ k-ft}$$
$$M_{lt} = 1.0M_W = 1.0(525 \text{ k-ft}) = 525 \text{ k-ft}$$

$$P_{nt} = 1.2P_D = 1.2(320 \text{ kips}) = 384 \text{ kips}$$
$$P_{lt} = 1.0P_W = 0 \text{ kips}$$

Step 3 - Compute the amplification factor

The equation for the total moment is:

$$M_r = B_1 M_{nt} + B_2 M_{lt}$$

B_1 does not need to be calculated since $M_{nt} = 0$. B_2 is calculated as:

$$B_2 = \frac{1}{1 - \alpha P_{story}/P_{estory}} \qquad \text{(Eqn.A-8-6)}$$
$$\alpha = 1.00 \qquad \text{(for LRFD)}$$

We calculate P_{story} by summing the factored axial forces in all the columns.

$$P_{story} = 1.2(320 \text{ kips}) + 1.2(170 \text{ kips}) = 588 \text{ kips}$$

continued on next page

Example Continued

Next we calculate P_{estory} by summing the buckling loads, P_e, of all the columns in the frame. Care must be taken when doing this calculation. By definition, the buckling loads for computing P_{estory} are those determined by sidesway buckling analysis - meaning that the KL used when computing P_e must be the effective length assuming a sidesway buckling mode.

$$P_{estory} = 2\left[\frac{\pi^2 EI}{(KL)^2}\right] = 2\left[\frac{\pi^2 (29000 \text{ ksi})(3010 \text{ in.}^4)}{[(2.1)(15 \times 12 \text{ in.})]^2}\right] = 12047 \text{ kips}$$

Note: It is not conservative to take $K = 1.0$ when considering frame translation. In the calculation above, a value of 2.1 was used for K [see Case (e) of Table C-A-7.1 on page 16.1-511] since this is sidesway buckling analysis.

$$B_2 = \frac{1.0}{1 - (1.0)(588 \text{ kips})/(12047 \text{ kips})} = 1.05$$

Step 4 - Get the ultimate demands for the left column

$$M_r = B_1 M_{nt} + B_2 M_{lt} = 0 + (1.05)(525 \text{ k-ft}) = \mathbf{551} \text{ k-ft}$$
$$P_r = P_{nt} + B_2 P_{lt} = (384 \text{ kips}) + (1.05)(0) = \mathbf{384} \text{ kips}$$

You Should Know

- What is the difference between a δ deflection and a Δ deflection?
- Is B_2 easier or more difficult to calculate that B_1?
- Why will K always be greater than 1.0 when calculating P_e to be used to get $P_{e\,story}$?

10.9 Moment Frame Column Demands

The previous sections have covered all of the things that are required for computing demands in beam-columns. This section on demands will provide one final example to demonstrate how everything comes together. This example illustrates the most time consuming type of beam-column demand problem - a column in a moment resisting frame.

Example 10.10 Computing Demands in a Moment Frame Column

Compute the demands M_r and P_r for the critical column under load combination 4.

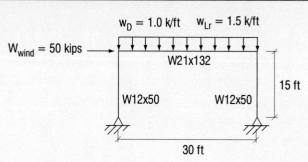

Example Continued

Step 1 - Calculate Ps and Ms from first-order analysis

The first-order effects need to be determined for each different type of load: dead, live, and wind. Since the frame is indeterminate, the analysis will be done using the stiffness method.

Under the dead load only, the member free-body diagrams are:

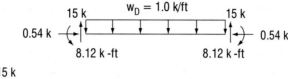

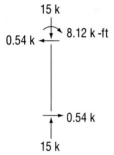
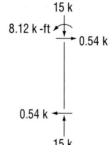

For the right column:

$$M_D = 8.12 \text{ k-ft}$$
$$P_D = 15 \text{ kips}$$

And under the live loads only, the member free-body diagrams are:

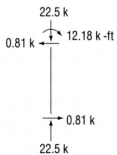
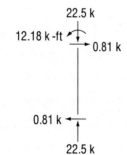

For the right column:

$$M_L = 12.18 \text{ k-ft}$$
$$P_L = 22.5 \text{ kips}$$

continued on next page

Finally, under the wind load only the member free-body diagrams are:

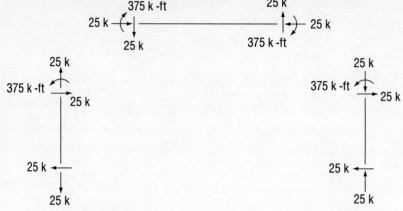

Observe that the right column is critical because the effects from the dead, live, and wind loads all act in the same directions for the right column.

$M_W = 375$ k-ft

$P_W = 25$ kips

Step 2 - Sum first-order effects using load combination 4

M_{nt}, M_{lt}, P_{nt}, and P_{lt} are the first-order effects that we want to get for the right column. Using the rules from page 246 and the load factors from combination 4:

$M_{nt} = 1.2M_D + 0.5M_L = 1.2(8.12 \text{ k-ft}) + 0.5(12.18 \text{ k-ft}) = \mathbf{15.8}$ k-ft

$M_{lt} = 1.0M_W = 1.0(375 \text{ k-ft}) = \mathbf{375}$ k-ft

$P_{nt} = 1.2P_D + 0.5P_L = 1.2(15 \text{ kips}) + 0.5(22.5 \text{ kips}) = \mathbf{29.3}$ kips

$P_{lt} = 1.0P_W = 1.0(25 \text{ kips}) = \mathbf{25}$ kips

Step 3 - Compute amplification factors

In this step we will compute the amplification factors B_1 and B_2. There are several things that go into the formulas for each, so there will be a number of other calculations. We actually need to start with B_2 because it is used to compute P_r which is required to compute B_1.

$$B_2 = \frac{1}{1 - (\alpha P_{story}/P_{estory})}$$

P_{story} is the sum of the factored effects in all the columns:

$$P_{story} = 2P_{nt} = 2(29.3 \text{ kips}) = 58.6 \text{ kips}$$

P_{estory} is the sum of P_e for the columns in the frame considering sidesway buckling. P_e for one column is calculated using a K factor of 2.0 [see Case (f) of Table C-A-7.1, recommended design value]:

$$P_e = \frac{\pi^2 (29000 \text{ ksi})(391 \text{ in.}^4)}{[2.0(15 \times 12 \text{ in.})]^2} = 862.6 \text{ kips}$$

$$P_{estory} = 2P_e = 2(862.6 \text{ kips}) = 1725 \text{ kips}$$

$$B_2 = \frac{1}{1 - (1.0)(58.6 \text{ kips})/(1725 \text{ kips})]} = 1.035$$

Example Continued

Now for B_1

$$B_1 = \frac{C_m}{1 - (P_r/P_{e1})} \geq 1$$

$$C_m = 0.6 - 0.4(M_1/M_2) = 0.6 - 0.4(0) = 0.6$$

$$P_r = P_{nt} + B_2 P_{lt} = 29.3 \text{ kips} + (1.035)(25 \text{ kips}) = 55.2 \text{ kips}$$

P_{e1} is calculated assuming no lateral translation (by definition) so $K = 1.0$:

$$P_{e1} = \frac{\pi^2 (29000 \text{ ksi})(391 \text{ in.}^4)}{[1.0(15 \times 12 \text{ in.})]^2} = 3450.6 \text{ kips}$$

$$B_1 = \frac{0.6}{1 - (55.2 \text{ kips}/3450.6 \text{ kips})} = 0.61 \geq 1$$

But it can't be less than 1 so:

$$B_1 = 1.0$$

Step 4 - Compute the ultimate load effects

Once the amplification factors have been calculated, all that remains is to apply them to compute the ultimate load effects.

$$M_r = B_1 M_{nt} + B_2 M_{lt}$$
$$M_r = (1.0)(15.8 \text{ k-ft}) + (1.035)(375 \text{ k-ft}) = \mathbf{404} \text{ k-ft}$$

$$P_r = \mathbf{55.2} \text{ kips}$$

You Should Know

- If Example 10.10 had been done using load combination 2, what would have been the values for M_{lt} and P_{lt}?
- What would have been the values for M_{nt}, M_{lt}, P_{nt}, and P_{lt} for the **beam** in Example 10.10 (using load combination 4)?

    M_{nt}

    M_{lt}

    P_{nt}

    P_{lt}

- Why is B_1 usually equal to 1.0 for columns in moment-resisting frames?

This page blank.

10.10 Interaction Equations

In previous chapters, we determined the capacities of members subject to axial loads *or* bending. The capacities were deemed adequate if they were greater than the demands. For example:

$$P_u \leq \phi_c P_n \qquad \text{or} \qquad M_u \leq \phi_b M_n.$$

Now in preparation for the discussion that follows, consider the following two things. First, the flexural demand-capacity equation could be written more explicitly for flexure about the strong and weak axes:

$$M_{ux} \leq \phi_b M_{nx} \qquad \text{and} \qquad M_{uy} \leq \phi_b M_{ny}$$

Second, we can re-write the demand-capacity equations in the following way, by dividing both sides by the capacity:

$$\frac{P_u}{\phi_c P_n} \leq 1 \qquad \text{and} \qquad \frac{M_{ux}}{\phi_b M_{nx}} \leq 1 \qquad \text{and} \qquad \frac{M_{uy}}{\phi_b M_{ny}} \leq 1$$

Now, the three equations above are valid for beams or columns, but they are not valid for beam-columns because the axial load effects and flexural load effects have some interaction. In other words, the flexural effects will impact the ability of a cross-section to carry axial loads; and the axial load will impact the ability of the cross-section to carry flexural loads.

An *interaction equation*, combines the three equations above, but rather than the demand-capacity ratio for *each effect* needing to be less than 1, the *sum* of the demand-capacity ratios needs to be less than 1. This approach is reasonable, but in order to prevent it from being overly conservative, additional factors (equal or less than 1.0) are added as indicated in the general formula below.

$$(\text{axial factor})\left(\frac{P_u}{\phi_c P_n}\right) + (\text{flexural factor})\left(\frac{M_{ux}}{\phi_b M_{nx}} + \frac{M_{uy}}{\phi_b M_{ny}}\right) \leq 1$$

The equation above is the general form of the beam-column interaction equation. There are two specific forms of the beam-column interaction equation given in the Specification.

Study the Manual

Turn to Chapter H of the Specification (page 16.1-73) and read the text prior to H1.

Read §H1.1 including the part that continues on to page 16.1-74. Notice there are two interaction equations given.

- What is the criteria for determining which interaction equation will apply?

As you look at the interaction equations, you will notice that the notation is somewhat different than we used in the general interaction equation above. The terms P_r and M_r are used for demands, as was explained in the previous sections on beam-column demands. The terms P_c, M_{cx}, and M_{cy} are general capacity terms with specific forms depending on whether you are using LRFD or ASD design.

Look at the section on page 16.1-74 with the heading "For design according to Section B3.3 (LRFD)." This is where the definitions of P_c and M_c are given.

- For LRFD design, what is P_c?

The terms M_{cx} and M_{cy} are equal to $\phi_b M_{nx}$ and $\phi_b M_{ny}$ for LRFD design. The term $\phi_b M_{nx}$ is simply the factored flexural capacity of a beam about its strong axis, and the term $\phi_b M_{ny}$ is the factored flexural capacity about the weak-axis.

If a particular shape satisfies the beam-column interaction equations (if the left side of the equation is less than or equal to one), that means the demand-capacity ratio is less than 1.0 and the member is adequate (the capacity is greater than the demand). The following example illustrates how interactions equations are applied.

Example 10.11 Using Beam-Column Interaction Equations

A W14×82 member is to be checked as a beam-column.
The demands on the member are:

$P_r = 90$ kips, and $M_r = 250$ k-ft.

The capacities of the W14×82 are:

$\phi P_n = 257$ and $\phi M_{nx} = 521$ k-ft.

Does the W14×82 have adequate capacity for the demands?

Step 1 - Identify the applicable interaction equation

In order to determine which interaction equation applies, we must compute the ratio P_r/P_c. Now P_r is simply the factored axial load effect (the previous sections have discussed how to compute P_r).

$P_r = 90$ kips (given)

P_c is the compression capacity of the member. For LRFD design P_c is (by definition) $\phi_c P_n$.

$P_c = \phi_c P_n = 257$ kips (given)

so

$$\frac{P_r}{P_c} = \frac{P_r}{\phi_c P_n} = \frac{90 \text{ kips}}{257 \text{ kips}} = 0.35$$

Since the ratio is greater than 0.2, Eqn H1-1a will apply.

Step 2 - Use the interaction equation

The left side of Eqn H1-1a can be written in LRFD terms as:

$$\frac{P_r}{P_c} + \frac{8}{9}\left(\frac{M_{rx}}{M_{cx}} + \frac{M_{ry}}{M_{cy}}\right) = \frac{P_r}{\phi_c P_n} + \frac{8}{9}\left(\frac{M_{rx}}{\phi_b M_{nx}} + \frac{M_{ry}}{\phi_b M_{ny}}\right)$$

Now all we need to do is plug in the given values for the various terms. In this example, a value for M_r was given, but there was no indication whether it was about the x- or y-axis. It is reasonable to assume the bending is about the strong axis so the given M_r is M_{rx}, and $M_{ry} = 0$ (making $\phi_b M_{ny}$ irrelevant). Substituting in the given values for the other terms yields:

$$\frac{90 \text{ kips}}{257 \text{ kips}} + \frac{8}{9}\left(\frac{250 \text{ k-ft}}{521 \text{ k-ft}} + 0\right) = 0.35 + 0.42 = 0.78 \text{ (<1, OK)}$$

The interaction equation gives a result less than 1.0, meaning that the capacity exceeds the demand. **The W14×82 is adequate** for the beam-column.

In the example above, checking the interaction equation was simple because all the pertinent inputs were given. In practice, determining the inputs is what takes the most time.

Example 10.12 Checking Capacity of Beam-Columns

Are the columns adequate for the indicated loads?

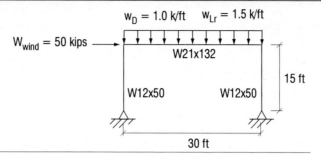

Step 1 - Determine the factored load effects

By far, the most time-consuming task in beam-column checks is computing the factored demands, P_r and M_r (usually M_{rx}). For the columns in the given frame, these calculations were performed in Example 10.10 (and took nearly four pages).

$P_r = 55.2$ kips (from Example 10.10)
$M_{rx} = 404$ k-ft (from Example 10.10)
$M_{ry} = 0$ k-ft (no out-of-plane loads indicated)

Step 2 - Determine the column compression capacity

The methods for determing the compression capacity for a wide flange shape were covered in Chapter 6. The fastest way to determine $\phi_c P_n$ for a wide-flange is to look it up in Table 4-1.

For a W12×50 with $KL_x = KL_y = 15$ ft:

$\phi_c P_n = 355$ kips

Step 3 - Determine the column flexural capacity

The methods for determing the flexural capacity for a wide-flange shape were covered in Chapter 8. The unbraced length of the column in this example is 15 ft. The capacity of the column (if $C_b = 1.0$) can be looked up in Table 3-10. For a W12×50 with $L_b = 15$ ft (page 3-128):

$\phi_b M_{n,Cb=1} = 221$ k-ft

Since the moment diagram for the member is not uniform, C_b will be greater than 1.0 and the moment capacity read from the Table will be adjusted upward. For an unbraced span with a triangular moment distribution, $C_b = 1.67$ (refer to Table 3-1 and Example 8.24):

$\phi_b M_n = C_b(\phi_b M_{n,Cb=1}) \le \phi_b M_p$
$\phi_b M_n = (1.67)(221\text{k-ft}) = 369$ k-ft ≤ 270 k-ft
$\phi_b M_n = 270$ k-ft (plastic limit state governs rather than LTB)

Step 4 - Use the appropriate interaction equation

With the input parameters determined in the previous steps, we are ready to check the interaction equation.

$$\frac{P_r}{P_c} = \frac{P_r}{\phi_c P_n} = \frac{55.2 \text{ kips}}{355 \text{ kips}} = 0.16$$

Since the ratio is less than 0.2, Eqn H1-1b will apply.

continued on next page

Example Continued

In LRFD form, Eqn. H1-1b is:

$$\frac{P_r}{2\phi_c P_n} + \left(\frac{M_{rx}}{\phi_b M_{nx}} + \frac{M_{ry}}{\phi_b M_{ny}}\right) \leq 1$$

Substituting values from the previous steps we have:

$$\frac{55.2 \text{ kips}}{2(355 \text{ kips})} + \left(\frac{404 \text{ k-ft}}{270 \text{ k-ft}} + 0\right) = 0.078 + 1.5 = 1.58 \ (>1, \text{ No Good})$$

The interaction equation gives a result greater than 1.0, meaning that the demand exceeds the capacity. **The W12×50 is not adequate** for the beam-column.

Note: we could have seen that the W12×50 would not work immediately after computing the flexural capacity. If the flexural capacity is less than the flexural demand, then the demand-capacity ratio for flexural effects alone will be above 1. Adding in the demand-capacity ratio for axial effects will only make things worse.

You Should Know

- Why do we need an interaction equation to check beam-column capacity?
- How do you know which interaction equation applies?
- What is the difference between the two interaction equations?

10.11 Capacity Table

The previous example showed how Tables 4-1 and 3-10 were used to get compression and flexural capacities required to check the beam-column capacity. Another table is provided in the Manual that is designed to provide the same information but in a way that is more convenient for beam-column checks.

Study the Manual

Turn to page 6-3 in the Manual and read the information under the heading "Table 6-1. W-Shapes in Combined Flexure and Axial Force."

- How is the value for p calculated in Table 6-1? What are the units?

- How is the value for b_x calculated in Table 6-1? What are the units?

The parameters p, b_x, and b_y are defined, such that the interaction equation H1-1a can check rapidly after they have been determined. Read the information on page 6-3 under the heading "Combined Flexure and Compression."

- How does Eqn 6-1 relate to Eqn H1-1a?

Study the Manual

Turn to Table 6-1 in the Manual (page 6-7). In essence, Table 6-1 is a combination of the information in Tables 4-1 and 3-10, packaged in a form that is convenient for checking interaction equations.

Table 6-1 lists values for p, b_x, and b_y for shapes that are commonly used for beam-columns. The values of p, b_x, and b_y can then be used to quickly check the interaction equations. The columns in the table give p as a function of the effective length (KL_y) and b_x as a function of the unbraced length (L_b). You enter in from the left of the table with either KL_y OR L_b, depending on whether you are looking up p or b_x.

- For a W44×335 with KL_y = 20 ft, what is p?

- For a W44×335 with L_b = 15 ft, what is b_x?

The value for b_y is not a function of unbraced length (since the plastic limit state always governs for bending about the weak-axis, regardless of the beam length). It is listed at the bottom of the table with "Other Constants and Properties."

- For a W44×335 with L_b = 15 ft, what is b_y?

Notice that the values listed in the table are not really p, b_x and b_y.

Rather, they are $p \times 10^3$, $b_x \times 10^3$, and $b_y \times 10^3$. So the answer to the questions above are p = 0.000319 kips⁻¹, b_x = 0.000152 k-ft⁻¹, and b_y = 0.001 k-ft⁻¹.

Example 10.13 Checking Capacity of Beam-Columns Using Table 6-1

Does a W14×48 (KL_y = 30 ft, L_b = 10 ft, and C_b = 1) have adequate capacity to resist the following load effects: P_r = 37 kips, and M_r = 197 k-ft (x-axis)? Use Table 6-1.

Step 1 - Look up p and b_x in Table 6-1

For the W14×48 the following values are read from Table 6-1:

$$p \times 10^3 = 11.2 \text{ kips}^{-1} \text{ (for } KL_y = 30 \text{ ft)}$$
$$b_x \times 10^3 = 3.30 \text{ (kip-ft)}^{-1} \text{ (for } L_b = 10 \text{ ft, } C_b=1)$$

Now p and b_x are obtained by multiplying the above values by 10^{-3}:

$$p = 0.0112 \text{ kips}^{-1}$$
$$b_x = 0.0033 \text{ (kip-ft)}^{-1}$$

Step 2 - Check which interaction equation will apply

To check which interaction equation applies, we multiply p by P_r.

$$pP_r = (0.0112\text{kips}^{-1})(37 \text{ kips}) = 0.414 \text{ kips } (>0.20)$$

This **is** $P_r/\phi_c P_n$. Equation H1-1a applies, and p and b_x can be used directly.

Step 3 - Check the interaction equation

Equation H1-1a is checked by:

$$pP_r + b_x M_{rx} = (0.0112\text{kips}^{-1})(37 \text{ kips}) + (0.0033\text{kip-ft}^{-1})(197 \text{ kip-ft})$$
$$= 0.414 + 0.650 = 1.06 \ (>1.0, \text{ No Good})$$

The W14×48 does not have adequate capacity.

The previous example showed how Table 6-1 could be used when H1-1a was the appropriate interaction equation and when $C_b = 1$. The values for p, b_x, and b_y from Table 6-1 can still be used if H1-1b applies or $C_b > 1$ but some modifications are required.

Study the Manual

Turn to page 6-3 in the Manual and look at Eqn. 6-2.

- When does Eqn. 6-2 apply?

- What is the difference between Eqn. 6-2 and Eqn. 6-1? How does it relate to the difference between Eqn. H1-1a and Eqn. H1-1b?

Read the information at the bottom of page 6-4 under the heading "Determination of b_x when $C_b > 1$."

- What is b_{xmin}? Where do you look it up?

- In what ways is the procedure given by Eqn. 6-5 similar to what was done in Step 3 of Example 10.12?

Example 10.14 Checking the Capacity of Beam-Columns Using Table 6-1

Does a W14×48 ($KL_y = 20$ ft, $L_b = 10$ ft, and $C_b = 1.3$) have adequate capacity to resist the following load effects: $P_r = 35$ kips, and $M_r = 197$ k-ft (x-axis). Use Table 6-1.

Step 1 - Look up p and b_x in Table 6-1

For the W14×48 the following values are read from Table 6-1:

$$p \times 10^3 = 4.96 \text{ kips}^{-1} \text{ (for } KL_y = 20 \text{ ft)}$$
$$b_{x(C_b=1.0)} \times 10^3 = 3.30 \text{ (kip-ft)}^{-1} \text{ (for } L_b = 10 \text{ ft, } C_b=1)$$

Now p and $b_{x(C_b=1.0)}$ are obtained by multiplying the above values by 10^{-3}:

$$p = 0.00496 \text{ kips}^{-1}$$
$$b_{x(C_b=1.0)} = 0.0033 \text{ (kip-ft)}^{-1}$$

Step 2 - Check which interaction equation will apply

To check which interaction equation applies, we multiply p by P_r.

$$pP_r = (0.00496 \text{ kips}^{-1})(35 \text{ kips}) = 0.174 \text{ kips } (<0.20)$$

This is $P_r/\phi_c P_n$. Equation H1-1b applies so the interaction is checked using Eqn 6-2.

Step 3 - Calculate bx

Since $C_b > 1$, Eqn. 6-5 is used to determine $b_{x(C_b>1.0)}$.

$$b_{x(C_b>1.0)} = \frac{b_{x(C_b=1.0)}}{C_b} \geq b_{xmin}$$

The value for b_{xmin} is read from Table 6-1 at $L_b = 0$ ft.

$$b_{xmin} = 0.00302$$

Example Continued

so

$$b_{x(C_b>1.0)} = \frac{0.0033}{1.3} \geq 0.00302$$
$$b_{x(C_b>1.0)} = 0.00254 \geq 0.00302$$
$$b_{x(C_b>1.0)} = 0.00302$$

Step 4 - Check the interaction equation

Equation H1-1b is checked using Eqn 6-2:

$$(\frac{1}{2})pP_r + (\frac{9}{8})b_xM_{rx} =$$
$$(\frac{1}{2})(0.00496 \text{ kips}^{-1})(35 \text{ kips}) + (\frac{9}{8})(0.00302 \text{ kip-ft}^{-1})(197 \text{ kip-ft}) =$$
$$0.0868 + 0.669 = 0.76 \ (<1.0, \text{ OK})$$

The W14×48 does have adequate capacity.

This concludes the discussion on beam-column capacity. In retrospect, we only really covered one new idea (interaction equations) and one new table (Table 6-1). The next section addresses beam-column design.

You Should Know

- Why is there a beam-column table, if compression and flexural capacities can be looked up in other tables?
- Which interaction equation is the default for the table values?
- What value of C_b is assumed in the tabulated values of b_x?
- How is b_x adjusted if $C_b > 1$?
- How can Table 6-1 be used if H1-1b governs?

10.12 Design

Now that you know how to compute demands and capacities for beam-columns, we are ready to discuss design. Recall that the general steps for design are:

1. Compute demands.
2. Pick a shape to try.
3. Compute the capacity of the shape and compare with demands.
4. Finalize the design or iterate to find a better design.

The steps above will not work for beam-column design because the demands depend on the shape (Step 2 would have to be performed prior to Step 1). There are two reasons why beam-column demands depend on the shape. First, beam-columns are often found in indeterminate structures, where the demands (load effects) cannot be computed until after shapes have been selected. Second, beam-column demands depend on second-order effects, which cannot be calculated until after the shape is known.

A basic strategy in beam-column design is to begin with approximate demands, find a shape that will probably work, and then calculate precise demands later. The steps are:

1. Estimate demands.
2. Pick a shape to try.
3. Check interaction equation using approximate demands.
4. Verify the shape, or iterate to find a better one.

The following examples will illustrate how these steps are applied for beam-column design.

Example 10.15 Designing a Beam-Column

Find a shape that will work as the "beam" in the frame. The top and bottom flanges of the beam are braced at the third points so that KL_y=10 ft and L_b=10 ft.

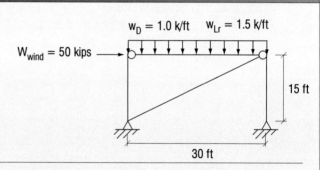

$w_D = 1.0$ k/ft $w_{Lr} = 1.5$ k/ft

$W_{wind} = 50$ kips

15 ft

30 ft

Step 1 - Estimate demands

The first step in beam-column design is to estimate the demands on the member. This is done by, first, calculating axial load effects and bending moments from first-order analysis; second, estimating which load combination will govern; and finally, estimating P_r and M_r by assuming the influence of the second-order effects.

1a - Get P and M from first-order analysis

The load effects on the "beam" from first-order analysis are:

$$M_D = \frac{w_D l^2}{8} = \frac{(1.0 \text{ k/ft})(30 \text{ ft})^2}{8} = 112.5 \text{ k-ft} \qquad P_D = 0 \text{ kips}$$

$$M_{Lr} = \frac{w_{Lr} l^2}{8} = \frac{(1.5 \text{ k/ft})(30 \text{ ft})^2}{8} = 168.8 \text{ k-ft} \qquad P_{Lr} = 0 \text{ kips}$$

$$M_W = 0 \text{ k-ft} \qquad P_W = 50 \text{ kips}$$

Example Continued

1b - Guess the governing load combination

The member we are designing has load effects from dead loads (D), roof live loads (L_r), and wind loads (W). By inspection, either load combo 3 or load combo 4 will govern. We will compute M_{nt} and P_{nt} for each combination to help us guess which might govern.

Load Combination 3
$$M_{nt} = 1.2M_D + 1.6M_{Lr} + 0.5M_W$$
$$= (1.2)(112.5 \text{ k-ft}) + (1.6)(168.8 \text{ k-ft}) + 0 = \textbf{405} \text{ k-ft}$$
$$P_{nt} = 1.2P_D + 1.6P_{Lr} + 0.5P_W = 0 + 0 + 0.5(50 \text{ kips}) = \textbf{25} \text{ kips}$$

Load Combination 4
$$M_{nt} = 1.2M_D + 1.0M_W + 0.5M_{Lr}$$
$$= 1.2(112.5 \text{ k-ft}) + 1.0(0) + 0.5(168.8 \text{ k-ft}) = \textbf{219.4} \text{ k-ft}$$
$$P_{nt} = 1.2P_D + 1.0P_W + 0.5P_{Lr} = 1.2(0) + 1.0(50 \text{ kips}) + 0.5(0) = \textbf{50} \text{ kips}$$

It is not obvious which will govern because combo 3 gives the highest moment and combo 4 gives the highest axial force. Since the member seems more like a beam, than a column, we might guess that combo 3 (which has the highest moment) will govern. We will proceed by assuming combo 3 governs (and check that assumption later).

1c - Estimate P_r and M_r by assuming the influence of second order effects

P_r and M_r are computed using Eqns. A-8-1 and A-8-2.
$$M_r = B_1 M_{nt} + B_2 M_{lt}$$
$$P_r = P_{nt} + B_2 P_{lt}$$
At this point, we can compute P_r exactly since we know P_{nt}, and $P_{lt} = 0$.

$$P_r = P_{nt} = \textbf{25} \text{ kips (assuming load combo 3)}$$

We cannot compute M_r because we don't know B_1 (and cannot know it until after we pick a shape). We will proceed by estimating B_1. In a previous example, B_1 turned out to be 1.09. For this problem let's estimate it will be around 1.10.
$$M_{r,est} = B_{1,est} M_{nt} = (1.10)(405 \text{ k-ft}) = \textbf{446} \text{ k-ft } (M_{nt} \text{ from combo 3})$$

Step 2 - Pick a shape to try

Now that we have an estimate of the demands, we can pick a shape to try. The member we are designing is more like a beam than a column so it is helpful to turn to the beam tables to get a rough idea of what shapes might be reasonable.

We need to pick a shape with flexural capacity somewhat greater than 446 k-ft, because some of the flexural capacity will be lost due to the axial load effects.

From Table 3-10 (page 3-122) we can identify a few shapes that have a flexural capacity of at least 446 k-ft for an unbraced length of 10 ft.

W12×62	W14×74	W16×67
W21×62	W18×71	W10×100
W14×82	W21×68	W16×77

continued on next page

Example Continued

Some of the above shapes are better suited for beam-columns than others. The deeper shapes (W18 and W21) may not be good picks because they will have a low axial capacity. The shallower shapes (W10, W12) seem a little too shallow for a 30 ft span, although they might work. The W14 and W16 shapes are the best bets, although it is not obvious which of those is the best.

We will try the **W16×67** and see if it works.

Step 3 - Check interaction equation using approximate demands

We can check the W16×67 using Table 6-1 (page 6-60).

For KL_y=10 ft.

$$p = 0.00135 \text{ kips}^{-1}$$

For L_b=10 ft.

$$b_x = 0.00188 \text{ k-ft}^{-1}$$

This value of b_x assumes C_b=1.0. No adjustment is necessary for this example since C_b is essentially 1.0 for the center unbraced span of the beam (see Table 3-1, uniform load on beam with restraints at third points).

We can determine which interaction equation applies by looking at pP_r.

$$pP_r = (0.00135 \text{ kips}^{-1})(25 \text{ kips}) = 0.034 \ (<0.20 \text{ so H1-1b will govern}).$$

Checking the interaction equation using Eqn. 6-2 and the approximate demands gives:

$$\left(\frac{1}{2}\right)pP_r + \left(\frac{9}{8}\right)b_xM_{rx} =$$

$$\left(\frac{1}{2}\right)(0.00135 \text{ kips}^{-1})(25 \text{ kips}) + \left(\frac{9}{8}\right)(0.00188 \text{ k-ft}^{-1})(446 \text{ k-ft}) =$$

$$0.0168 + 0.943 = 0.96 \ (<1.0)$$

This preliminary check, with our estimated demands, suggests that the W16×67 has adequate capacity. If the check had suggested insufficient capacity, we would have gone back to Step 2 and selected a different shape to try.

Step 4 - Verify the shape or iterate to find a better one

To get to this point we made two assumptions. First, we assumed that load combo 3 governed. Second we assumed that B_1 was 1.1. We need to verify both assumptions before we can finalize the design.

We can verify that load combo 4 does not govern by checking the interaction equation using P_r and M_r based on load combo 4 :

$$\left(\frac{1}{2}\right)(0.00135 \text{ kips}^{-1})(50 \text{ kips}) + \left(\frac{9}{8}\right)(0.00188 \text{ k-ft}^{-1})[(1.1)(219.4 \text{ k-ft})] =$$

$$0.034 + 0.51 = 0.54 \ (<0.96, \text{ combo 4 does not govern})$$

With a shape selected we can also calculate the exact value for B_1.

Example Continued

$$B_1 = \frac{C_m}{1 - \alpha(P_r/P_{e1})} \qquad \text{(Eqn. C2-2)}$$

$\alpha = 1.00$ (for LRFD)

$C_m = 1.00$ (for beam-column with transverse loading)

$P_r = 25$ kips (since load combo 3 governs)

Extra care must be taken when computing P_{e1}. Recall from Section 10.6 of *Build With Steel* that P_{e1} is the Euler buckling load for the member with respect to the axis of flexural bending. For the beam in this example, the dead and live loads are causing bending about the strong axis of the beam. Therefore, when computing P_{e1}, we need to use the moment of inertia for the x-axis. The other thing to be careful about is the effective length. In this problem the beam is restrained out-of-plane at the third points, but in-plane the only restraints are at the ends. Since there are no mid-span restraints against strong-axis bending, KL is 30 feet when computing P_{e1}.

$$P_{e1} = \frac{\pi^2 EI}{(KL)^2} = \frac{\pi^2 (29000 \text{ ksi})(954 \text{ in.}^4)}{(30 \times 12 \text{ in.})^2} = 2105 \text{ kips}$$

so

$$B_1 = \frac{1.0}{1 - (1.0)[25 \text{ kips}/2105 \text{ kips}]} = 1.012$$

Since this is less than the value assumed in Step 1, our shape will still work. The calculations below simply show the interaction equation using the actual (not estimated) demands.

$$M_r = B_1 M_{nt} = (1.012)(405 \text{ k-ft}) = 410 \text{ k-ft}$$
$$(\frac{1}{2})(0.00135 \text{ kips}^{-1})(25 \text{ kips}) + (\frac{9}{8})(0.00188 \text{ kip-ft}^{-1})(410 \text{ kip-ft}) =$$
$$0.0168 + 0.867 = 0.88 \ (<1.0, \text{ OK})$$

We have demonstrated that the W16×67 works for the critical load combination and the calculated value for B_1.

Use **W16×67**.

The next example (begining on the following page) is the more challenging case of a column in a moment resisting frame. Notice how the same steps are applied, but more work is required for the analysis.

Example 10.16 Designing a Beam-Column

Find a shape that will work for the columns in the frame. For side-sway buckling, $KL_x = 27$ ft.; for no sidesway $KL_x = KL_y = L_b = 13$ ft.

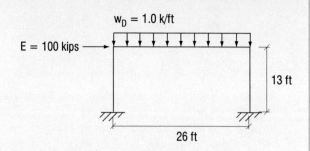

Step 1 - Estimate demands

The first step in beam-column design is to estimate the demands on the member. This is done by first estimating axial load effects and bending moments from first-order analysis; second, estimating which load combination will govern; and finally, estimating P_r and M_r by assuming the influence of the second-order effects.

1a - Estimate P and M from first-order analysis

Since the system is indeterminate, the load effects from the dead and earthquake loads cannot be determined using the stiffness method unless the member sizes are known. To get things started, we need to assume something about the *relative* stiffness of the beams and columns in the frames. If we assume the moment of inertia is the same for the beams and columns ($I_b = I_c$) we can use the stiffness method to determine the member free-body diagrams under the dead loads:

The dead load effects for all members are indicated below:

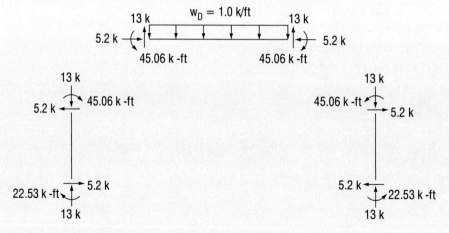

For the right column:

$$M_D = 75.12 \text{ k-ft} \qquad P_D = 13 \text{ kips}$$

Example Continued

Under only the earthquake loads the member free-body diagrams are:

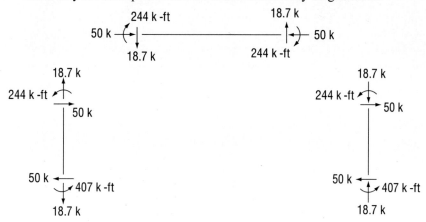

For the right column:

$$M_E = 407 \text{ k-ft} \qquad P_E = 18.7 \text{ kips}$$

1b - Determine the governing load combination

The column we are trying to size has load effects from dead loads (D) and earthquake loads (E). By inspection, load combo 5 will govern for the right column in the frame since the dead and earthquake axial loads both cause compression and the moments are additive.

We will determine M_{nt}, M_{lt}, P_{nt}, and P_{lt} using load combo 5. Recall that the dead load effects contribute to M_{nt} and P_{nt} because they (alone) do not cause the ends of the column to translate relative to each other. However, the earthquake load effects contribute M_{lt} and P_{lt} because they do cause the column ends to translate relative to each other. Finally, notice by inspection that the maximum moment under the combined loads will be at the bottom of the column, so we will get M_{nt} and M_{lt} for that location.

Load Combination 5
$$M_{nt} = 1.2M_D = 1.2(22.53\text{k-ft}) = 27.0 \text{ k-ft}$$
$$M_{lt} = 1.0M_E = 1.0(407\text{k-ft}) = 407 \text{ k-ft}$$
$$P_{nt} = 1.2P_D = 1.2(13 \text{ kips}) = 15.6 \text{ kips}$$
$$P_{lt} = 1.0P_E = 1.0(18.7 \text{ kips}) = 18.7 \text{ kips}$$

1c - Estimate P_r and M_r by assuming the influence of second order effects

P_r and M_r are computed using Eqns. A-8-1 and A-8-2.

$$M_r = B_1 M_{nt} + B_2 M_{lt}$$
$$P_r = P_{nt} + B_2 P_{lt}$$

At this point, we cannot compute M_r and P_r exactly since we do not know B_1 and B_2 (and cannot know them until after we pick a shape).

We will proceed by estimating B_1 and B_2. From previous examples, these factors have not exceeded 1.1. We will assume a value of 1.1 for both, and then compute a precise value after a shape has been selected.

$$M_{r,est} = (1.1)(27.0 \text{ k-ft}) + (1.1)(407 \text{ k-ft}) = \mathbf{477} \text{ k-ft}$$
$$P_{r,est} = (15.6 \text{ kips}) + (1.1)(18.7 \text{ kips}) = \mathbf{36.2} \text{ k-ft}$$

continued on next page

Example Continued

Step 2 - Pick a shape to try

Now that we have an estimate of the demands, we can pick a shape to try. The member we are designing is probably more like a beam than a column, since the axial load effects are relatively small. Therefore, it is helpful to turn to the beam tables to get a rough idea of what shapes might be reasonable.

It is also helpful to recognize that C_b will be high for the member because there is significant moment gradient over the unbraced length. This means that the flexural capacity of the shape will likely be governed by plastic hinge formation, rather than lateral-torsional buckling. For that reason, we will go to the Zx Table (Table 3-2) to get ideas for possible shapes.

From Table 3-2 (page 3-24) we can identify a few shapes that have a plastic moment capacity, $\phi_b M_p$, a little higher than 477 k-ft.

W21×57	W16×67	W12×87
W18×65	W24×55	W14×82
W21×62	W18×71	W12×96

Some of the above shapes are better suited for beam-columns than others. The W18, W21, and W24 shapes may not be good picks because they will have a low axial capacity and columns deeper than W14 are less common in practice.

We will try the **W12×87** and see if it works.

Step 3 - Check interaction equation using approximate demands

3a - Read p and b_x from Table 6-1

We can check the W12×87 using Table 6-1 (page 6-79).

For KL_y=13 ft.

$$p = 0.00105 \text{ kips}^{-1}$$

For L_b=13 ft.

$$b_x = 0.00184 \text{ k-ft}^{-1}$$

This value of b_x assumes C_b=1.0. This column actually has a significant moment gradient so we will compute C_b and adjust b_x.

3b - Compute C_b

C_b is calculated using Eqn. F1-1 in the Specification (page 16.1-46). Recall that C_b is unit-less and depends on the *shape* of the moment diagram, not the actual values of the moments. It is a bit of work to compute C_b precisely, and such work is often not necessary if we can come up with a conservative value. We know that if one of the column end moments were zero, then C_b=1.67. Since we have moments at both ends and double curvature, we know the moment gradient is steeper than the zero-end-moment case, and C_b would be somewhat greater than 1.67. We will conservatively use a value of 1.67 for C_b.

3c - Calculated adjusted b_x

Since $C_b > 1$, Eqn. 6-5 is used to determine $b_{x(C_b>1.0)}$.

$$b_{x(C_b>1.0)} = \frac{b_{x(C_b=1.0)}}{C_b} \geq b_{xmin}$$

The value for b_{xmin} is read from Table 6-1 at $L_b = 0$ ft.

$$b_{xmin} = 0.00180$$

so

$$b_{x(C_b>1.0)} = \frac{0.00184}{1.67} \geq 0.00180$$

$$b_{x(C_b>1.0)} = 0.00110 \geq 0.00180$$

$$b_{x(C_b>1.0)} = 0.00180$$

Note that it would have been a waste of time to compute C_b precisely (in Step 3b) because b_{xmin} governs by a large margin even with the conservative estimate of C_b. This will generally be the case for columns in moment frames.

3d - Check interaction equation with estimated demands

We can determine which interaction equation applies by looking at pP_r.

$$pP_r = (0.00105 \text{ kips}^{-1})(36.2 \text{ kips}) = 0.038 \ (<0.20 \text{ so H1-1b will govern}).$$

Checking the interation equation using Eqn. 6-2 and the approximate demands:

$$(\frac{1}{2})pP_r + (\frac{9}{8})b_xM_{rx} =$$

$$(\frac{1}{2})(0.00105 \text{ kips}^{-1})(33.6 \text{ kips}) + (\frac{9}{8})(0.00180 \text{ k-ft}^{-1})(477 \text{ k-ft}) =$$

$$0.0190 + 0.966 = 0.99 \ (<1.0)$$

This preliminary check, with our estimated demands, suggests that the W12×87 has adequate capacity. If the check had suggested insufficient capacity, we would have gone back to Step 2 and selected a different shape to try.

Step 4 - Verify the shape or iterate to find a better one

To get to this point we made some assumptions. First, we assumed that the moment of inertia for the beams and columns in the frame were the same. If we were designing the beam too, we could pick the beam size to satisfy this assumption. Second we assumed that B_1 and B_2 were 1.1. Now that we have picked a shape we can compute B_1 and B_2 and verify the design.

4a - Calculate B_2:

We will actually calculate B_2 first (since it is required for P_r which is required for B_1).

$$B_2 = \frac{1}{1 - \frac{\alpha P_{story}}{P_{estory}}} \geq 1 \qquad \text{(Eqn. A-8-6)}$$

$$\alpha = 1.0 \text{ (LRFD)}$$

continued on next page

For P_{story} we need to sum all the vertical loads on the frame. In this case, it will be equal to sum of P_{nt} for the two columns.

$$P_{story} = 2P_{nt} = 2(15.6 \text{ kips}) = 31.2 \text{ kips}$$

The term P_{estory} is determined by summing the sidesway buckling capacity of the two columns. Since we are calculating for the sidesway case, we will use KL_x associated with the sidesway case, given as 27 ft. For one column, the sidesway buckling load is:

$$P_e = \frac{\pi^2 (29000 \text{ ksi})(740 \text{ in.}^4)}{(27 \times 12 \text{ in.})^2} = 2015 \text{ kips}$$

For the story, we sum the buckling loads of the two columns:

$$P_{estory} = 2P_e = 2(2015 \text{ kips}) = 4030 \text{ kips}$$

$$B_2 = \frac{1}{1 - \dfrac{(1.0)(31.2 \text{ kips})}{(4030 \text{ kips})}} = 1.01$$

4b - Calculating P_r:

Now that B_2 is known, P_r can be computed precisely:

$$P_r = P_{nt} + B_2 P_{lt} = (15.6 \text{ kips}) + (1.01)(18.7 \text{ kips}) = \mathbf{34.5} \text{ k-ft}$$

4c - Calculating B_1:

Now we can calculate B_1:

$$B_1 = \frac{C_m}{1 - \alpha(P_r/P_{e1})} \geq 1 \qquad \text{(Eqn. A-8-3)}$$

$$\alpha = 1.00 \qquad \text{(for LRFD)}$$

The term C_m is computed based on the first-order moments not associated with lateral translation.

$$C_m = 0.6 - 0.4(M_1/M_2)$$

We can get values for M_1 and M_2 from the member free-body diagram under the dead load effects.

$$M_1/M_2 = 22.53 \text{ k-ft}/45.06 \text{ k-ft} = 0.5 \text{ (positive for reverse curvature)}$$
$$C_m = 0.6 - 0.4(M_1/M_2) = 0.6 - 0.4(0.5) = 0.4$$

Extra care must be taken when computing P_{e1}. When doing calculations associated with B_1 we assume no sidesway of the frame, so KL is 13 feet when computing P_{e1}.

$$P_{e1} = \frac{\pi^2 EI}{(KL)^2} = \frac{\pi^2 (29000 \text{ ksi})(740 \text{ in.}^4)}{(13 \times 12 \text{ in.})^2} = 8694 \text{ kips}$$

We now have all the required information to compute B_1 using Eqn. A-8-3:

$$B_1 = \frac{0.4}{1 - (1.0)(34.5 \text{ kips}/8694 \text{ kips})} = 0.40 \geq 1$$

$$B_1 = 1.0$$

4d - Calculating M_r:

$$M_r = B_1 M_{nt} + B_2 M_{lt} = (1.00)(27 \text{ ft}) + 1.01(407 \text{ k-ft}) = 438 \text{ k-ft}$$

Example Continued

4e - Checking interaction equation with the final demands:

Since M_r and P_r turned out to be less than what we assumed, the W12×87 will still work. The calculations below simply show the interaction equation using the actual (not estimated) demands.

$$(\frac{1}{2})(0.00105 \text{ kips}^{-1})(34.5 \text{ kips}) + (\frac{9}{8})(0.00180 \text{ kip-ft}^{-1})(407 \text{ kip-ft}) =$$
$$0.0181 + 0.82 = 0.84 \ (<1.0, \text{ OK})$$

We have demonstrated that the W12×87 works for the column in the frame. There may be lighter shapes that work, but we would need to repeat Steps 2 through 4 to demonstrate it.

Use **W12×87**.

You Should Know

- Why do the general steps for design need to be modified for beam-columns?
- What are reasonable initial estimates for B_1 and B_2?
- How do you know if a shape has adequate capacity as a beam-column?

Remember This

- Beam-columns are members that have both axial forces and bending moments.
- The combination of axial forces and bending moments generates additional bending moments called second-order moments.
- Second-order moments that occur without end translation are called P-δ moments and may be accounted for by the amplification factor B_1.
- Second-order moments caused by end translation are called P-Δ moments and may be accounted for by the amplification factor B_2.
- Interaction equations are used to check beam-column capacity.
- In beam-column design, demands must be estimated initially, because they cannot be determined precisely until after a shape is selected.
- After a beam-column has been selected, the demands must be calculated precisely to ensure it is adequate.

A welder attaches a shear tab to a steel plate embedded in a concrete wall. Welded connections have been used in steel structures since the 1970s, but field welding is usually minimized to control costs.

Beams are welded to columns when moments need to be transmitted.

11. Welded Connections

Consider This

- What is arc welding? Are there different ways to do it?
- What are the different types of welds?
- How do I specify welds on plans? What is standard weld notation?
- How do I calculate the strength of a weld?
- What are the minimum and maximum weld sizes for different configurations?
- What weld proportions result in the best economy?

11.1 Arc Welding

Welding is a process of fusing materials by melting the edges and often adding molten filler metal. There are various ways to melt metals including gas flame, an electric arc, and friction. Electric arc welding is commonly used in steel construction.

During welding, the molten metal must be protected from the atmosphere. Without protection, oxygen from the air will oxidize the molten metal, resulting in porous and brittle welds. Modern welding processes use inert gases to shield the molten metal.

An electric arc is a like a continuous spark, resulting from electric current flowing through the air. Electric arcs can generate very high temperatures capable of melting most materials. Electric arc furnaces are used for melting scrap metal during steel production. Electric arc welding is commonly used to join steel pieces.

Advances in welding technology since the 1950s have facilitated the use of welding in steel building construction. Shielded metal arc welding (also known as stick welding) was developed in the 1950s and quickly became a popular arc welding process. In the late 1950s, automatic welding processes were developed which make high volume welding more economical. Welding began to be used for steel building construction in the 1970s.

The figure below illustrates some of the features common to all arc welding processes.

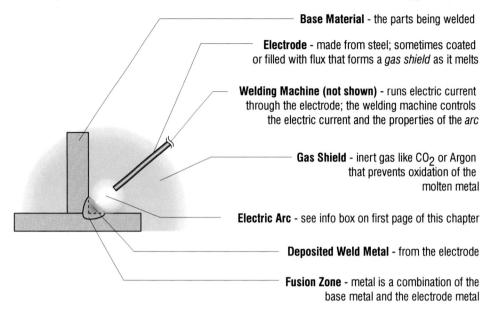

Base Material - the parts being welded

Electrode - made from steel; sometimes coated or filled with flux that forms a *gas shield* as it melts

Welding Machine (not shown) - runs electric current through the electrode; the welding machine controls the electric current and the properties of the *arc*

Gas Shield - inert gas like CO_2 or Argon that prevents oxidation of the molten metal

Electric Arc - see info box on first page of this chapter

Deposited Weld Metal - from the electrode

Fusion Zone - metal is a combination of the base metal and the electrode metal

There are several different arc welding processes. Shielded metal arc welding (SMAW), commonly called "stick welding" is called a manual method because as the electrode is melted and deposited, a new electrode is manually reloaded. In SMAW, the electrode is coated with flux that melts to form the inert gas shield.

In contrast to this manual method, there are three automatic arc welding processes, all of which involve an electrode that is spooled and fed automatically. What differs among the three automatic processes is the way the gas shield is generated. In gas shielded metal arc welding (GMAW), commonly called "MIG welding", the gas shield is provided by blowing gas on the weld. In submerged arc welding (SAW), the gas shield is generated as granular flux that covers the joint melts. In flux core arc welding (FCAW), flux within the electrode melts to form the gas shield.

Stick welding (SMAW) is used for low-volume applications and where portability of equipment is important. Automatic welding processes are used for applications where significant volumes of electrode need to be deposited.

Example 11.1 Strength of Electrode Material

How strong is typical electrode material?

The electrodes used in welding are generally stronger than the base materials being joined. The most common electrode for structural steel welding is designated E70 and has a 70 ksi ultimate strength.

You Should Know

- Why and how are inert gasses used in welding?
- Were there welded steel buildings in the 1960s?
- What is the difference between MIG welding and stick welding?

11.2 Types of Joints and Welds

There are four types of joints that are frequently used in steel structures. These are: butt joints, lap joints, tee joints, and corner joints.

There are three families of welds that can be used in these joints: groove welds, fillet welds, and plug and slot welds. The figures below illustrate joints with these different types of welds. Fillet welds tend to be the least expensive and most common because they require less preparation of the parts.

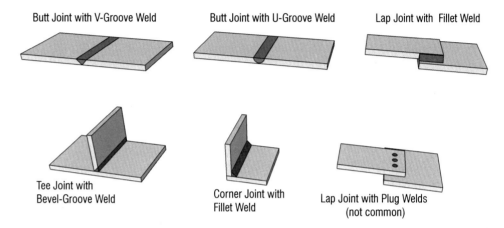

Butt Joint with V-Groove Weld   Butt Joint with U-Groove Weld   Lap Joint with Fillet Weld

Tee Joint with
Bevel-Groove Weld   Corner Joint with Fillet Weld   Lap Joint with Plug Welds (not common)

Example 11.2 Different Types of Welds

What is the difference between a V-groove weld and a bevel-groove weld?

In a V-groove weld, both of the pieces being connected have a beveled edge. In a bevel-groove weld, only one of the edges being connected is beveled.

Study the Manual

Chapter 8 in the Manual provides information on welded connections. The second page of Table 8-2 (page 8-35) summarizes the various types of welds and the symbols for each.

- What is the symbol for a fillet weld?

- What is the symbol for a V-groove weld?

The rest of Table 8-2 provides parameters for each of the different types of welds for various joints. For example, look at page 8-37 which gives information for square groove welds. Look at the table below the upper figures to answer the following questions.

- When SMAW welding is used for the butt joint shown on the left, how big should the root opening, R, be?

- What is the maximum thickness of the plate, T_1, that is pre-qualified?

11.3 Standard Notation

Engineers need to know how to properly specify welds on plans. There are a few components of weld notation that are common for most welding. The basic components are: the arrow, the reference line, the weld size, the weld symbol, and the length.

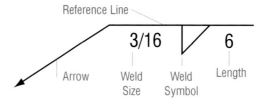

The **arrow** points to a location that should be welded. The arrow head should touch the lines or joint where the weld is intended. It is okay for the arrow tail to have multiple legs (when plans get crowded it can be difficult to find a convenient spot for the weld information). The arrow should point to the weld in roughly the same way the electrode might approach (not through a part).

The **reference line** is always horizontal and may appear to the right or left of the arrow. Information may be written above or below the reference line. Information that is written below the reference line refers to the location that the arrow is pointing to. Information that is written above the reference line refers to the "other side" from where the arrow is pointing. For parts that are welded on both sides, there will be information written both above and below the reference line.

The **weld size** is always the left-most information item. It is always specified in inches, so units are not written. Weld sizes are specified to the 16th of an inch.

The **weld symbol** indicates the type of weld. The symbol for a fillet weld is a right triangle. The weld symbol is always written such that the part of the symbol that is perpendicular to the reference line is always on the left.

The **weld length** appears to the right of the weld symbol. It is always specified in inches, so units are not written. If no weld length is written, it is presumed that the entire edge is to be welded.

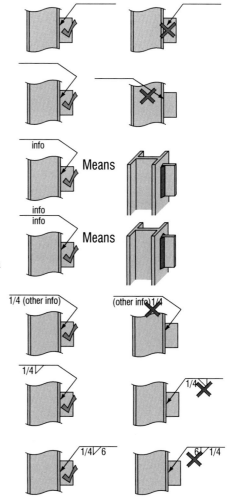

11.4 Simple Connections

Now that you know some basic information about welds, the rest of this chapter will discuss demands, capacities, and design. This section will discuss demands.

When a member is connected to another using welds, the welds must resist the load effects that are present at the end of the member. In general, these may include a bending moment, M_u, and a force which is the resultant of P_u and V_u. A *simple* welded connection is one in which the demands may be represented as a single force acting through the centroid of the weld.

Example 11.3 Recognizing Simple Connections

Is this a simple welded connection?

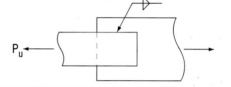

The centroid of the weld is indicated by the + in the figure to the right. Since the demand on the weld is a single force passing through the centroid of the weld, it is a simple welded connection.

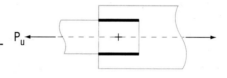

Example 11.4 Recognizing Simple Connections

Is this a simple welded connection?

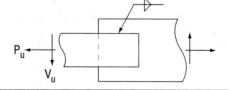

The resultant of the demands is shown on the figure to the right. The resultant force does not pass through the centroid of connection, so this is NOT a simple connection.

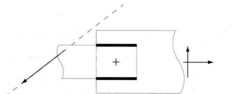

Simple welded connections are typically found at the ends of members that have only axial load effects (tension members or compression members). The factored demand on such welded connections is typically designated P_u.

Example 11.5 Calculating Demands for Simple Welded Connections

Member BE is a double angle welded to the top and bottom chords. What is the factored demand for the welded connection at each end of member BE?

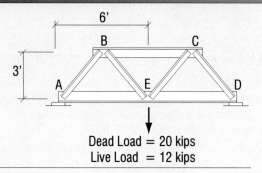

Dead Load = 20 kips
Live Load = 12 kips

Step 1 - Calculate loads

The dead and live loads are given, so no additional calculation is required.

Step 2 - Calculated load effects

The dead load effect in member BE is easily determined by the method of sections. Summing forces in the y-direction for the free-body diagram to the right:

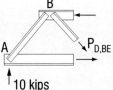

Free-Body Under Dead Loads Only

$$(\cos 45)P_{D,BE} = 10 \text{ kips}$$
$$P_{D,BE} = 14.1 \text{ kips}$$

Similarly for the live load effect:

$$(\cos 45)P_{L,BE} = 6 \text{ kips}$$
$$P_{L,BE} = 8.5 \text{ kips}$$

Step 3 - Factor loads

By inspection, load combination 2 will govern:

$$P_{u,BE} = 1.2P_{D,Be} + 1.6P_{L,BE}$$
$$P_{u,BE} = 1.2(14.1 \text{ kips}) + 1.6(8.5 \text{ kips}) = \mathbf{30.5} \text{ kips}$$

Step 4 - Recognize the connection demand

In the previous steps we computed the factored load effects in member BE. The connections at each end of BE must be capable of resisting the factored load effects in the member. Therefore, the demand on the welded connection at each end of BE is: $P_u = \mathbf{30.5}$ kips.

You Should Know

- How can you tell if a welded connection is "simple"?
- Where might you find simple welded connections in structures?
- How do you compute, P_u, for simple welded connections?

11.5 Limit States

Fillet welds are the most common weld for all joints except butt joints, where groove welds are the only type that will work. The next three sections will discuss how to compute the capacity of fillet welded connections.

Consider the lap joint below. If it were loaded to failure, we might envision two possible types of failures. The first type is weld failure. The second type is base metal failure.

Lap Joint with Load

Weld Metal Failure

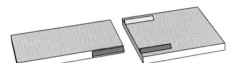

Base Metal Failure

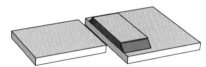

Study the Manual

Turn to Chapter J in the Specification.

- What is the name of the Chapter?

- Which section addresses welds?

Turn to §J2.4 in the Specification. This section gives the formulas for computing the nominal capacity for base metal failure (Eqn J2-2) and weld metal failure (J2-3).

- How are the two equations alike?

- How are the two equations different?

Computing the capacities for welded connection limit states consists of determining the failure areas and metal strengths (in ksi) and multiplying the two.

You Should Know

- What are the two types of failures that should be considered when determining weld capacity?
- What part of the Specification addresses weld capacities?

11.6 Fillet Weld Capacity

To compute the capacity for weld metal failure we need to know the area of weld that is failing. This area is designated the *effective area* of the weld, A_{we}. When computing A_{we}, we consider the weld failing through the throat as illustrated to the right. The throat width depends on the weld size, a, and the slope of the fillet. If the fillet weld slopes at 45°, the throat width will be $(\cos 45°)a = 0.707a$. Once the throat width is known, A_{we} is calculated by multiplying the throat width by the length of the weld.

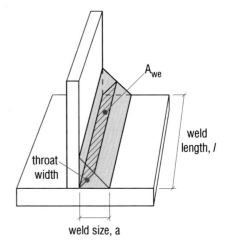

Besides A_{we}, the other piece of information that is required to compute the weld metal limit state is the nominal strength of the weld metal, F_{nw}. For simple connections, F_{nw} can be determined from Eqn. J2-5.

Study the Manual

Look at Eqn. J2-5 in §J2.4 of the Specification (bottom of page 16.1-115).

The first part of the equation, $0.6F_{EXX}$, is the shear strength of the electrode material. F_{EXX} is the tensile strength of the electrode, and can be determined from the electrode designation. For example, E70 electrode has $F_{EXX} = 70$ ksi.

- Compute $0.6F_{EXX}$ for an E70 electrode.

The second part of Eqn J2-5 (in parentheses), is a factor that depends on the orientation of the welds relative to the direction of loading. For loading parallel to the direction of the welds, $\theta = 0°$ and the factor will be 1.0. For loading perpendicular to the direction of the welds, $\theta = 90°$ and the factor will be 1.5; experiments have shown that welds are stronger when loaded perpendicular to the longitudinal axis of the weld. The following example will illustrate how to apply Eqn. J2-5.

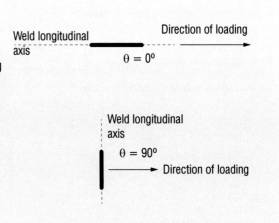

Example 11.6 Computing Capacity for Weld Failure Limit State

What is the capacity of the weld metal to resist the indicated load?

direction of loading

3/16   3
3/16   3

Step 1 - Calculate weld failure area, A_{we}

From the detail we note that the total length of weld is 6 in. (3 in. on each side of the plate). For the weld metal failure limit state, we consider the weld to fail through the throat. The assumed failure planes are indicated on the figure to the right. The weld failure area is calculated as:

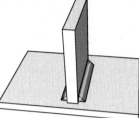

$$A_{we} = (0.707a)l$$
$$A_{we} = (0.707)(3/16 \text{ in.})(6 \text{ in.}) = 0.795 \text{ in.}^2$$

Step 2 - Compute the weld failure stress, F_{nw}

The weld strength depends on the orientation of the welds relative to the direction of loading. In this case, the two welds run in a direction that is perpendicular to the direction of loading, so:

$$\theta = 90°$$

$$F_{nw} = 0.6F_{EXX}(1.0 + 0.5\sin^{1.5}\theta)$$
$$F_{nw} = 0.6(70 \text{ ksi})(1.0 + 0.5\sin^{1.5}90°)$$
$$F_{nw} = 0.6(70 \text{ ksi})(1.5) = 63 \text{ ksi}$$

Step 3 - Compute the factored capacity for weld metal failure

The nominal capacity is:

$$R_n = F_{nw}A_{we} = (63 \text{ ksi})(0.795 \text{ in.}^2) = 50.1 \text{ kips}$$

The ϕ factor for fillet weld metal failure is:

$$\phi = 0.75$$

so:

$$\phi R_n = 0.75(50.1 \text{ kips}) = \mathbf{38 \text{ kips}}$$

You Should Know

- Why do we use the throat width, rather than the weld size, when computing A_{we}?
- How does the direction of loading change the capacity of the weld material?
- How do you compute ϕR_n for weld metal failure?

11.7 Weld Groups

Welds with different orientations can be used in the same connection. For example, consider the connection shown to the right. Two of the welds will be loaded in the direction of their longitudinal axis ($\theta = 0°$) and one will be loaded perpendicular to its axis ($\theta=90°$). When welds with different orientations are used together, §J2.4(c) applies.

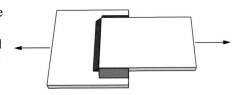

Study the Manual

Read §J2.4(c) of the Specification (beginning on the bottom of page 16.1-116).

- How is R_{nwl} calculated?

- How is R_{nwt} calculated?

- Note, that using F_{nw} as defined in Table J2.5 ($0.6F_{EXX}$) is the same thing as assuming $\theta = 0°$ in Eqn. J2-5.

- For the connection in the figure at the top-right corner of this page, which would be greater: J2-10a or J2-10b?

Note: It is often more convenient to use Eqn. J2-10a, even if it gives lower values for R_n.

Example 11.7 Computing Capacity of Weld Metal

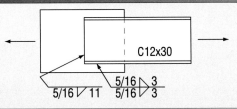

What is the capacity of the weld metal to resist the indicated load?

Step 1 - Calculate R_{nwl} and R_{nwt}

We first compute the capacity for the longitudinal and transverse welds separately, using $F_{nw} = 0.6 \times 70$ ksi for both.

$$R_{nwl} = (0.6 \times 70 \text{ ksi})[(0.707)(5/16 \text{ in.})(6 \text{ in.})] = 55.7 \text{ kips}$$
$$R_{nwt} = (0.6 \times 70 \text{ ksi})[(0.707)(5/16 \text{ in.})(11 \text{ in.})] = 102.1 \text{ kips}$$

Step 2 - Evaluate Eqn J2-10

With R_{nwl} and R_{nwt} determined, we can evaluate Eqns. J2-10a and J2-10b.

$$R_n = R_{nwl} + R_{nwt} = 55.7 \text{ kips} + 102.1 \text{ kips} = 157.8 \text{ kips} \quad \text{(Eqn J2-10a)}$$
$$R_n = 0.85R_{nwl} + 1.5R_{nwt}$$
$$= 0.85(55.7 \text{ kips}) + 1.5(102.1 \text{ kips}) = 200.5 \text{ kips} \quad \text{(Eqn J2-10b)}$$

We are permitted to use the greater of the two, so $R_n = 200.5$ kips, and:

$$\phi R_n = (0.75)(200.5 \text{ kips}) = \textbf{150.4 kips}$$

From the weld calculations we have done, you may have noticed that several things are usually the same: the 0.6, the 70 ksi, and the 0.707. Since it is always conservative to assume $\theta = 0°$ (the basis for Eqn. J2-10a), the strength of the weld metal in any simple connection with E70 electrode can be written as:

$$\phi R_n = (0.75)(0.6 \times 70 \text{ ksi})[(0.707)(D/16)l] = \mathbf{1.392}Dl$$

where D is the weld size in sixteenths of an inch, and l is the total weld length in inches.

Study the Manual

Turn to page 8-8 of the Manual and read the section titled "Available Strength."

- Which equation did we derive above?

- How is the equation modified if all the welds are loaded transversely, rather than longitudinally?

Example 11.8 Weld Capacity Using Condensed Equation

What is the capacity of the weld metal to resist the indicated load?

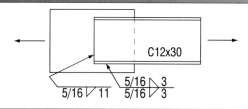

C12x30

5/16 11   5/16 3
           5/16 3

A conservative value for the capacity is:
$$\phi R_n = 1.392Dl = 1.392(5)(17) = \mathbf{118} \text{ kips}$$

You Should Know

- When welds in a group have different orientations relative to the load, can you sum the capacities of the individual welds as determined from Eqn. J2-5?
- In what situations would Eqn. J2-10a give a higher value than Eqn. J2-10b? Would this be common or rare?
- What assumptions are built into the equation $\phi R_n = 1.392Dl$?
- For a 7/16 inch weld size, what is the value for D?

11.8 Base Metal Capacity

The previous two sections discussed failure of the weld metal. The other limit state that needs to be considered for welded connections is failure of the base metal.

The base metal capacity depends on the area that would fail and whether the failure is in tension or shear. The first step for determining both of these things is to envision the failure mode that is being calculated.

Example 11.9 Envisioning Base Metal Failure Modes

How might the base metal fail for the connection shown? For each mode, indicate whether the base metal is failing in shear or tension.

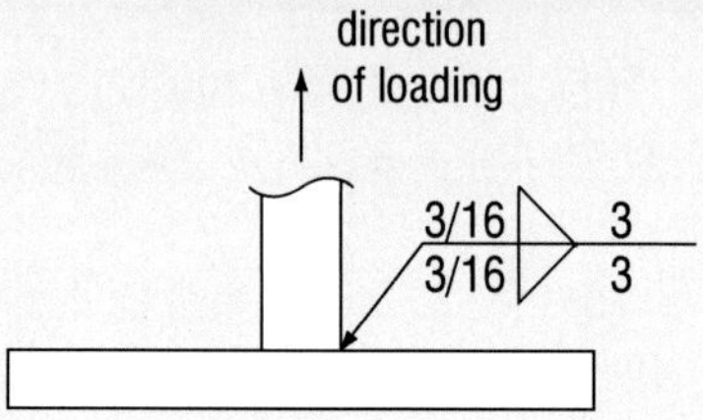

direction of loading

3/16 — 3
3/16 — 3

Step 1 - Imagine how the base material might fail

One way the base material could fail is shown to the right. For this mode of failure, the top plate fails right above the welds. The base metal is **failing in tension**.

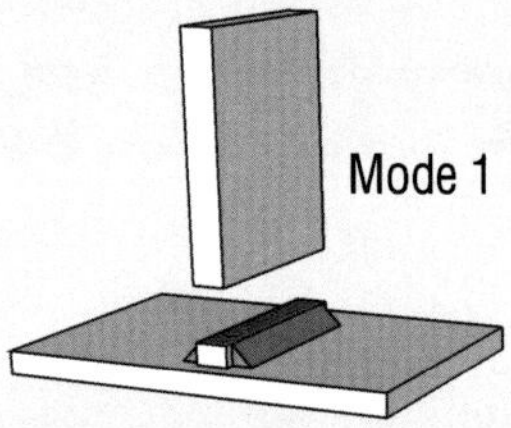

Mode 1

Step 2 - Imagine another way that base material might fail

Usually there are at least two different base material failure modes because fillet welds are always connecting two parts.

The figure to the right illustrates another base material failure mode. Here, the bottom plate is failing on two planes. The base metal is **failing in shear**.

Mode 2

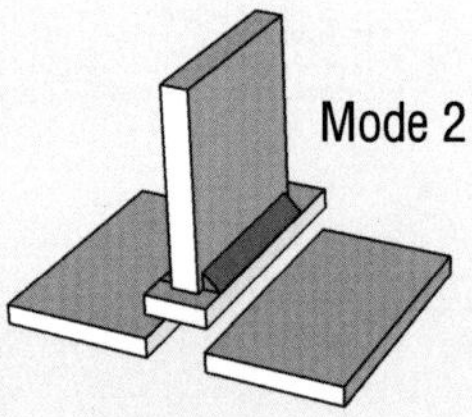

Once the base material failures have been envisioned, the capacities associated with each type of failure can be computed using equations in §J4 of the Specification. The equations in §J4 are specific forms of Eqn. J2-2.

Study the Manual

Read §J4.1. of the Specification (page 16.1-128). This section applies when base material is failing in tension, as illustrated in Mode 1 of Example 11.9.

- How many equations are given for R_n in §J4.1?

- What is the difference between them?

When applying the equations, A_g and A_e are taken as the area of the base material that is failing, A_{BM}.

In many cases A_g and A_e are the same, so the only differences between Eqns. J4-1 and J4-2 are the ϕ factor and the stress. For A36 steel: $0.9F_y = 0.9(36 \text{ ksi}) = 32.4$ ksi, and $0.75F_u = 0.75(58 \text{ ksi}) = 43.5$ ksi. Since 32.4 is less than 43.5, Eqn. J4-1 will always govern for A36 steel (if $A_e = A_g$). This is also true for A992 steel.

Read §J4.2. of the Specification (page 16.1-129). This section applies when base material is failing in shear, as illustrated in Mode 2 of Example 11.9.

- How many equations are given for R_n in §J4.2?

- What is the difference between them?

In comparing, Eqns J4-3 and J4-4, the areas will be the same (in the context of fillet weld calculations). For A36 steel: $1.0(0.6F_y) = 1.0(0.6 \times 36 \text{ ksi}) = 21.6$ ksi, and $0.75(0.6F_u) = 0.75(0.6 \times 58 \text{ ksi}) = 26.1$ ksi. Since 21.6 is less than 26.1, Eqn. J4-3 will always govern for A36 steel. For A992 steel, though, Eqn. J4-4 will govern.

Example 11.10 Computing Capacity for Base Metal Failure Limit State

Compute the factored capacity for base metal failure for the connection of Example 11.9, given that A_g for Mode 1 is 0.68 in², and A_{gv} for Mode 2 is 1.4 in².

Step 1 - Calculate the capacity for Mode 1

We will assume the plates are A36 steel. For Mode 1 the base metal is failing in tension. Eqns J4-1 and J4-2 apply; for A36 material Eqn. J4-1 will govern (see discussion above).

$$\phi R_n = (0.9)(36 \text{ ksi})(0.68 \text{ in.}^2) = 22 \text{ kips}$$

Step 2 - Calculate the capacity for Mode 2

For Mode 2 the base metal is failing in shear. Eqns J4-3 and J4-4 apply; for A36 material Eqn. J4-3 will govern (see discussion above).

$$\phi R_n = (1.0)(0.6)(36 \text{ ksi})(1.4 \text{ in.}^2) = 30 \text{ kips}$$

Step 3 - Summarize governing mode and capacity

The governing mode for base metal failure is Mode 1 with $\phi R_n = \mathbf{22}$ kips.

A final example will illustrate how weld metal failure and base metal failure are both considered in order to determine the capacity of a simple welded connection.

Example 11.11 Computing Capacity for Base Metal Failure Limit States

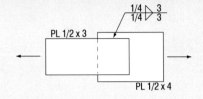

Compute the capacity of the lap joint loaded as shown.

PL 1/2 x 3

PL 1/2 x 4

Step 1 - Calculate the capacity for weld failure limit state

$$\phi R_n = 1.392Dl = 1.392(4)(6) = 33.4 \text{ kips}$$

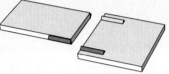

Step 2 - Compute the capacity for base metal failure limit state

The most obvious base metal failure mode is illustrated to the right. We can tell by inspection that base metal failure of the bottom plate will not govern. We will calculate the illustrated mode.

Since the base metal is failing in tension, Eqns J4-1 and J4-2 apply. Assuming A36 plate, Eqn. J4-1 will govern.

$$\phi R_n = 0.9(36 \text{ ksi})[(0.5 \text{ in.})(3 \text{ in.})] = 48.6 \text{ kips}$$

Step 3 - Summarize the governing limit state and capacity

Failure of the weld metal governs.

$$\phi R_n = \textbf{33.4} \text{ kips}$$

You Should Know

* Why is there more than one base metal failure mode?
* How do you determine the capacity of a welded connection?

11.9 Sizing Requirements

Now that we know how to compute demands and capacities for welded connections, we are ready to discuss design. Before we apply our usual design steps, there are some basic rules for weld sizing that should be discussed.

Study the Manual

Turn to §J2.2b of the Specification (page 16.1-111) and read the first paragraph.

- For a connection involving a 1/2 in. thick part and a 1/4 in. part, what is the minimum size that can be used for the filled weld?

Turn to the commentary for §J2.2b (page 16.1-389 to 16.1-390) and read the first two paragraphs in the subsection.

- Why is there a **minimum** fillet size requirement?

Study the Manual

Turn to §J2.2b of the Specification (page 16.1-111) and read the paragraphs about the **maximum** size of fillet welds.

For thin plates (1/4 in. or less), provision (a) is simply stating the obvious limit for how big a fillet weld can be.

The fillet weld on the edge of a plate cannot be bigger than the plate.

Provision (b) gives the limit that will apply to most plates.

- What is the maximum fillet weld size along the edge of plates that are 1/4 in. or thicker?

Turn to the commentary for §J2.2b (page 16.1-390) and read the first paragraph and study the pictures.

- Why is the thickness minus 1/16 in. the maximum fillet size for thicker plates?

It is helpful to clarify that these maximum weld sizes pertain to welding along the thickness of a plate. For butt, tee, or corner joints, these rules do not apply.

It is fine for the weld size to be greater than the plate thickness in situations like this.

Design

In addition to the requirements for minimum and maximum weld sizes, there are two other things to keep in mind when sizing welds. First, the largest fillet weld that can be deposited in a single pass is a 5/16 in. fillet weld. Larger welds will require multiple passes and significantly more labor. Second, it is generally more efficient to use smaller fillet weld sizes and longer lengths, as compared to large weld sizes and shorter lengths.

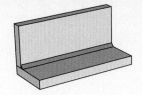

If the weld is 5/16 in. or smaller, it can be deposited in a single pass.

If the weld is larger than 5/16 in. it must be "built-up" over multiple passes.

Example 11.12 Principles for Sizing Welds

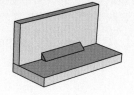

Which is better, a 3/16 in. weld that is 6 in. long, or a 6/16 in. weld that is 3 in.?

Step 1 - Calculate weld failure area for each case, A_{we}

We can begin by comparing the failure area for each weld. In general, the failure area is computed as:

$$A_{we} = (0.707a)l$$

For the small-long weld:

$$A_{we} = (0.707)(3/16 \text{ in.})(6 \text{ in.}) = 0.795 \text{ in.}^2$$

For the bigger-shorter weld:

$$A_{we} = (0.707)(6/16 \text{ in.})(3 \text{ in.}) = 0.795 \text{ in.}^2$$

Since the two welds have the same A_{we} they will have the strength. From the standpoint of strength the welds are equal.

Step 2 - Compute the weld volumes

The volume of a fillet weld (the amount of filler metal) is equal to:

$$V_w = (a \times a)\frac{1}{2}l = \frac{a^2 l}{2}$$

For the small-long weld:

$$A_{we} = \frac{(3/16 \text{ in.})^2(6 \text{ in.})}{2} = 0.105 \text{ in.}^3$$

For the bigger-shorter weld:

$$A_{we} = \frac{(6/16 \text{ in.})^2(3 \text{ in.})}{2} = 0.21 \text{ in.}^3$$

We see now that the bigger-shorter weld will have **double** the volume. While the cost of the extra filler metal may be insignificant, the double volume indicates double the labor to make the weld and represents a significant increase in cost. This cost is in addition to the extra labor involved with multiple passes for welds bigger than 5/16 in.

- Why is there a minimum size for fillet welds? Where is it specified?
- Why is there a maximum size for fillet welds? Where is it specified?
- Why is 5/16 a popular weld size?
- When you double the size of a weld, how much do you increase the volume (if the length is the same for both cases)?

11.10 Length Requirements

Section J2.2b of the Specification discusses several requirements regarding fillet weld lengths.

Turn to §J2.2b in the Specification. Read the last paragraph on page 16.1-111.

- If you are using a fillet weld size of 1/2 in., what is the minimum length of the weld (if you don't want a penalty)?

- Suppose you use a 1/2 in. fillet weld that is only 1 in. long. How do you compute the capacity of the weld?

Read the first four paragraphs on page 16.1-112 of the Manual.

For some long welds the demand cannot be assumed to be evenly distributed over the weld, even if the resultant demand passed through the centroid.

- When does an effective length need to be calculated?

- How is the effective length of a weld calculated?

Intermittent welds may be used to stitch together built-up shapes. The column shown to the right is a built-up section made from four plates stitched together.

- What is the minimum length for stitch welds?

Read the paragraph on lap slices on page 16.1-112. For each connection below - indicate what is wrong.

11.11 Design

The general steps for design apply to welded connections. They are:
1. Compute demands.
2. Pick a weld to try (size and length).
3. Compute capacity and compare with demands.
4. Finalize the design or iterate.

In Step 2, we can pick a combination of size and length such that we are sure the connection will be adequate for the weld metal failure limit state. All that is left to check in Step 3 is base metal failure. Usually iteration is not required.

Example 11.13 Fillet Weld Design

Design the welds for the lap splice. Indicate the welds on a sketch of the connection using correct weld notation.

$P_D = 26$ kips
$P_L = 11$ kips

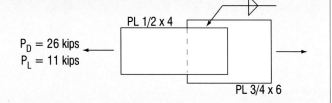

PL 1/2 x 4

PL 3/4 x 6

Step 1 - Compute demands

Load combination 2 governs, by inspection:

$$P_u = 1.2P_D + 1.6P_L = 1.2(26 \text{ kips}) + 1.6(11 \text{ kips}) = 48.8 \text{ kips}$$

Step 2 - Pick a weld (size and length)

2a - Determine the minimum weld size

The minimum weld size is read from Table J2.4 and is based on the thickness of the thinner part joined. In this example, the thinner part is 1/2 in. thick, so the minimum weld size is: 3/16 in.

2b - Determine the maximum weld size

The maximum weld size is t-1/16 in. for plates that are 1/4 in. or thicker. The maximum weld size is: 1/2 in. - 1/16 in. = 7/16 in..

2c - Pick a weld size

We will need to pick a size within the bounds set by the minimum and maximum determined in Steps 2a and 2b. Smaller weld sizes result in less material and labor. Try **3/16 in.** weld size.

2d - Determine the required length

$$\phi R_n \geq P_u$$

Using Eqn. 8-2a:

$$1.392Dl \geq 48.8 \text{ kips}$$

$$l \geq \frac{48.8 \text{ kips}}{1.392(3) \text{ kips/in}}$$

$$l \geq 11.7 \text{ in.}$$

Try **6 in.** of weld on each side of the plate.

Example Continued

Step 3 - Check the capacity against demands

The only thing that remains to be checked is failure of the base metal. Only one mode is feasible (illustrated to the right) and needs to be checked. Since the base metal would fail in tension, Eqns. J4-1 and J4-2 apply. Since the material is A36 and $A_e = A_g$, Eqn. J4-1 will govern.

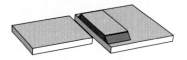

$$\phi R_n = (0.9)(36 \text{ ksi})(4 \text{ in.} \times 1/2 \text{ in.}) = 68.4 \text{ kips } (> 48.8 \text{ kips, OK})$$

Step 4 - Finalize the design

The design is specified using appropriate weld notation.

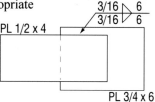

You Should Know

- In weld design, which is decided first: the weld size or the weld length?
- What things are considered when determining the weld size?

11.12 Centroids of Weld Groups

The definition of a "simple" welded connection is that the resultant demand passes through the centroid of the welds. It is helpful to review how the centroid of a weld group might be calculated.

Example 11.14 Calculating the Centroid of a Weld Group

Relative to the datum, where is the centroid of the weld group?

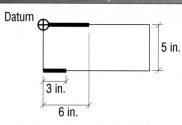

$$\bar{x} = \frac{\bar{x}_1 l_1 + \bar{x}_2 l_2}{l_1 + l_2} = \frac{(3 \text{ in.})(6 \text{ in.}) + (1.5 \text{ in.})(3 \text{ in.})}{6 \text{ in.} + 3 \text{ in.}} = 2.5 \text{ in.}$$

$$\bar{y} = \frac{\bar{y}_1 l_1 + \bar{y}_2 l_2}{l_1 + l_2} = \frac{(0 \text{ in.})(6 \text{ in.}) + (5 \text{ in.})(3 \text{ in.})}{6 \text{ in.} + 3 \text{ in.}} = 1.7 \text{ in.}$$

Design

Example 11.15 Fillet Weld Proportioning

The 2L3×2×1/4 needs 14 inches of weld at the connection. Proportion the welds so that the centroid of the weld corresponds with the centroid of the double angle.

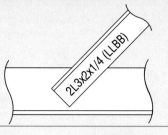

Step 1 - Determine the centroid of the double angle

The location of the centroid for the double angle cross-section is easily determined. It will lie on the axis of symmetry (by inspection), and the distance $\bar{y}$ will be the same as $\bar{y}$ of an individual L3×2×1/4.

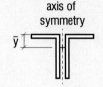

axis of symmetry

$$\bar{y} = 0.980 \text{ in (from Table 1-7)}$$

Step 2 - Ensure alignment in the x-direction

The objective in this problem is to proportion the welds so that the centroid of the welds corresponds with the centroid of the double angle. For the x-direction the approach is obvious.

By using the same welds for each angle, we are guaranteed that the centroid of the group will lie on the axis of symmetry. Provide **7 in.** of weld for each angle (resulting in a total of 14 in. for the connection).

Step 3 - Ensure alignment in the y-direction

To align the centroid of the welds in the y-direction, we must proportion the 7 in. of weld for each angle such that $\bar{y}$ will be equal to 0.980 in. (see Step 1).

This is accomplished by solving a system of equations with the two unknowns l_1 and l_2, which are the lengths of the weld segments for one of the angles. The first equation is based on the result from Step 2.

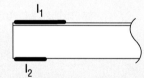

$$l_1 + l_2 = 7.0 \text{ in.}$$

The second equation is that $\bar{y}$ of the two welds must match $\bar{y}$ of the angle (see previous page for a reminder on how to calculate the centroid of a weld group).

$$0.980 \text{ in.} = \frac{(l_1)(0 \text{ in.}) + (l_2)(3 \text{ in.})}{l_1 + l_2}$$

Solving these two equations for the two unknowns, l_1 and l_2 yields:

$$l_1 = 4.71 \text{ in.}$$
$$l_2 = 2.28 \text{ in.}$$

Step 4 - Specify the welds

For the design we will round the weld lengths to the nearest 1/4 in. The detail communicates the design with appropriate weld notation.

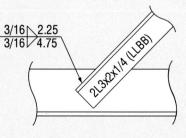

You Should Know

- How do you compute the centroid of a weld group?
- How do you proportion welds such that the centroid lies in a particular location?

Remember This

- All arc welding processes involve an electrode and a gas shield. The differences in welding processes have to do with the form of the electrode and how the gas shield is generated.
- There are four types of joints (butt, lap, tee, and corner) and three families of welds (groove, fillet, and plug).
- Welds should be specified using standard notation.
- Simple welded connections resist a resultant force that acts through the centroid of the group.
- The capacity of a welded connection may be limited by weld metal capacity or base metal capacity.
- Weld metal capacity depends on the orientation of the weld relative to the loading. Welds are stronger when the loading is transverse to the longitudinal axis of the weld.
- Base metal failures may occur in the connected parts, away from the weld. They are shear or tensile failures through a section of the connected part.
- There are minimum and maximum *sizes* for fillets welds. There are also minimum *lengths* for fillet welds, and a penalty if the weld length exceeds 100 times the size.
- In fillet weld design, the weld size is often selected first, and then the necessary length is determined.

Index

C

cast iron, xii, 1
element, the, 1, 5
wrought iron, 1

L

Labor, minimizing, 28
Lateral force resisting systems, 241
Lateral torsional buckling (LTB). *See* Buckling, lateral torsional (LTB)
Length
unbraced. *See* Unbraced length
Limit states
defined, 25
for beams, 161
for bolts, 69, 72
for tension members, 36
serviceability, 160
Live loads
defined, 18
minimums, 20
office example, 20
reduction, 88–90, 147–148
Load and Resistance Factor Design (LRFD), 17, 22
Load combinations, 242
ASD, 28
determining the governing, 24
for beam columns, 245
LRFD, 22–24
truss example, 23
Load effects, 86
beam-columns, 242, 243–247
beams, 149, 150–151
defined, 21
truss members, 21
Load factors, 17, 22–23
Loads, 16, 18, 21
average area, 19
exterior wall, 91–93, 119, 156
point loads, 152
seismic, 241
uniform, 86
wind, 241
Long-slotted holes, 66

M

Manual, the, 12, 13, 14, 15, 19, 23, 28, 41, 59, 106, 108, 149, 170, 171, 173, 175, 209, 215, 266, 267, 268. *See* Steel Construction Manual

MEP (Mechanical, electrical, plumbing), 19
Metal deck, 146
Mises yield criterion, 3
Modulus of elasticity, 5, 95, 160, 205. *See also* Young's modulus of elasticity
Moment gradient, 172, 179–182, 189, 253
Moment of inertia, 95, 160, 162, 173
Moment resisting frames, 240, 242

N

Net area, 39–43. *See also* Effective net area
Neutral axis, 162. *See also* Plastic neutral axis
Nominal capacity, 25, 36
Non-compact element, 183. *See also* Buckling, local
Notation. *See* Standard notation

O

Oversized holes, 66. *See also* Bolt holes

P

Parthenon, 84
P-delta effects. *See* Second-order effects (bending moments)
Pinned connections, 145
Pipes, 96, 97, 100, 173
Plastic hinge, 161, 165, 170, 203–207
Plastic moment, 164–169, 170
Plastic neutral axis (PNA), 203–207
Plastic section modulus (Z), 168, 171
Plate girders, 14, 144, 200
Plates, 5, 9, 12, 14. *See also* Standard shapes; *See also* Plate girders
Preferred Materials, 13, 110
Professional Engineering (PE) Exam, ix

R

Radius of gyration, 59, 62, 98–100. *See also* Slenderness
Rain loads, 18
Recycling, 6
Reduced live load. *See* Live load, reduction
Reduction, chemical, 5
Repeatability, 28
Residual stress, 104
Resistance factors, 17, 26, 36, 51, 73, 105, 170
Rivets, 65
Roof live loads, 151
defined, 18

Rupture in the net section (fracture limit state), 36, 38–51, 62, 81

S

Safety factor, 27
Second-order effects (bending moments), 242, 250–252
Serviceability limit state, 160
Service center, 8
Shape factor, 169
Shear center, 125
Shear forces, 21, 143, 149, 185, 241
Shear lag, 38, 44–50
Shear yielding, 161
Short-slotted holes, 66
Simple connections
   bolted, 67. See also Bolted connections
Slab-on-metal deck, 199. See also Metal deck
   overhang, 156
   weight, 19
Slender element, 112, 183. See also Buckling, local
Slenderness, 36, 59, 62–63
Slenderness ratio, 98–101, 104, 106
Slip, at beam interface, 203
Slip critical connections, 75. See also Bolted connections
Slotted holes, 66. See also Bolt holes
Smelting, 5
Snow loads, 18
Spacing, bolt, 77–78
Spandrel beams. See Beams, spandrel
Specification, the, xi, 5, 36, 39, 44, 105, 114, 126, 185, 209, 210, 213, 217, 235, 246, 251, 254, 263. See also AISC 360-10
Staggered bolts, 41–44
Standard notation, 21, 25, 26
Standard shapes, 13
   american standard (S-shapes), 14
   angles (L-shapes), 14, 15
   channels (C- and MC-shapes), 14
   pipes, 11
   tubes (hss shapes), 11
   wide flange (W-shapes), 12, 15
Steel
   ductility, 1, 4
   strength, 1
Steel Construction Manual, ix, x
Stiffened elements, cross-section, 112
Stiffness method, 259

Stories, building, 88
Strain
   from tensile test, 2
   hardening, 2, 36
Strength, 1, 30
   shear, 3
   ultimate, 2, 4
   yield, 2, 4, 95
Stress
   Euler, buckling, 104
   from tensile test, 2
   in beams, 162, 185
   in composite beams, 207
   residual, 104
   shear yield, 3
   tensile yield, 2, 11, 13, 104
   ultimate, 2, 11, 13, 38, 69
Stress-strain diagrams, 2, 5
Strong axis, 100
Structural analysis, 242, 243
Structural design, ix, 29
Studs, 199–200, 205–207
   resultant force, 207–209
   shear capacity, 208, 213–218
   spacing requirements, 235
Sweep, 15

T

Tees, 123, 124, 126
Tensile test, 2
Tension members
   capacity, 36–58
   demands, 33–35
   design, 59–63, 79–82
Threads, bolt, 69, 70. See also Bolted connections
Tolerances, 15
Tributary area, 33–34, 86–87, 147
Tributary width, 147, 150, 201–202
Truss analysis
   examples, 21–22
Trusses
   compression members, 123
   connections, 124
Twist-off bolt, 66

U

Unbraced length, 95, 103, 172, 174
Uniformly distributed loads. See Loads, uniform

Unstiffened elements, cross-section, 112

W

Y

Made in the USA
San Bernardino, CA
06 January 2016